CW01082186

Women and Ireland as Beckett's Lost Others

Women and Ireland as Beckett's Lost Others

Beyond Mourning and Melancholia

Rina Kim

© Rina Kim 2010

All rights reserved. No reproduction, copy or transmission of this publication may be made without written permission.

No portion of this publication may be reproduced, copied or transmitted save with written permission or in accordance with the provisions of the Copyright, Designs and Patents Act 1988, or under the terms of any licence permitting limited copying issued by the Copyright Licensing Agency, Saffron House, 6–10 Kirby Street, London EC1N 8TS.

Any person who does any unauthorized act in relation to this publication may be liable to criminal prosecution and civil claims for damages.

A section from Chapter 1 has appeared in *Samuel Beckett Today/ Aujourd'hui* (2005), and part of Chapter 2 has been published in *Journal of Beckett Studies* (2007). I thank the respective publishers for permission to reprint here. I am also grateful to Edward Beckett for permission to quote from unpublished manuscripts. Excerpts from Samuel Beckett's 'Psychology Notes' (TCD MS 10971) and from his 'Super conquérent' (UoR MS 2934) are reproduced by kind permission of the Estate of Samuel Beckett c/o Rosica Colin Limited, London © The Estate of Samuel Beckett.

The author has asserted her right to be identified as the author of this work in accordance with the Copyright, Designs and Patents Act 1988.

First published 2010 by
PALGRAVE MACMILLAN

Palgrave Macmillan in the UK is an imprint of Macmillan Publishers Limited, registered in England, company number 785998, of Houndmills, Basingstoke, Hampshire RG21 6XS.

Palgrave Macmillan in the US is a division of St Martin's Press LLC, 175 Fifth Avenue, New York, NY 10010.

Palgrave Macmillan is the global academic imprint of the above companies and has companies and representatives throughout the world.

Palgrave® and Macmillan® are registered trademarks in the United States, the United Kingdom, Europe and other countries.

ISBN-13: 978–0–230–23047–7   hardback

This book is printed on paper suitable for recycling and made from fully managed and sustained forest sources. Logging, pulping and manufacturing processes are expected to conform to the environmental regulations of the country of origin.

A catalogue record for this book is available from the British Library.

A catalog record for this book is available from the Library of Congress.

10 9 8 7 6 5 4 3 2 1
19 18 17 16 15 14 13 12 11 10

Printed and bound in Great Britain by
CPI Antony Rowe, Chippenham and Eastbourne

For my parents,
Boksu and Sechang Kim

Contents

Acknowledgements   ix

List of Abbreviations   xi

Introduction   1

**1 Severing Connections with Ireland: Women and the Irish
Free State in Beckett's Early Fiction**   23
   I   Introduction   23
  II Ireland-as-woman   24
 III Woman-as-Ireland   34
 IV 'The comic exaggeration of what elsewhere is expressed
     in elegy'   42

**2 Memories and Melancholia in Beckett's Early
French Fiction**   48
   I   Introduction   48
  II Mourning and melancholia   49
 III Women and Ireland as lost objects   57
 IV Analysing away   64

**3 The Gendering of Mourning and Melancholia in Beckett's
Early Drama**   76
   I   Introduction   76
  II Alternation between mourning and melancholia in
     All That Fall   79
 III Farewell to love: *Krapp's Last Tape*   90
 IV 'All the others ... Throttling the dead in his head':
     Embers and *Eh Joe*   97

4 Beyond Mourning and Melancholia: Kleinian Approaches   107
   I   Introduction   107
  II Recuperating the female voice in *Happy Days*   115
 III Mania and the female castration anxiety in *Happy Days*   121
 IV Flight from the 'self so-called': *Play* and *Film*   131

5 **The Kleinian Work of Mourning in Beckett's Late Works**   **140**
   I   Introduction   140
   II   Restoring the abject entity in *Not I*   142
   III 'Seek well': search for the lost (m)other in *Footfalls*
      and *...but the clouds...*   153
   IV   'On the Sense of Loneliness' and *Company*   161
   V   'Foreknell': *Ill Seen Ill Said* and *Rockaby*   169

Conclusion: *Stirrings Still*   **179**

Notes   185

Bibliography   197

Index   205

Acknowledgements

This book would not have been accomplished without the immense support, encouragement, insight and academic excellence of my PhD supervisor, Dr Elizabeth Barry. She has guided me throughout, helping develop the initial project idea into its completed book form. I am tremendously grateful for her enthusiasm and the faith she has shown in my work as well as for being inspiring, admirable and personable. Liz has been an amazing friend and colleague, offering me a safety net – in every sense of the phrase – throughout my time at Warwick. In a Beckettian sense, I do not think I will ever be able to find the words that can express my sincerest gratitude to her.

I am also greatly indebted to my colleague, Dr Claire Westall, who was a huge inspiration during the revision of this project. I am extremely grateful for her brilliant and sharp feedback on the entire book as well as for years of friendship and support. Christabel Scaife at Palgrave Macmillan and Barbara Slater, Editorial Services Consultant, have been exceptionally helpful and I want to thank them for their efficiency, precision and hard work. I am also immensely grateful to Professor Karen O'Brien for her critical suggestions and timely interventions. I am indebted to the Department of English at Warwick and especially support from Professor Thomas Docherty, Professor Michael Bell, Professor Tony Howard and Professor Jacqueline Labbe.

I would like to express special thanks to Dr Matthew Feldman for his enthusiasm about my project. He kindly allowed me to consult his invaluable transcriptions of Samuel Beckett's 'Psychology Notes', and the contribution of the transcriptions to this project is inestimable. I am indebted to Thomas Mansell and Dr Mark Nixon who generously assisted me with the transcriptions of 'Beckett-Thomas MacGreevy Correspondence' and the doctoral thesis that discusses Beckett's 'German Diaries', respectively. I am also grateful to Professor Anna McMullan and Professor Janelle Reinelt for their invaluable feedback on my monograph and for their ongoing support. I would like to express my cordial gratitude to Dr Marsha Gontarski and Professor S.E. Gontarski whose support spurred me on and gave me the additional strength I needed to complete my monograph. I also would like to thank Professor James Knowlson and Professor Lois Oppenheim for their helpful comments on my monograph and encouragement about this book project, and also to Professor Kwangsook Chung for her continuous support as well as for introducing me to the world of Beckett.

From a more personal perspective, I am so grateful to my friends, Edith Andrees, Salama Belghali, Adela Macarie and Claudia Lozada-Can whose precious friendship, hospitality and support helped me feel at home in Europe throughout. I also would like to thank Rita McCann, Claire Nally, Kumiko Kiuchi, Danielle Wait Roegele, Patricia Silva McNeill and Mercedes Sanjose for their long-lasting friendship. Tocil residential staff, Dr James Shields, Dr Red Chan and Ruth Leigh in particular, offered me a strong sense of community at Warwick. Also, my friends, Nicola Wilson, Dimitar Angelov, Letizia Gramaglia, Cristiano Coppola, Kerstin Oloff, James Graham, Katsura Sako and Juyoung Kim enriched my life at Warwick. I would like to thank my friends in Korea, Seoin Shin, Yookyung Yoon, Sanghee Lee, Heeju Yang and Heagin Choi whose friendship means much to me. They have supported me in numerous ways while I have been away from home. I am also immensely grateful to Dr Stephen van Vlack, whose unwavering support began before my studies in Ireland, for his enormous encouragement and guidance in life. Sabrina Piras's friendship is also invaluable, and I would like to express my heartfelt gratitude to Sabrina for designing the cover of this book. I also want to thank Edith, Claire, Rita, Stephen, Red and Kumiko for reading parts of this monograph and offering valuable comments. Any mistakes are, of course, my own responsibility and reflect solely on myself.

My greatest debt is owed to my family, who vastly supported me throughout my study here. I would like to thank my siblings Mina, Gina and Shinyeup Kim as well as Won Jung, Taeyong Lee, Hyunjung Park, Eunhye Cho, Kyunglim, Kyungsook and Kyunglan Kim, Dalwon Lee and Chulnam Yang for their love and support. I am also extremely grateful to my aunt, Duksu Kim, for her encouragement and faith in me. Most of all, I would like to state my deepest gratitude to my parents, Boksu and Sechang Kim, who never fail to believe in me, supporting me mentally and financially. Their strength, faith, encouragement and love guided me to where I am, and though it can never be repaid, I dedicate this work to my parents.

List of Abbreviations

Works of Samuel Beckett

C	*Company*
CDW	*The Complete Dramatic Works*
CSP	*The Complete Short Prose 1929–1989*
D	*Disjecta: Miscellaneous Writings and a Dramatic Fragment*
DFMW	*Dream of Fair to Middling Women*
E	*Eleutheria*
ISIS	*Ill Seen Ill Said*
LSB	*The Letters of Samuel Beckett: 1929–1940*
M	*Murphy*
MPTK	*More Pricks Than Kicks*
P	*Proust and Three Dialogues with Georges Duthuit*
T	*Three Novels: Molloy, Malone Dies, The Unnamable*
W	*Watt*

Library archives

UoR	Beckett International Foundation Archives, University of Reading Library
TCD	Trinity College Dublin Library, Department of Manuscripts

Other works

DF	James Knowlson, *Damned to Fame: the Life of Samuel Beckett*
LGR	Melanie Klein, *Love, Guilt and Reparation and Other Works 1921–1945*

Introduction

'Time and grief and self so-called'

Samuel Beckett's nonverbal television play, *Quad* (1982), shows four players rapidly moving across the diagonals of a square, 'each following his particular course' (*CDW*, 451). Beckett explained the movements to Martha Fehsenfeld in rehearsal:

> [As] the figures approach the centre, each makes a 'jerky turn to his left as a diversion away from it.' It may first appear that 'they were avoiding one another, but gradually one realizes they were avoiding the centre. There was something terrifying about it ... It was danger.'
>
> (Cited in Gontarski 1985, 180)

The 'danger zone' (ibid.), as Beckett puts it in an unpublished type-script, might refer to any kind of perilous situation that can be drawn from personal experience. Yet, we might wonder why more than one player is needed. As Beckett's own comment indicates, the players' ini-tial misconception and the subsequent realization that they were avoid-ing 'the centre' not 'one another' is crucial in understanding *Quad*. As one of Beckett's late plays, *Quad* provides a good point of departure for a study of the self in flight and the role of 'others', the psychic representa-tions of the people significant to the subject in the development of the self. I would suggest that the 'danger zone' not only represents the self that is unknown and strange to the subject, but also the self that has incorporated others and has mistakenly conceived them as real objects.[1] It can be argued that Beckett, in this short but symbolic choreography, envisages the complex psychological process whereby the characters

1

realize that they are in flight from the 'self so-called' (*CSP*, 265): the self that has internalized other people and projects its fear onto others. The self that Beckett's works depict is more strongly subject to these psychic others than it first appears.

As Beckett told Morton Feldman in 1976, 'there was only one theme in his life' – his search for the self: 'to and fro in shadow | from inner to outer shadow | from impenetrable self to impenetrable unself | by way of neither' (*DF*, 557).[2] Indeed, Beckett's works often present characters casting doubt on the self and puzzling over the 'impenetrable' and incomprehensible self. As they are uncertain about the self, so are the people surrounding them in what is an equally uncertain physical world. Beckett seems to question the self 'by way of' negating the conventional way of forming such self-identity through national and parental origins, and effacing the traces of such origins. In portraying the quest for the self in his early fiction, such as *More Pricks Than Kicks* (1934) and *Murphy* (1938),[3] Beckett's home country, Ireland, and women are often positioned as objects that the male protagonists reject. As Mary Bryden convincingly shows in *Women in Samuel Beckett's Prose and Drama: Her Own Other*, Beckett's early fiction posits women as material and menacing others resisted by the male subject. Similarly, Ireland, as J.C.C. Mays claims, is 'most important to Beckett as an inheritance to deny' (Mays 1984, 21). Even though Mays's view needs to be amended because the representation of Ireland changes in Beckett's later works, in his early fiction Irish cultural and literary heritage is indeed denied and criticized as John Harrington asserts in *The Irish Beckett*. If both women and Ireland exist in Beckett's early fiction as psychological objects that the male protagonists attempt to expel in search of the self, it can also be argued that they become the objects of loss, the 'lost others'[4] in the later works written after his exile. Proposing that Beckett's self-imposed exile to France in 1937 influenced his representation of women and Ireland, this book examines changes and correlations in this representation in Beckett's oeuvre.

According to Leslie Hill, 'the loss' in Beckett's works 'has always already taken place', and 'does not derive from an event that may be named or determined as an origin' (Hill 1992, 15). As Hill claims, Beckett's oeuvre displays a 'poetics of grieving' (15): the last lines of Beckett's last short prose piece, *Stirrings Still* (1988), for instance, are 'Time and grief and self so-called. Oh all to end' (*CSP*, 265), and his first novel, *Dream of Fair to Middling Women* (1932)[5] cites over 300 entries from Robert Burton's *Anatomy of Melancholy* (1621), a work that analyses the melancholic tradition in literature.[6] Beckett's engagement with the melancholic tradition is not limited to quoting Burton nor to Beckett's own private work on what he called the 'Journal of a Melancholic',[7] an abortive project that he began in Germany in 1936. Beckett also demonstrated his awareness of the literary heritage when he asked Duncan Scott whether Scott 'had ever detected the influence of Burton's *Anatomy of Melancholy* in his own works' (cited in Knowlson and Knowlson 2006, 217).

While such evidence indicates Beckett's participation in the melancholic tradition, it is difficult to entirely agree with Hill's argument that Beckett's position in the 'poetics of grieving' can be mainly 'described as a melancholy one' (Hill 1992, 15). According to Hill, in Beckett's works 'there is no single event that may be identified as the cause of loss' (15), a primary condition of melancholia in Freud's theory. Whereas Beckett's characters do seem to display symptoms that correspond to Freud's model of melancholia, we see that these symptoms are most noticeable in Beckett's works written shortly after his exile, such as his early French fiction, four *Nouvelles/Novellas* (1946) and *Molloy* (1947).[8] In contrast to Hill's claim, all the narrators in these works talk obsessively about the single finite event, the moment of departure from home and their experience in a new place. According to Freud, the patient in melancholia 'cannot consciously perceive what he has lost' as well as the cause of loss (Freud 1991, 253). However, in Beckett's later works, such as *Krapp's Last Tape* (1958), written some time after his exile, the lost loved object is often identified as a woman. Thus, Krapp's symptoms and those of other protagonists do not entirely fit into Freud's model of melancholia. Beckett's 'poetics of grieving' then is not merely limited to the 'melancholy' without any cause or event, nor is it completely independent from one of the key events in his life – exile.

Yet, Beckett's studies of psychoanalytic melancholy, his attempts to incorporate Burton's text into his own works and to write his 'Journal of a Melancholic' significantly reveal his interests in melancholic symptoms even before his exile. These studies of psychoanalysis prefigure not only his consequent research into and interests in psychoanalysis but also his exploitation of such knowledge in his works. It is well known that Beckett undertook psychoanalytic therapy three times a week for two years at the Tavistock Clinic[9] in London between Christmas 1933 and late 1935. During this period,[10] Beckett also intensively studied psychology and psychoanalysis, taking 'a corpus of some 20,000 words of typewritten notes' from 'nine psychological texts' in his 'Psychology Notes'.[11] As Matthew Feldman's thorough examination of the 'Psychology Notes' in *Beckett's Books* highlights, 'much of this material was directed toward a systematic understanding of psychology and psychoanalysis', and also focuses 'on (mainly) psychosomatic symptoms that Beckett thought might be the cause of his physical maladies at this time' (Feldman 2006, 14). The aim of this study is, then, to show that Beckett, knowing psychology and psychoanalysis in depth, uses such concepts and theories in his works, particularly focusing on his exploration of the self and the psychic development of the self in relation to the lost others, and that these lost others are manifested in his works as women and Ireland. If the loss seems to have always already taken place in Beckett's works, the reason, I argue, can be found in part in the very early psychic and emotional development of the infant and the experience of the loss of the first love-object, which continuously affects the adult's psychic processes. Beckett's self-imposed exile to France can be regarded as an event that reactivates and intensifies the sense of loss that is closely linked to his relationship with the first love-object, his mother.

Beyond mourning and melancholia

Beckett's 'intentional, deliberate, [and] calculated' (O'Hara 1997, 9) use of psychology and 'elaborate presentation of materials taken from Freud' (11) have been demonstrated in J.D. O'Hara's *Samuel Beckett's Hidden Drives* and Phil Baker's *Beckett and the Mythology of Psychoanalysis*. In addition to the intertextual evidence, Beckett's knowledge of Freudian psychoanalysis and concepts is also apparent in his 'Psychology Notes': the section entitled 'Id, Ego & Superego' summarizes Freud's Lecture XXXI in *New Introductory Lectures on Psychoanalysis* (1933). Two sections extensively cover books by Freud's chief disciple, Ernest Jones – 'Freudchen [Little Freud]' as Beckett puts it – and the section on Jones's *Papers on Psycho-Analysis* (1923) explores 'Freud's Psychology'.[12] However, as Feldman rightly points out, existing psychoanalytic literary criticism on Beckett's texts tends to concentrate on his engagement with Freudian ideas (and some Jungian theory) even though his 'Psychology Notes' 'display much more interest in psychoanalysis as such rather than solely Freudian conceptions' (Feldman 2006, 81).[13] With regard to the subject of loss and grieving in Beckett's writing, this tendency is persistent, as critics like Hill focus on Freudian melancholia in which the lost object is effaced.[14] Baker also persuasively shows the Freudian models of mourning and melancholia represented in Beckett's works. While Freud's 1917 essay 'Mourning and Melancholia' is also important to this study, I contend that critical discussion of Beckett's representations of loss must move beyond the Freudian binary distinction of mourning and melancholia. As the following passage from Beckett's own notes taken from Freud's theory of melancholia under the section of Jones's *Papers on Psycho-Analysis* demonstrates, Beckett was not simply absorbing psychoanalytic theories, but actively interpreting them:

> Melancholia: After some deprivation connected with loved object the subject has withdrawn his love from that object, but instead of transferring it to some new one, as the normal person would, or introverting it on to unconscious fantasies, as the neurotic does, or on to the ego, as the paraphrenic does, he replaces it by narcissistic [love] of himself with former object, thereby no doubt regressing to original narcissism of his love-making. Thus the ego becomes split, the conscious part criticising, abusing & hating the unconscious part formed by fusion with idea of object. It is this ability to treat oneself as object that leads to suicide. Freud places fixation point of melancholia at oral phase of libido. (So that a baby denied the breast at 2 months might reasonably become a melancholic.)[15]

When comparing Beckett's summary with the original text by Jones, it becomes evident that the notes were taken according to Beckett's interests. Jones's summary of Freud's theory of melancholia, for example, starts with descriptions of general symptoms of melancholia, rather than the ego's response to the lost loved object. Beckett's understanding of Freud's melancholia, described in the first sentence, colours the characterization in his early French fiction, the *Novellas* and *Molloy*, when the male narrators refuse to 'transfer' a loved object 'to some new one' after the loss occurs.

What is most fascinating, however, is Beckett's comment in parentheses where he attempts to apply Freud's idea of melancholia to the infant's psychic development. Whereas the original text by Jones explains that the 'fixation-point characteristic of melancholia' can be placed in the 'oral phase of the libido' (Jones 1923, 63), Freud's essay does not spell out the link so clearly; he only briefly comments on the process whereby the ego incorporates the loved object 'in accordance with the oral or cannibalistic phase of libidinal development'.[16] Freud's point here is to suggest the cannibalistic oral phase as the prototype of a process of identification that can be associated with melancholia rather than to claim that 'a baby denied the breast at 2 months might reasonably become a melancholic'. This is, however, crucial in Melanie Klein's theory, in which the infant's defence mechanisms (melancholia among them) against the loss of its first love-object, the mother's breast, are not only comparable to the adult's reaction to their loss of the loved one, but are also 'revived whenever grief is experienced in later life' (*LGR*, 344), and so continuously affect the adult's psychic development. As Chapter 4 will show, in Beckett's *Film* (1963) the male protagonist, in experiencing the impending death of his mother, visits her house, and looks at the photograph of his mother and himself when he was an 'infant' (*CDW*, 333). Klein's theory, therefore, is helpful in examining the way in which Beckett reveals the link between characters' symptoms in relation to the loss of the loved ones and their infantile experiences.

Even though Beckett's therapist was Wilfred Ruprecht Bion, a prac-titioner who was later to be deeply influenced by Klein and who has been called her 'most original follower' (Hinshelwood 1989, 61), Beckett studies tend to minimize the Kleinian aspect[17] within Beckett's works because Bion, as Lois Oppenheim asserts, was not yet qualified as a psychoanalyst, and 'only had two years of training when Beckett came to the Tavistock Clinic' (Oppenheim 2008, 432). Since Bion joined the group of Kleinian analysts only in 1946, Steven Connor claims, it is unlikely that the psychoanalyst with whom Beckett worked in the mid-1930s was a Kleinian,[18] and that Bion (or Beckett) would have been exposed to Klein's theory and method before this time. *The Grove Companion to Samuel Beckett*, however, states that 'Bion recommended to SB [Samuel Beckett] *The Psycho-Analysis of Children* (1932)' (Ackerley and Gontarski 2004, 299) written by Klein, although no evidence of Beckett's response to this text has been found.[19] Furthermore, Beckett's letter to Nuala Costello on 27 February 1934 suggests that he was famil-iar with Klein as well as with Karin Stephen, the author of *Psychoanalysis and Medicine: a Study of the Wish to Fall Ill* (1933; hereafter *The Wish to Fall Ill*, following the running headline in Stephen's book and Beckett's own heading in his notes), notably the first book summarized in his 'Psychology Notes'.

In this letter, Beckett puts Stephen's name alongside Klein's, suggest-ing that in his mind they are connected. While listing 'animal houses in Regent's Park Zoo', Beckett includes the names of practitioners whose consulting rooms, according to Martha Fehsenfeld and Lois Overbeck, 'might be found in the vicinity of nearby Harley Street' (*LSB*, 191): '[...] I spoke of <u>changing</u> for Harley Street and the Zoological Gardens. Of course one does not change, one <u>alights</u>. Alight for Monkey Hill, alight for the Wild Asses House, Small Rodents House [...] alight for Karin Stephen, Melanie Klein, Creighton Miller [for Crichton-Miller] and Burt White, alight to them that sprawl in darkness and in the shadow of – resurrection'[20] (*LSB*, 186, Beckett's emphasis). Although both Stephen and Crichton-Miller, the founder of the Tavistock Clinic, had their consulting rooms in Harley Street,[21] Klein's was located in 42 Clifton Hill as Phyllis Grosskurth's biography of Klein shows (Grosskurth 1987, 200). Also, Beckett does not add the most obvious name to his list, 'Freudchen', Ernest Jones, the President of the International Psycho-Analytic Association, who had his consulting rooms in Harley Street, and whose work Beckett summarized in his 'Psychology Notes'. This suggests that Beckett's list is not simply one of practitioners whose consulting rooms are in geographical proximity to one another, but rather that his stream of consciousness is making the necessary connections, triggered by the word 'alight' and the association of the caged animals (presumably in relation to the constrained libido) with psychoanalysts' (ill-fated) aim. Together with his intriguing comment 'alight to them that sprawl in darkness and in the shadow of – resurrection', the list hints at Beckett's own interests and even perhaps his reading at that time.

Karin Stephen, who is a less well-known psychoanalyst and more familiar to Virginia Woolf scholars as Adrian Stephen's wife, offers a useful link between Klein and Beckett here, and is worthy of attention specifically because the relationship between Klein and Stephen's works has not yet been fully explored. Until the recent dispute among British psychoanalysts regarding whether or not Stephen supported Klein's theory, the relation between their works had been documented only in a few brief reports: in 1925 Klein's six lectures given at 'the house of Karin and Adrian Stephen fired a pre-existing interest in child analysis' (Taylor 1994, 627–8). According to R.D. Hinshelwood, Karin Stephen 'is really very respectful and acknowledges the importance of Klein's contribution to the nature and origins of the superego', and he disagrees with Michael Brearley's comment that Stephen is opposed to Kleinian notions of 'internal objects' (Hinshelwood 2000, 290). Hinshelwood and Brearley's debates focus on Stephen's paper, 'Relations between the Superego and the Ego' (2000), published fifty-five years after it was originally given to the British Psycho-Analytical Society. However, when studying her works in detail, including *The Wish to Fall Ill*, it becomes clear that Stephen is influenced by Klein particularly in regard to the concepts that are crucial in this study, such as infantile sadism, guilt and rage, and to Klein's ideas of introjection and projection. The titles of Stephen's following papers, for instance, indicate the closeness of her interests to Klein's; 'Introjection and Projection: Guilt and Rage' (1934) – which begins by remarking Klein's *The Psycho-Analysis of Children* – and 'Aggression in Early Childhood' (1939). Moreover, Stephen, quoting

The Psycho-Analysis of Children, praises Klein as 'a leading pioneer' whose research of 'conscious and unconscious reactions of young children' has 'added a fresh field to psychoanalytic research', and writes that such views 'were regarded as the most important contribution since Freud' (Stephen 1933, 195). Also, Hinshelwood, when talking about the reception of *The Psycho-Analysis of Children* in Britain, puts Stephen in the list of the 'future members of the non-aligned, independent group' who 'were as respectful [to this book] as [Klein's] own followers' (Hinshelwood 1997, 877).

By closely examining the Kleinian concepts explored in Stephen's *The Wish to Fall Ill* alongside Beckett's own transcriptions of the book, this study introduces important ideas from Klein's theory that will be shown to be imperative to Beckett's works. Even though Stephen's text was written earlier than Klein's major essays, such as 'Mourning and its Relation to Manic-Depressive States' (1940) in which she established her theory of loss, I argue that the most important ideas in Stephen's text are not only developed from *The Psycho-Analysis of Children*, but also share much in common with Klein's theory. I attempt to read Klein through Stephen and through Beckett's reading of Stephen because Klein added significantly to Freud's theory of mourning and melancholia, and developed her theory of loss further than Freud to include symptoms such as mania and paranoia as reactions to the loss of the loved object. While Freud's models of mourning and melancholia are pertinent in certain works of Beckett, many of his characters' responses to their lost loved ones do not entirely fit in either of these models. However, Klein's essays, 'A Contribution to the Psychogenesis of Manic-Depressive States' (1935) and 'Mourning and its Relation to Manic-Depressive States', are useful in exploring paranoia in Beckett's *Film* and Winnie's 'manic'[22] – in Beckett's own word – symptoms in *Happy Days* (1961) as responses to the loss of the loved ones.

'I am what her savage loving has made me.'

Shortly after the death of his father, William Beckett, in 1933, Samuel Beckett suffered from night sweats, sensations of suffocation, panic attacks accompanied by palpitations and, 'when his condition was at its most severe, total paralysis'.[23] His doctor friend, Geoffrey Thompson thought that Beckett's symptoms (accompanied by a number of other physical symptoms, such as 'a cyst') might be of psychosomatic origin, and advised Beckett to attend the Tavistock Clinic in London (*DF*, 167). In the opening session, Beckett presented himself to his psychotherapist,

Wilfred Bion, with 'severe anxiety symptoms' (169). Given the circumstances, it is not surprising that Beckett's intensive study and note-taking of psychoanalysis started with Stephen's *The Wish to Fall Ill* whose title suggests its concentration on such psychosomatic symptoms. Beckett underlined the thesis of Stephen's book at the beginning of his summary: 'Thesis: <u>Psychogenic symptoms are defences designed to prevent anxiety from developing when repression threatens to give way</u>' (cited in Feldman 2006, 108, Beckett's emphasis).

Given Beckett's transcriptions from Stephen's book, his interests in anxieties and their relation to the infant's psychic development must have grown out of his close reading of *The Wish to Fall Ill*. It is important to note that Beckett's introduction to psychoanalytic texts began with Stephen who was 'never comfortable with anything orthodox' (Orr 2004, 22). Even though Stephen uses Freudian theory, she makes clear that she is modifying Freudian views, as does Klein. For instance, immediately after introducing Melanie Klein as 'a leading pioneer' who has undertaken 'considerable modifications' on the origins of 'neurotic guilt', specifically referring to *The Psycho-Analysis of Children*, Stephen introduces 'the older' (meaning Freudian) 'psychoanalytic view on the subject of guilt and conscience': 'they were derived from the punishments inflicted by parents and nurses for "naughty" behaviour' (Stephen 1933, 195). On the following page, however, Stephen claims:

> This old theory of guilt, however, is not adequate to explain all the facts; guilt cannot all be due to harsh training, since it appears as strongly, or even more strongly, in children who have been brought up with great lenience. The view now being taken is much more that the root of the trouble is *the child's own destructive impulses*, with which it reacts to frustration.
>
> (Stephen 1933, 196, emphasis added)

Klein and Stephen's view of infantile aggression as innate and of guilt as a product of the infant's own destructive impulses rather than the influence of the super-ego inflicted upon it by parents clearly deviates from Freud's theory and this view is also significant to this study. Beckett's first exploration (at least in terms of his first serious research on psychoanalytic concepts) of the Oedipus complex and the castration fear which is closely related to the concept of 'neurotic guilt' also starts with Stephen who, again like Klein, takes a different stance from Freud's.

The castration complex, which is closely linked with the Oedipus complex, is often found in Beckett's works. The differences between the theories of Freud and of Klein and Stephen about those two concepts are essential and worthy of greater explanation. According to Freud, the Oedipus complex plays a fundamental part in the structuring of the personality: the boy's incest wishes are frustrated through fear of castration by the father, and consequently 'a severe super-ego is set up as its heir' (Laplanche and Pontalis 1980, 437), as Beckett observed in his 'Psychology Notes'.[24] Stephen, however, attempts to correct the 'misunderstanding' of the popular view on 'these notorious "incest wishes" and the famous "Oedipus complex"' by stating that 'it is not because the first attempts at love are usually "incestuous" that they sometimes result in the neurotic repudiation of sexuality' (Stephen 1933, 182–3). Rather, 'this first "incestuous" love' is critical in the child's psychic development because 'in so far as it seeks satisfaction in a physical sexual sense, it is doomed to disappointment' (183). She continues to argue that this 'mixes rage with the original love, giving rise to conflict and tension which may lead to repression, with the result that emotional development becomes arrested' (183). That is, in Stephen, as in Klein, the main reason why the Oedipal period is critical is not because the 'incest-barrier' causes repression through the 'instruments of castration', but because the infant's first ambivalent feelings, created by the mixed feelings of disappointment, rage, fear and original love affect our emotional development.

While the Freudian concept of the male castration complex introduced in Stephen's book and transcribed by Beckett is pertinent in his early fiction, his portrayal of unusual female castration anxiety – manifested in *Happy Days* in Winnie's traumatic childhood memory of being bitten by a mouse – can also be argued as a concept that he acquired from Stephen and Klein. The female castration fear not traceable to Freud is visible in Klein and Stephen since in their theories what is more important than the paternal threat is infantile sadism, the wish to attack the mother's body.[25] As Beckett noted, 'the child desires father's penis to be taken from him or it & the mother's genital to be injured' (TCD MS 10971/7/3). The child's aggressive wish to attack its parents and the consequent 'fear of their revenge' produce 'Fears of genital attack from [its] parent[s]' (10971/7/3). Using these ideas, Chapter 4 contends that Winnie's 'Mildred' story reveals a hidden anxiety that is the counterpart of the castration anxiety and a manifestation of the infantile persecutory fear that is found in Klein's theory. Infantile aggression plays a very important role in Klein and Stephen's theory because 'the child's own omnipotent destructive fantasies' (10971/7/4) towards its parents cause not only anxiety, 'fear of explosion of anger (suffocation) or of retaliation' (10971/7/2), but also a sense of guilt. Furthermore, the baby's rage, mixed with its original love towards the mother, provokes an emotional ambivalence. In Klein and Stephen's theory, such emotional ambiguity, rather than sexuality or desire, is the overriding problem with which the infant and later the adult both have to cope. The infant's conflict, which stems from fluctuating emotions of love and hate, becomes the cause of acute anxiety and is at the root of what Klein terms the 'depressive position', which shares symptoms with melancholia. Beckett also pays much attention to 'ambivalent emotion' and its relation to melancholia: 'Excessive self-control, resulting from excessive parental control of excretory functions, tends to inhibit aggression & produce loss of initiation & power to stand up to circumstances, as well as to turn the aggression in upon the subject & produce melancholia' (10971/7/2).[26]

What is remarkable, then, is how far Beckett's notes, even though melancholia is not central to Stephen's book, summarize a theory that is identical to Klein's theory of melancholia, the depressive position in relation to the infant's parent: 'introjection of parent, producing internal conflict, self-hatred, -love, -denial, -fear, & perhaps melancholia & suicide' (10971/7/3). These notes show how both Stephen and Klein's texts have contributed to Beckett's own understanding of melancholia and impelled him to highlight the connection between melancholia and the infant's psychic development when summarizing Freud's ideas on melancholia in the later section of the 'Psychology Notes'. Beckett's interests in the infant's ambivalent relationship with its parents and the symptoms of melancholia are likely to be derived from his own troubled relationship with his mother. As James Knowlson's biography of Beckett, *Damned to Fame*, suggests, Bion's 'analysis must have focused on the intensity of his mother [May Beckett]'s attachment to him and his powerful love-hate bond with her' (*DF*, 172). While it is not my intention to diagnose the symptoms which Beckett is said to have exhibited, it does seem important to point out how such symptoms affected 'his interest and the intensity of his personal involvement' (172) in exploring psychoanalytic texts during his psychotherapy sessions.

When undergoing sessions centring on his relationship with his mother, ideas such as 'Parent imagos, fantastic creations reflecting the child's own intentions' (TCD MS 10971/7/4) must have appealed to Beckett; helping him to distinguish his 'real' mother from the maternal imago, as his detailed summary on the concept in his 'Psychology Notes' suggests. In Klein's theory, the infant builds up its inner relationship with parent imagos rather than with its real parents. Also, 'the idea of them [parents] to be split, into the familiar easy person & the terrifying sexual monster' (10971/7/3) is one of the earliest defence mechanisms to be brought into play against the loss of the first love-object. Paraphrasing Klein's theory through Beckett's notes, in the infant's 'phantasy'[27] it is not just the mother who is fragmented and split into good and bad objects, but 'the breast his first love-object' (10971/7/1) is also perceived as split and polarized: as a 'good object' when the infant is satisfied by feeding, and as a 'bad object' when the infant's desire is frustrated. It is also important to note that the super-ego, which constitutes the persecutory fear, is formed through not only the stern real parents and 'excessive parental control' but also through harsher 'introjected'[28] parents. So, 'no matter how mild the real parents', 'the Imagos of an aggressive self-assertive child are terrifyingly primitive' (10971/7/4). The imago is an internalized representation of a parent or 'unconscious prototypical figure', which forms an 'emotionally charged personal stereotype', and is 'built up on the basis of the first real and phantasied relationships within the family environment'.[29] It can be argued that Beckett's maternal imago manifested in his works is closely linked to his own psychoanalytic knowledge, yet the 'emotionally charged' nature of this imago inevitably influences the representation of the mother.

Writing of Beckett and his mother, Knowlson reports that it is 'difficult to know exactly what precipitated their final and most bitter quarrel, which caused Beckett to leave Cooldrinagh and Ireland, never to live there again' (*DF*, 251). Beckett's letters to Thomas MacGreevy dated 28 September and 6 October 1937 reveal his 'angry yet hurt' feelings caused by the separation from his mother:

> I was wrong in thinking I was well enough to deal with her and with myself in relation to her. Now I give up une fois pour toutes [once and for all]. [...] I am what her savage loving has made me, and it is good that one of us should accept that finally.
>
> (*DF*, 252)

The words 'savage loving' epitomize Beckett's ambivalent emotions towards his real mother; they also imply that his maternal imago is both terrifying and loving. What is also intriguing is that after these remarks he continues 'And if a telegram came now to say she was dead, I would not do the Furies the favour of regarding myself even as indirectly responsible. Which I suppose all boils down to saying what a bad son I am. Then Amen. It is a title for me of as little honour as infamy' (*LSB*, 553). What we see here is Beckett's comparison of his separation from his mother with Orestes's matricide. However, it is not the first time that Beckett has made this allusion. In his first published fiction, *More Pricks Than Kicks*, a story entitled 'Ding Dong' describes the male protagonist Belacqua's flight from Dublin. Here, the narrator describes himself and Belacqua as 'Pylades and Orestes' (*MPTK*, 40). Belacqua's compulsion 'to move constantly from place to place' is to give 'the Furies the slip by merely setting himself in motion' (39). The mother figure is absent from the fiction, but the influence of Beckett's maternal imago is there, and Belacqua's flight from the introjected mother is implied. With this in mind, the next section outlines male protagonists' 'projection'[30] of their fear onto female characters and their consequent flights from women as seen in Beckett's early fiction. These ideas will be considered in greater detail in Chapter 1.

Women and Ireland as Beckett's lost others

According to *Damned to Fame*, one of the biggest conflicts Beckett had with his mother especially around the period when he wrote his early fiction, *More Pricks Than Kicks* and *Murphy*, was related to her 'dislik[ing]'[31] and not understanding his artistic style as well as to her demands for him to get a proper job. While this is not to suggest that Murphy's girlfriend, Celia, is Beckett's maternal imago, it is interesting to note that she is given the role of 'trying to wheedle Murphy into seeking gainful employment' (*DF*, 203). It is also telling that 'she quotes the exact words that Beckett's mother used to him' when she is said to be attempting 'to make a man of him' (203). As Knowlson points out, 'Murphy's reply vents the frustration and tension that had built up between Beckett and May' (203). The plot of the novel can be broadly summarized as the story of Murphy, suffering the Cartesian split between the body and the mind, and attempting to find a sense of self by expelling Celia. At the beginning of the novel Murphy claims, 'I distinguish. You, my body and my mind. [...] In the mercantile gehenna [hell], [...] to which your words invite me, one of these will go, or two, or all' (*M*, 39–40). Murphy detests the material world or the 'big world' as he puts it, and what he pursues is 'his mind' represented as the 'little world' (178). Nevertheless, since Murphy cannot ignore his bodily desires, he is also attached to Celia. Murphy's identification of his body with Celia is thus presented as 'The part of him that he hated craved for Celia, the part that he loved shrivelled up at the thought of her' (8). Because Murphy cannot be free from his sexual desire and Celia, he tries to join the big world that her 'words [urging him to get a job] invite'.

In the end, however, Murphy manages to reject Celia, who stands for the body, and the following indicative example reveals a psychologically critical process of introjection, projection and abjection. Some time after Murphy has left Celia, she says:

> 'At first I thought I had lost him because I could not take him as he was. Now I do not flatter myself.' A rest. 'I was a piece out of him that he could not go on without, no matter what I did.' A rest. 'He had to leave me to be what he was before he met me, only worse, or better, no matter what I did.' A long rest. 'I was the last exile.' A rest. 'The last, if we are lucky.'
>
> (*M*, 234)

Celia 'was a piece out of him', the object that was expelled from Murphy. His struggle to expel Celia, however, also significantly shows that she has been first introjected, as his identification of his body with her suggests. In this novel we see Murphy, in the first place, move to London, 'wandering to find home' (*M*, 4) to escape from another female character, Miss Counihan. Celia is associated with sexuality, so too Miss Counihan is portrayed as sexually provocative, as the one who attempts to entrap Murphy in 'Cork County [where he felt] Depraved' (6). Even though Murphy's conflicts originate with his own sexual desire, he projects his dread and need of it onto the female characters as if it is only women who push him to engage with the body. In *More Pricks Than Kicks* this tendency whereby the female characters are portrayed by the narrator as devouring and menacing is persistent. Like Murphy, Belacqua is presented as being torn between the mind and the body and in constant flight, attempting in this case to escape the confines of Dublin city centre.

It is also notable that both Belacqua and Murphy's quests for the self, their acts of separation from the female characters, equate with leaving the geographical spaces in which the women reside. Murphy leaves Miss Counihan and Cork to go to London, and as Celia's wishful words show, Celia and London could be 'the last exile', the last exile in the big world at least. However, in so far as Murphy also longs for the body, he cannot successfully pursue the quest for the self and the mind. This conflict can only be resolved through his death, by expelling his body and Celia, and leaving the physical world. The male protagonist's attempt to seek the self through expelling the woman and also expelling himself from where she belongs, then, can be compared to Julia Kristeva's notion of abjection. As Anna McMullan points out in her 'Irish/postcolonial

Beckett', 'in order for the bounded identity of the self/nation to be defined' the other 'is abjected or disidentified with', and 'Beckett's early work posited women as material and often suffocating others' in such a sense (McMullan 2004, 105). What McMullan highlights here is the similarity in the process of forming identity of the self and nation, that is, by way of abjecting the other. In this psychologically significant process, according to Ernesto Laclau, 'political or national borders are founded in order to offer an imaginary coherence and identity which will mask the lack or loss at the heart of our fantasies of identity' (McMullan 2004, 105).

Agreeing with McMullan, I also argue that in *More Pricks Than Kicks* and *Murphy* the male protagonists, in the constitution of their identity, attempt to abject the others that are represented as women and Ireland. As Chapter 1 demonstrates, Beckett emphatically resists the search of the Irish Free State for its national identity and literary tradition by 'Gaelicising' (Watson 1994, 30) itself and 'through an externalization of the other via drawing of political frontiers' (McMullan 2004, 105). Neither Belacqua nor Murphy seem to succeed in forming the desired identity, even in 'fantasies', as what are displayed are their struggles and attempts to sever their relationships with both women and Ireland in order to search for the self by way of negating them. Yet, Ireland and women do not appear as lost objects in Beckett's early fiction since the male protagonists are unaware of having lost something important. Murphy, after having left Celia, thinks 'how her efforts to make a man of him had made him more than ever Murphy; and how by insisting on trying to change him she had lost him, as he had warned her she would. '"You, my body, my mind [...] one must go"' (*M*, 190). Murphy emphasizes that Celia has lost him, evading the realization that the reverse was also true: that he too had lost her.

While the main intention of this study is to explore women and Ireland as lost others in Beckett's works using a psychoanalytic frame-work, it is also important to show the intricate correlations between the detailed representation of women and Ireland. Consequently, Chapter 1 concentrates on how closely women and Ireland in *More Pricks Than Kicks* and *Murphy* are bound up with one another, both existing as objects that the male protagonists need to expel for their quest for the self. It can be further argued that Beckett's desire for exile is manifested through the male protagonists' attempts to detach themselves from the females in his early fiction. Conversely, in Beckett's later works, written after his exile, Ireland tends to stand for a place in which the male protagonists left their loved ones behind. More importantly, as if recalling the memory of Ireland also invokes that of the lost loved one, the characters display similar emotional reactions to both women and Ireland.

Memory is one of the central themes in Beckett's oeuvre and much Beckett scholarship has delved into the subject. As H.P. Abbott claims in *Beckett Writing Beckett: the Author in the Autograph*, memory in Beckett's works needs to be considered beyond the autobiographical elements. Abbott writes that 'Beckett's work can be best understood as self-writing or [...] autographical action', that 'responds to writing not as a mode of recovery or reconstruction or even fictionalizing of the past but as a mode of action taken in the moment of writing' (Abbott 1996, ix–x). The aim and emphasis of this book similarly rely neither on merely identifying biographical facts nor on claiming that what Beckett does is to tell the story of his life, but on examining what is manifested in his texts. However, the act of recollecting memories, even for a writer like Beckett whose artistic practice largely concerns controlling emotion, inevitably evokes emotions; even more so if the memory is related to the lost object. The caustic representations of women that are in part resonant with biographical experience in Beckett's early fiction seem to provoke an emotional response and to affect the writing and representation of women in his later works. Narrative attempts to repress the memories of women and Ireland in Beckett's early French fiction, for instance, can be read as a melancholic disavowal of the loss of the loved ones and therefore as an emotional reaction.

What is excluded and abjected from oneself, however, 'can never be fully obliterated but hovers at the borders of our existence' and threatens 'the apparently settled unity of the subject with disruption and possible dissolution' (Grosz 1989, 71), as Kristeva's notion of abjection suggests. Beckett's French fiction written shortly after his exile displays just such a troubled self, a self which is disturbed by the lost others that are abjected from the male narrator. The *Novellas* and *Molloy* show a fascinating tension that arises from the narrators' contradictory feelings towards fading yet haunting memories of both Ireland and women; between their attempts to exorcize the memories and their compulsion to repeat the story. Karin Stephen pays attention to something rather like the concept of Kristeva's abjection: 'what was once desired is often transformed into an object of aversion' (Stephen 1933, 125). Like Kristeva, Stephen uses the idea of 'infantile excretory processes', and shows that excrement is 'both dreaded & desired by the subject' (TCD MS 10971/7/2) as Beckett notes.

Kristeva's abjection is going to be useful in exploring Beckett's *Premier amour/First Love*[32] where the male narrator's confused state after having expelled Lulu is represented in an excremental vision[33] of him contaminated by 'cowshit' (*CSP*, 34). However, the use of the term 'abjection' – or rather, of the concept of abjection – in this study has been slightly modified from Kristeva, following my reading of Stephen and Klein's theories. In Kristeva's theory, the infant forms its sense of the self by repressing its earlier stage as an 'undifferentiated being' or what Kristeva refers to as the '*chora*'[34] and through the act of expelling and abjecting the mother's body. Rather than considering the *chora* as representing the status quo, it seems important to emphasize that, as Klein claims, the infant is an undifferentiated being as a result of the process of projection, or 'projective identification in which the baby projects itself onto the mother and then re-identifies with her' (Minsky 1996, 7), and that it eventually introjects her inside of itself in phantasy. Such Kleinian concepts will be helpful when applying abjection to the ongoing psychic development of both adults and Beckett's characters, wherein the infant's first experience of abjecting the mother influences later reactions to the loss of the loved objects through a similar process of introjection and projection.

Love, guilt and reparation

In Beckett's plays written before *All That Fall* (1956), women are either absent, as in *En attendant Godot/Waiting for Godot* (1952/1954), or when they are present, as in his early fiction, they are vehemently resisted by the male protagonists. In Beckett's later drama, however, as both Bryden's *Women in Samuel Beckett's Prose and Drama* and McMullan's *Theatre on Trial* persuasively show, women are no longer posited as silenced others. Instead, women start to speak in their own voices in his plays from *All That Fall* onwards. As Bryden observes, Beckett's works display 'a progressive tendency [...] from rigid gender polarity towards a radically destabilised gender base' (Bryden 1993, 1). (Indeed, Beckett's fascinating writing, which disturbs the rigid boundary between the speaking subject and object, is an outcome of his persistent efforts to create a new voice and experiment with language. These are some of the many factors which contribute to his being one of the greatest writers of the twentieth century.) Beckett's 'destabilised gender base' and the move to the female subject in his later drama can be considered as the outcome of his interest in women's historically marginalized position.[35] As McMullan states, 'perhaps, in the same way that Beckett shifted from English to the French language in order to dispossess himself of his English textual heritage, he adopted the historically excluded female position in his drama in order to explore the alienation of the female subject in relation to self, language and representation' (McMullan 1993, 74). In his later drama, Beckett attempts to restore the others who have been abjected from the self, and to embrace and understand these lost others by adopting the female position. Moreover, Beckett's later works, as Chapter 4 and 5 demonstrate, recuperate not only culturally and historically marginalized women in general, but also the female who was ridiculed and expelled in his early fiction.

Such an intertextual element in Beckett's works is also suggested by Stephen Connor in *Samuel Beckett: Repetition, Theory and Text*. Drawing attention to 'the internal allusions to and citations from [Beckett's] own texts', Connor claims that 'characters and situations, ideas and phrases, recur irresistibly between fiction and drama, as well as between the different forms of drama that Beckett has produced since the 1960s'[36] (Connor 1988, 2). Certain repetitions in Beckett's drama since the 1960s are cohesively related to what I would call his project of revision: restoring the female subject that has been damaged and abjected in his early fiction. As his biographer, Anthony Cronin, observes, Beckett's 'moral torment' – from which he suffered until late in life – is closely linked to the hostile 'portrait' of women such as Smeraldina Rima, a reminiscence of his cousin and first love, Peggy Sinclair (Cronin 1997, 578). Born of this sense of guilt, I argue, in his later works such as *Footfalls* (1975) and *Rockaby* (1980) Beckett attempts to reconstruct the female subject that has been damaged and silenced in his early works.

The sense of guilt in Klein's theory plays a crucial part in the creative impulse. The creative urge, for Klein, is closely associated with the child's aggressive wishes and 'a destructive attack on or by persecutors – its introjected parents – in phantasy' (Hinshelwood 1989, 263). Out of guilt and remorse, the baby attempts to restore the damaged objects through the process of what Klein calls 'reparation', through repairing the damaged objects and restoring them as good objects within the self. Klein's theory of artistic creation will be useful in understanding Beckett's urge to create female characters in his later plays and in discussing his writing from the 1960s onwards as an act of recuperating the voice of the lost objects, the females who are abjected from the self, as well as restoring them. Situations, ideas and phrases that recur irresistibly in Beckett's texts need to be considered not just as simple repetition, but as recreations of similar situations in order to revise them, as Connor's emphasis on 'the junction of difference and repetition' in Beckett's use of repetition suggests (Connor 1988, 11).

Since Beckett's manuscripts offer valuable opportunities further to locate the close relations between the representations of the female in his works, this study explores his manuscripts as well as his texts. S.E. Gontarski's study of the evolution of Beckett's dramatic manuscripts in *The Intent of Undoing in Samuel Beckett's Dramatic Texts* and Rosemary Pountney's *Theatre of the Shadows* will also be useful in serving this purpose. The aim of *The Intent of Undoing* is to show Beckett's artistic tendency towards abstraction by 'undoing' and 'vaguening'[37] personal, cultural and historical material during his creative process; in this study it will be of value in disclosing a psychologically important motivation behind the process of undoing. For example, the first three pages of 'J.M. Mime' – a piece that Beckett abandoned in 1963 and reshaped as *Quad* – indicate various geometric patterns of movement moving across the diagonals of a square. 'The mime aspect of the play', however, is evidently dropped, and from page four it 'introduces a dialogue between a mother and her son'.[38] Such evidence suggests that Beckett had a mother in mind at the inception of *Quad*, and makes it possible to argue that at the core of the 'danger zone' which the self fears lies the internalized '(m)other'.

As James Olney's *Memory & Narrative: the Weave of Life-Writing* convincingly tells us, memories are inescapably suffused with emotion, and Beckett had to find ways to control emotion in his writing, such as through writing in French. Olney claims, 'It was with the intention, I believe, of clothing memories in a language that had for him no tentacular roots in memory, a language that was therefore safer, more formal and abstract than the intensely charged medium of English, that Beckett decided, when memory became in all ways central to his work, to write in French' (Olney 1998, 347). Beckett's early French fiction written shortly after his exile exemplifies Olney's view. If, as Adam Piette claims, Beckett's works tend to 'mock memories' (Piette 1996, 198) as an act of 'fabricated remembering' (201), this is particularly the case with his early French fiction written when the emotional affect of recent exile was at its greatest. Such intense emotion seems to influence Beckett's representation of memory in the French fiction where the male narrators show melancholic repression of what they have lost. Beckett's French fiction, however, is not the only work in which memory is central: *Company* (1979), for example, concentrates on childhood memories drawn from Beckett's own life. If his plays do not seem to centre on memories, it is because, rather than talking about memories, he envisages his memories of the lost others on stage using a theatrical language that verbal language cannot offer. Theatre, as Michael Robinson asserts, 'allows Beckett a double freedom; the opportunity to explore the blank spaces between the words and the ability to provide visual evidence of the untrustworthiness of language' (Robinson 1970, 230). As the famous last scene of *Waiting for Godot* – 'Yes, let's go. [*They do not move.*]' (*CDW*, 88) – shows, what Beckett attempts to explore in his drama is not just how language betrays gestures. His drama also displays the emotions that his prose writing often betrays and represses.

Memories, emotions and theatre

This study began from a single point of observation: when Beckett's works have a woman as a protagonist or speaker, he goes back to the English language of Ireland and also often creates a more conspicuously Irish setting. *All That Fall* is one of the examples that I had in mind. *All That Fall* is Beckett's second work written in his mother tongue after having abandoned the language for nearly ten years.[39] It is suggested that Beckett wrote *All That Fall* in English because it was the BBC who invited him to write a radio play. Perhaps triggered by the use of his mother tongue, the play is 'flood[ed]' (*CDW*, 176), in Mrs Rooney's word, with childhood memories of Foxrock, his home town in Ireland. Mrs Rooney can be seen as the first female protagonist given a voice of her own, and I would argue that a female voice was Beckett's inevitable choice in order to assuage his uneasiness in expressing his own longing for Ireland.

In the Western literary tradition, as Juliana Schiesari claims, mourning and the expression of grief have received a negative response with the sole exception of the elegy. They have also been allocated to the female domain while melancholia and control over emotion have been regarded 'as a privileged form of male expression' in literary practice (Schiesari 1992, 12–13). Such a cultural/gendered codification of mourning, however, has also made it difficult for men to express their loss or grief. As Jahan Ramazani points out, many male writers borrow a female voice in order to relieve their anxiety in expressing their grief and in breaking the social and cultural codification of mourning (Ramazani 1994, 20–1). To some extent, Beckett's *All That Fall* corresponds to such a gendering of mourning and melancholia: whereas Mr Rooney – like the male narrators in Beckett's early French fiction – attempts to repress his emotion, and shows symptoms of melancholia, Mrs Rooney mourns openly for her loss and displays her grief through other kinds of pathological behaviours, such as hysteria. Borrowing her nostalgic voice, Beckett's childhood memories of Ireland are ventriloquized.

Beckett's first use of the female voice in *All That Fall* represents a seminal point in his works, triggering subsequent efforts to explore the female subject position as well as expanding the possibilities that theatre can offer him. On the one hand, as Hélène Cixous claims in 'Difficult Joys', theatre gives people a chance to explore a potentially uneasy topic through taking another person's position: 'They appear, although they say "I", as "she" or "he", but not "me" – which is the reason why, I feel, some people write for theatre, because they can be extremely violent and at the same time, not very violent' (Cixous 1990, 21). Cixous talks about violence, but her point can also be applied to emotion and to Beckett, who borrows the female voice to express feelings. On the other hand, taking up the female position also seems to offer Beckett the opportunity to understand his own significant others and to move away from the focus on the self and from the burden of 'searching for the non-pronounial' that avoids the subject pronoun, 'I'.[40] Hence, this study investigates not only the gender dynamics in Beckett's oeuvre but also his exploration of self and others.

Chapter 1 examines the ways in which Beckett's representation of the female in his early fiction is closely related to his resistance to the Irish Free State and the Celtic revival movement that is represented by the works of W.B. Yeats. Further, this chapter argues that the male protagonists' attempt to achieve detachment from the possessive women in Beckett's early fiction gives expression to the author's desire for exile as well as a desire to distance himself from the predominant literary nationalism. James Joyce's influence on Beckett's works, particularly in his early fiction, is unquestionable.[41] However, since Beckett does not show the change from earlier rejection to later embracing of Joyce's works that he does with respect to Yeats's works – a dynamic that is essential in this study – Joyce does not feature prominently here. By choosing self-imposed exile to Paris, Beckett also seems to follow a similar artistic path to that which Joyce chose rather than resisting his senior.

Chapter 2 explores Beckett's early French fiction, written shortly after his exile, and argues that the narrators' ambivalent attitudes towards memories of severance with Ireland and women correspond to Freud's model of melancholia. Within this model, Beckett's country is itself the lost object creating pathological symptoms of melancholia in the narrators. Chapter 3 investigates the ways in which the representation of the female and Ireland start to change in Beckett's English drama, written more than a decade after his exile. Although Beckett's male characters still show symptoms of melancholia towards their memory of the loss of women and their Irish homeland, they start to present signs of moving towards the work of mourning. Female voices allow Beckett to develop alternative ways of using memories by opening the opportunity for women to express nostalgia towards the past and to overtly mourn for their loss.

Chapter 4 argues that in his early 1960s drama Beckett turns significantly towards lost others and away from his earlier Freudian focus on the narcissistic self. Klein's emphasis on the inner world of the ego in relation to the lost object offers a helpful framework for a discussion of Beckett's study of the lost others in general and the mother in particular. Beckett's use of pathological symptoms such as mania and paranoia is discussed with the help of Klein's theory of the loss of the loved object. Chapter 5, using what Klein calls the 'reparation' process as a model, explores the ways in which Beckett recuperates the lost loved objects in his late works, and reconstructs the female subject that has been damaged and silenced in earlier writing. This chapter argues that through the reparation process, Beckett not only expresses his own sense of loss, but also attempts properly to understand and to embrace his lost others. By closely examining how the representation of Ireland and the female are bound up with one another throughout Beckett's oeuvre, using a psychoanalytic framework, this study aims to shed new light on Beckett's literary practice and to contribute to the fields of Irish and feminist studies.

1
Severing Connections with Ireland: Women and the Irish Free State in Beckett's Early Fiction

I Introduction

> 'Haven't we had enough of that in this festering coun-
> try. Haven't we had enough Deirdreeing of Hobson's
> weirds and Kawthleens in the gloaming hissing up
> petticoats of sororarrhœa?'
>
> *(DFMW,* 197)

So says the Alba, one of three young women with whom the male protagonist Belacqua liaises in Beckett's first novel, *Dream of Fair to Middling
Women* (1932). Here, the Alba is attacking the Celtic 'twilight' (197)
literary movement, specifically referring to two legendary Celtic hero-
ines, who are best represented in J.M. Synge's *Deirdre of the Sorrows*
(1910; Synge 1996), and W.B. Yeats's *The Countess Cathleen* (1892) and
Cathleen ni Houlihan (1902; Yeats 1952). The Alba savagely mocks the
Celtic 'twilight': '"The mist", she sneered, "an' it rollin' home UP the
glen and the mist agin an' it rollin' home DOWN the glen." Up, down,
hans arown ... Merde. Give me noon. Give me Racine.'[1] As the young
Beckett himself favoured Racine, so the Alba expresses her own prefer-
ence for the French playwright over contemporary Irish dramatists.[2]
When Beckett reworked the Alba story in his second fiction, *More Pricks
Than Kicks* (1934), he omitted these lines. Yet, they can be seen to
exemplify Beckett's female characterization in his early fiction, in both
More Pricks Than Kicks and *Murphy* (1938), as well as his attitude towards
the Irish literary tradition of the 1930s when these prose works were
written. In comparison to Beckett's other works, there are a considerable number of female characters in *More Pricks Than Kicks* and *Murphy*.
However, these women are represented as grotesque, devouring and

23

sexually provocative. This chapter examines the ways in which this form of representation is closely related to Beckett's resistance to the Irish Free State and the Celtic revival movement by showing that such characterization can be attributed to his impulse to satirize the Celtic revivalists' portrayal of the idealized Ireland-as-woman.

While the subsequent chapters concentrate on women and Ireland as Beckett's lost others, this chapter will focus on the ways in which his male protagonists' fear of devouring women in his early English fiction is inflected and influenced by his relationships with Ireland and the Anglo-Irish literary tradition. The representation of women in Beckett's early fiction continues to impact on his later female characterizations. In order to understand this issue, we need to trace Beckett's conscious relationships with the Anglo-Irish tradition and with the Irish Free State; relationships that underlie the hostile representation of women in his early work. Underneath Beckett's conscious resistance to woman-as-Ireland, there seems to be also a subconscious and psychologically complex resistance to the elements of women and home. Having already introduced Beckett's early female as the abject entity expelled from the subject in the formation of the self, this chapter will concentrate on establishing the relationship between women and Ireland in *More Pricks Than Kicks* and *Murphy*.

II   Ireland-as-woman

The Irish literary tradition of the 1930s

In order to approach Beckett's female representations in relation to Ireland and the Celtic revival movement, I will first investigate his attitude towards the existing literary tradition at the time when *More Pricks Than Kicks* and *Murphy* were written. According to J.C.C. Mays, 'Ireland is most important to Beckett as an inheritance to deny, or set of appearances to go behind, or a range of authorities to disagree with' (Mays 1984, 21). Based on Beckett's artistic theory in his essay *Proust* (1931) that the progress of an artist is one of rejection, Mays claims 'To sum up: the traces of Ireland and Irish writers in Beckett's writing are present in order to be denied' (25). Beckett's representation of Ireland and the Irish literary tradition cannot be summed up so simply, however, since the representation changes to one far less hostile in his later works. Yet, Mays's argument is particularly relevant to *More Pricks Than Kicks* and *Murphy*, in which the young Beckett applied the artistic theory of rejection argued in *Proust*. The Ireland of the 1930s, when those works were written, can be represented as standing in Beckett's work for what he saw as the 'insular and exclusionist cultural nationalism' (Harrington 1991, 57) of the new Catholic Free State. What the young Beckett resists, then, is the predominant nationalistic literary tendency adopted by the Celtic twilighters, and for him, the 'literary models most associated with the Celtic twilight, fairly or unfairly, were Synge and Yeats' (Harrington 1991, 63). During the Irish colonial period, W.B. Yeats and J.M. Synge were involved in nationalism, establishing a national literature symbolized by the Abbey Theatre and recovering legendary figures such as Cathleen ni Houlihan, Deirdre and Cuchulain. In Beckett's early fiction, it is this aspect of Yeats and Synge that is central to his critical engagement with their nationalistic legacy.

The representation of nation as woman is, of course, a classic feature of nationalist discourses. Yet, such a representation was particularly pervasive in the literary history of the Irish revival. As Marjorie Howes points out, figures such as Fair Erin, Cathleen ni Houlihan, Dark Rosaleen and *Cailleac Beare* (the Crone of Beare) became hallmarks of the revival movement, and 'often are treated as the one thing its various competing literary and political movements had in common' (Howes 1996, 44–5). This was precisely how the young Beckett diagnosed the Irish literary tendency of the 1930s. In his review of 'Recent Irish Poetry' (1934), Beckett attacks the emptiness of the theme advanced by 'the leading twilighters', writing that 'At the centre there is no theme. Why not? Because the centre is simply not that kind of girl, and no more about it' (*D*, 71). Considering 'that kind of girl' as particularly referring to the theme of a feminized Ireland imagined by Celticism, I argue that Beckett's hostile representation of the female in *More Pricks Than Kicks* and *Murphy* can be attributed in part to his resistance to a feminized Ireland. If the Celtic revivalists imagined and worshipped Ireland as an unliberated woman who would be set free through the sacrifice of male heroes, and who later on functioned as a republican icon on the political agenda of the Free State, Beckett in reaction exploits and ridicules such an allusion to Ireland-as-woman in order to satirize the Irish Free State, the literary revival in general, and Yeats in particular.

'Nobel Yeats' and Beckett

Yeats was actively engaged with Irish nationalism from his early allegiance to his final rejection of it. Importantly, his representation of women also changes as his relationship to Ireland evolves. While the later Yeats proclaimed his resentment towards the Catholic state and its censorship, what the young Beckett sees in Yeats is still the Celtic twilighter who contributed to establishing the Irish Free State in which the political successors to men like Yeats were setting up a Catholic conservatism that restricted cultural and sexual freedom as well as determining the literary tradition of the 1930s. In 'Recent Irish Poetry', Beckett categorizes 'contemporary Irish poets' by dividing them 'into antiquarians [who are] in the majority'[3] and 'others [who are] kindly noticed by Mr W.B. Yeats as "the fish that lie gasping on the shore", suggesting that they might at least learn to expire with an air' (*D*, 70). As his own categorization implies, the young Beckett diagnoses recent Irish poetry as being dominated by the antiquarians who marginalize 'the younger Irish poets' – working at something different – as 'others' (70). Yeats, to whom the 'others' are 'the fish that lie gasping on the shore', is the 'leading twilighter' (71) of the former group. When recollecting his article 'Recent Irish Poetry', Beckett described it as a review of 'late work by W.B. Yeats',[4] showing how central Yeats was to Beckett's understanding of the Irish literary landscape at this time. One of Yeats's late works mocked by the young Beckett is 'The Tower': '[Yeats's] bequest in "The Tower" of his pride and faith to the "young upstanding men" has something almost second-best bed' (72). By comparing the older poet's 'will' – which declares that his chosen 'upstanding men' 'shall inherit' his 'pride' and 'faith' – to Shakespeare's grudging and mean-spirited bequest to his wife, Beckett ridicules both Yeats and his chosen Irish people.[5]

It is interesting that later, while in exile, Beckett's response to the same poem shifts from mockery to admiration. According to Anne Atik, 'The Tower' was 'particularly significant for [Beckett]' and 'the congruence of language with visual imagery' in the poem 'made him turn to Yeats so often' (Atik 2001, 67–8). Beckett's admiration of the poem is reflected in the title of his play *...but the clouds...* (1976), which is a quote from 'The Tower'. Beckett's new found respect for Yeats is not merely limited to his poetry but also includes his drama. Deirdre Bair and Gordon Armstrong report that Beckett's earlier disinclination towards Yeats's poetry stood in contrast to his interest in Yeats's plays:

> In the past, [Beckett] had deliberately shunned Yeats's poetry and knew only his most famous poems – those which no Irishman living in Dublin could avoid – and had concentrated on the plays, for which he had great respect and admiration. There were lines in The *Countess Cathleen* that he knew by heart, and passages from *At the Hawk's Well* that never failed to move him.[6]

Beckett's 'great respect and admiration' for Yeats's plays, however, only appears in works written some time after his exile, when his attitude

towards Yeats had changed. Beckett, for instance, quotes the first line of
At the Hawk's Well (1917) in his play *Happy Days* (1961). The main character, Winnie, recalls 'unforgettable' (*CDW*, 160) lines from the classical
canon of English literature – Shakespeare, Milton and Keats. Compared
to the 'wonderful' (140), 'exquisite' (164), and 'immortal lines' (166)
from the rest of the classical canon, which Winnie fails to recall entirely,
Yeats's 'I call to the eye of the mind' (164) is evoked without any difficulty in order to 'call upon the spirit of Yeats to assist her' (Worth
1978, 256) when she tries to tell an emotionally charged story. As James
Knowlson observes, Beckett has scrupulously recorded the authorship
and location of Winnie's 'wonderful lines' in his production notebook
(Knowlson 1985, 144). According to Knowlson, those unforgettable
lines have clearly been chosen with considerable care and with concern
for their relationship with important themes of the play.

However, whereas Milton's 'Oh fleeting joys – [*lips*] – oh something
lasting woe' (*CDW*, 141) is presented in fragments, Yeats's line is quoted
intact. This suggests that Beckett plainly wanted the phrase from Yeats
complete in the play while Milton's line is a more arbitrary choice.
Instead of 'oh fleeting joys' from Milton's *Paradise Lost*, Beckett's early
typescript draft of *Happy Days* indicates with its note 'First words of
famous line – transitoriness of all things – Bible possibly' (cited in
Knowlson 1985, 144). This does not diminish the importance of the
attention Beckett pays to the rest of the canon. Yet, it does show
Beckett's particular familiarity with and interest in Yeats's works, hinting at a psychologically complex motivation behind Beckett's use of the
senior Irish poet. Yeats's line is not included in the part of the manuscripts where Beckett identifies the literary allusions – even if it exists
from the early stage of the manuscripts. The line is only 'included in
the list of allusions [that] Beckett sent to Alan Schneider' and in his
production notebook (Gontarski 1977, 77). Thus when the reference to
Yeats's works comes up again after two decades, it appears as though it
sprang unbidden to his mind in comparison with the more calculated
selection of Milton.

While Beckett's homage to Yeats as well as his curious and psychologically significant association of the 'woman lost' (Yeats 1996, 305) in
'The Tower' with Beckett's own 'woman lost' will be explored in later
chapters, here we will look at the ways in which the young Beckett's
resistance to Yeats centres on Yeats's early portrayal of the female as
abstract beauty. In *More Pricks Than Kicks* Beckett quotes from Yeats's
At the Hawk's Well in order to ridicule Yeats's romanticized descriptions
of woman, his 'embroideries' (*D*, 71), as Beckett puts it. In the story,

'A Wet Night' (*More Pricks Than Kicks* is comprised of a collection of ten short stories), the main protagonist Belacqua Shuah is supposed to join a party with the Alba, the woman he is pursuing. When he is killing time in a pub before going to the party, he reads an advertisement for a 'corset-builder' in a paper:

> 'A woman' he read with a thrill 'is either: a short-below-the-waist, a big-hip, a sway-back, a big-abdomen or an average. If the bust be too cogently controlled, then shall fat roll from scapula to scapula. [...] [The corset-builder] bestows stupendous diaphragm and hip support, it enhances the sleeveless backless neckless evening gown ...'
>
> (*MPTK*, 58)

As Susan Brienza has observed, while the magazine parodies women's figures as 'desperately need[ing] to be lifted or bound' (Brienza 1990, 94), the advertisement makes Belacqua curious as to whether the Alba's dress will be 'backless' since she, who is not a 'woman of flesh', has 'no waist, nor [does] she deign to sway', and is not 'to be corseted' (*MPTK*, 58). 'Unable to bear any longer his doubt as to the rig of the gown', he phones the Alba's house to find out what she will be wearing. The Alba's maid, Venerilla, answers the phone, and tells him that she is afraid of going to check this because the Alba is in a bad mood. Therefore, Venerilla has to try to recall the Alba's outfit and she calls here upon the spirit of Yeats to assist her: 'Venerilla requested him to hold on while she called it to the eye of the mind' (59). Here, as Brienza points out, the narrator 'delights in degrading and debasing his paramours' by overturning not only 'the literary convention of celebrating the lover's beauty' (Brienza 1990, 94) in general, but also, I would argue, Yeats's relationship with this tradition in particular.

Beckett's intentional mockery of Yeats is clear in another story, 'Walking Out'. Belacqua's fiancée Lucy is described with specific reference to Yeats: 'Indeed she was better than lovely, with its suggestion of the Nobel Yeats, with her jet of hair and her pale set face, the whipcord knee and the hard bust sweating a little inside the black jersey' (*MPTK*, 114). The tone of this passage suggests that the narrator does not admire Lucy's beauty, but rather rejects the word 'lovely' because of its association with Yeats and with regard to his idealization of the female body. Later on, we realize that the title 'Walking Out'[7] indicates Belacqua's attempt to escape from Lucy 'on the very eve of their nuptials' (116). By showing Belacqua's resistance to a woman with 'better than lovely' Nobel Yeatsian features, by devising an accident whereby

Lucy is crippled and noting that she 'expired [...] in the twilight' (118), Beckett simultaneously satirizes the Celtic twilight and Yeats's idealization of the female body – which the narrator refers to as 'itemis[ing] her poor body' (113).

The Countess Cathleen and *Cathleen ni Houlihan*

Beckett is not simply criticizing Yeats's glorification of female beauty, his target is Yeats's representation of Ireland-as-woman. As most critics agree, Yeats's early plays, *The Countess Cathleen* and *Cathleen ni Houlihan*, which were written while he was deeply involved in Irish nationalism and the discourse of Celticism, are outstanding examples of this figuration. In *More Pricks Than Kicks* and *Murphy*, then, the young Beckett ridicules the female characters who embody the personification and spirit of Ireland in order to attack and devalue the Catholic state's social and sexual conservatism, and much of the satire is directed towards Yeats's *The Countess Cathleen* and *Cathleen ni Houlihan*. To this end, Yeats's first play, *The Countess Cathleen*, whose lines Beckett 'knew by heart' (Bair 1993, 527), is his first target. The ten short stories in *More Pricks Than Kicks* concern Dublin in the 1930s, and as John Harrington states, the stories 'most integrally centre on protest to the images of the revival' (Harrington 1991, 62). Harrington argues that Beckett satirizes the Celtic twilight in the story 'Ding-Dong' 'in the form of pastiche Cathleen Ni Houlihan' (63), pointing out the parallels between Yeats's visionary and romanticized description of Cathleen and Beckett's abuse of the same style, which he assigns to a female pedlar. Harrington's detailed comparisons between the two works are helpful. Yet, 'Ding-Dong' shows more parallels with Yeats's other play *The Countess Cathleen* than *Cathleen ni Houlihan*.

Like the poet Aleel in *The Countess Cathleen*, in 'Ding-Dong' Belacqua is a poet both marginalized and ridiculed by people in the public house. While he is 'sitting paralysed and grieving in a pub', and 'wait[ing] for a sign', the 'mysterious pedlar' (*MPTK*, 46) suddenly appears to Belacqua as if in response to the desire for a sign, as if she will save him from his 'paralysed' state. The narrator's exaggerated description of the pedlar is indeed a parody of the Countess Cathleen, whom Aleel praises:

> Her speech was that of a woman of the people, but of a gentlewoman of the people. Her gown had served its time, but yet contrived to be respectable. [...] But her face, ah her face, was what Belacqua had rather refer to as her countenance, it was so full of light. This she lifted up upon him and no error. Brimful of light and serene,

serenissime, it bore no trace of suffering, and in this alone it might be said to be a notable face.

(MPTK, 46–7)

The pedlar's countenance, 'full of light', echoes specifically the last scene of *The Countess Cathleen* when she enters 'the gates of pearl [heaven]' while the 'light beats down [...] on her face' (Yeats 1952, 50). The narrator's overstated portrayal of the pedlar and his use of the 'sign' satirizes 'the Celtic twilight in the form of pastiche'.[8] The main plot of *The Countess Cathleen*, which is her saving of the Irish peasants' souls during a famine by sacrificing her life, is distorted and caricatured in 'Ding-Dong' when the pedlar woman reveals her mysterious identity as one who comes to sell 'Seats in heaven' (*MPTK*, 47). Her advertisement for 'Seats in heaven, tuppence apiece, four fer a tanner' (47) parodies the pervasive materialistic tendency in Dublin, echoing the peasant Shemus's cry, 'Money for souls, good money for a soul' in *The Countess Cathleen* (Yeats 1952, 22). Yet, in Beckett's story, it is the mocked Countess Cathleen herself who announces the 'Seats in heaven'. In addition, whereas the Catholic peasants haggle with the demons over the price of their souls in *The Countess Cathleen*, in Beckett's story the ridiculed Cathleen haggles with Belacqua in order to sell more seats. *The Countess Cathleen* once caused a riot because such scenes as the peasants' haggling over their souls 'inflamed Irish religious sensibilities' (Watson 1994, 66). By deliberately appropriating Yeats's Countess Cathleen, Beckett attacks the religious consciousness of the people of Dublin in the 1930s, deflates the religious principles of the theocratic government, and fails to allow for the possibility of an ideal Ireland beyond its materialistic people.

Yeats's most famous nationalistic play, *Cathleen ni Houlihan* feeds into Beckett's characterization of the female in *Murphy*. Beckett presents several variations on Yeats's characterization of Cathleen ni Houlihan, among them the barmaid 'Cathleen na Hennessey' (*M*, 46). This name is used in order to hint at the main characters' alcohol consumption in an 'underground café' at 'holy hour' (46) – a compulsory bar closing hour from 2.30 to 3.30 p.m. on Sundays following the Intoxicating Liquor Acts of 1927 introduced by the Catholic Free State:

> 'But by Mooney's clock,' said Wylie, 'the sad news is two-thirty-three.' [...] 'There there,' said Wylie. 'Needle knows no holy hour.' He led the way to an underground café close by, steered Neary into an alcove and called for Cathleen. Cathleen came. 'My friend Professor

Neary,' said Wylie, 'my friend Miss Cathleen na Hennessey.' [...] 'Two large coffees,' said Wylie. 'Three star.'

(*M*, 46)

As C.J. Ackerley notes, Hennessey's three-star brandy is 'the Alba's favorite painkiller' (Ackerley 1998, 49). Here, Yeats's Cathleen ni Houlihan, representative of the spirit of Ireland, is ridiculed by association with a brand of spirits and the characters' underhand violation of a law brought in by the new state. Moreover, it is Cathleen who serves the alcohol and helps to defy the ban, lending her once noble image to the act of undermining Catholic rule. By satirizing Yeats's image of the republican symbol of Ireland, Beckett criticizes the repressive regime of the Free State.

Miss Counihan, another character in *Murphy*, is also considered as 'the contemporary embodiment of Cathleen ni Houlihan' (Ackerley 1998, 10), as the closeness in their names shows, Miss Counihan's name being an abbreviated version of Cathleen ni Houlihan. Mays argues that Miss Counihan is 'Ireland's Kathleen Ni Houlihan, whom the novel's characters chase round in circles at a distance from anything central' (Mays 1984, 23). As Yeats's Cathleen impels the protagonist, Michael, to join the French army to fight against England in order to set her free, so in *Murphy* Miss Counihan drives male characters like Neary and Wylie to chase after Murphy. Yet, Miss Counihan is motivated by something more selfish than Cathleen ni Houlihan's patriotism and determination to gain independence. Rather, Beckett uses Miss Counihan in order to raise sensitive moral questions about the Catholic state, presenting her characteristics in opposition to those of Yeats's Cathleen. Miss Counihan, like Cathleen ni Houlihan, is described as being loved by many men. However, unlike Cathleen ni Houlihan who is represented as a pure virgin and herself declares 'With all the lovers that brought me their love I never set out the bed for any' (Yeats 1952, 84), Miss Counihan appears to have affairs with both Wylie and Neary, even though she still claims to love Murphy. For example, while chapter 10 starts with the announcement that 'MISS COUNIHAN and Wylie were not living together!' (*M*, 195), the narrator nonetheless hints at their affair. Later in the same chapter, she is found on Neary's bed, again with the implication of an affair. Such representations of the contemporary embodiment of Cathleen ni Houlihan further highlight Beckett's attempt to raise moral issues pertinent to the Catholic state. After the lengthy description of Miss Counihan and Wylie's 'oyster kiss' (117) in Wynn's Hotel, the narrator reveals his intention: 'The above passage is carefully calculated to deprave the cultivated reader' (118). This is Beckett's riposte to the Irish Censorship of Publications Act of 1929 on 'Evil Literature' which mentions literature 'inciting to sexual immorality or unnatural vice or likely in any other similar way to corrupt or deprave' (*D*, 84) as quoted by Beckett in his 'Censorship in the Saorstat'. By juxtaposing the representations of Miss Counihan as a satirized version of Yeats's Cathleen ni Houlihan and as a lustful female figure who is 'just like any other beautiful Irish girl' (*M*, 118), Beckett contrives to attack both the Catholic state and its excessive censorship laws.

Developing this theme, the relationship between Miss Counihan and Wylie also satirizes the political situation in Ireland when *Murphy* was written. The narrator uses the metaphor of Partition – with its notable political resonance – while hinting at Miss Counihan and Wylie's affair: 'the partition of Miss Counihan and Wylie had more concrete grounds' (*M*, 195). This alludes to the conflict between the Free State and Northern Ireland as a result of Irish Partition after the Civil War. Whereas Yeats's Cathleen ni Houlihan appeals for her freedom as a symbol of Irish independence, Beckett's caricatured Cathleen celebrates the 'partition', and claims she 'had to be free to twist Wylie and this was perhaps her best reason for keeping him at a distance' (196). In his describing these 'concrete grounds' for Miss Counihan and Wylie's 'partition', however, the narrator reveals their dirty tricks: how they 'bribed and browbeat Cooper' (196), who is their agent and informer, in order to get information about Murphy. Immediately after describing in detail their tricks – cheating and betrayal – the narrator observes that: 'Such were the chief grounds for the partition, which was not however so inflexible that they could not contrive, now and then after supper, to meet on neutral ground and compare notes and ruts' (*M*, 197).

Meeting on neutral ground and comparing notes is what Irish politicians did during the Partition period. The narrator caricatures the political situation of Ireland by juxtaposing the Irish Partition with Miss Counihan and Wylie's 'partition' which is achieved by cheating, bribing and browbeating. Allusion to the Partition continues when Wylie comments on Miss Counihan after discovering her affair with Neary: 'I continue to regard [...] Miss Counihan as the only nubile amateur to my certain knowledge in the Twenty-six Counties who does not confuse her self with her body, and one of the few bodies, in the same bog equal to the distinction' (*M*, 216–17). Certainly Miss Counihan does not confuse 'her self with her body' since she claims her love for Murphy while having affairs with both Wylie and Neary. Here the narrator again identifies 'nubile' Miss Counihan as a representative of women in Ireland, thus ridiculing the image of Cathleen ni Houlihan as a personification of Ireland, yet also distinguishing between the Irish Free State and Northern Ireland. By clearly asserting 'Twenty-six Counties' (thereby excluding the six counties of Northern Ireland), the narrator of *Murphy* shows that his target is the Catholic Free State. Using this political allusion in the disclosure of Miss Counihan's affairs with other male characters, Beckett again emphatically resists the Catholic state, particularly in terms of what it saw as immoral.

Beckett continues his demolition of Yeats's Cathleen. Towards the end of *Murphy*, he parodies the famous last line of Yeats's *Cathleen ni Houlihan* – 'I did not, but I saw a young girl, and she had the walk of a queen' (Yeats 1952, 88) – which refers to Cathleen's transformation from a withered hag to a radiant young queen. Here is a long passage about Miss Counihan's walk:

> Miss Counihan rose, gathered her things together, walked to the door and unlocked it with the key that she exiled for that purpose from her bosom. Standing in profile against the blazing corridor, with her high buttocks and her low breasts, she looked not merely queenly, but on for anything. And these impressions she enhanced by simply advancing one foot a pace, settling all her weight on the other, inclining her bust no more than was necessary to preserve her from falling down backwards and placing her hands upon her moons, plump and plain.
>
> (*M*, 219–20)

The phrase 'she looked not merely queenly, but on for anything' is particularly reminiscent of Cathleen's 'walk of a queen'. However, apart from the word 'queenly' the narrator's descriptions of her as 'on for anything' dismisses Yeats's idealized female's body and manner. Descriptive vocabulary such as 'high buttocks' and 'low breasts' is also intended to provoke 'the word "indecent"' which the Censorship Act listed in 'Part I' (*D*, 84). By making his satirized version of Yeats's Cathleen serve alcohol at 'holy hour', 'incite sexual immorality', and celebrate 'partition', the young Beckett unleashes a fierce attack on the female icon of republicanism.

As we have observed so far, the young Beckett's hostile representations of women are closely related to his resistance to the Irish Free State. By ridiculing Yeats's (female) personification of Ireland, Beckett works to undermine the Catholic state's policies as regards religious, social, cultural and political issues. On the other hand, as we will see in the next section, while criticizing the presentation of Ireland-as-woman, Beckett also mobilizes it himself when he expresses his desire for exile through male protagonists who are in pursuit of freedom from women.

III   Woman-as-Ireland

Cailleac Beare and Deirdre: devouring females

Yeats's *Cathleen ni Houlihan* provides a further intriguing analogy with those of Beckett's early female characters who are threatening, devouring and sexually provocative. *Cathleen ni Houlihan* is thought to have originated as *Cailleac Beare* – the 'Crone of Beare' (*D*, 71), a magically powerful old hag with whose legend the young Beckett was familiar. The *Cailleac Beare* is construed as one of the earliest representations of woman-as-Ireland. According to Celtic tradition, the *Cailleac Beare* is 'miraculously restored to youth and beauty' from her old, ugly and crazed status when she succeeds in persuading 'some intrepid male to make love to her' (Cullingford 1993, 67). In turn she offers the lover kingship, sovereignty of the land. Yet, as Elizabeth Cullingford points out, in *Cathleen ni Houlihan* 'Yeats's version of the *Cailleac* demands not sex but the death' (67) of a young male like Michael in order to free Ireland from its colonizers. In Beckett's early fiction, the threatening elements of the *Cailleac Beare* as a devouring female are pervasive in his female representations. However, whereas Yeats's Michael in *Cathleen ni Houlihan* chooses self-sacrifice for the motherland, Belacqua and Murphy are constantly attempting escape from female characters who use their sexuality to entrap the male protagonists in the earthly world, which is specifically defined as Ireland. Before discussing the male protagonists' attempts to detach themselves from the female characters as a manifestation of Beckett's desire for exile, I first examine his exploitation of the *Cailleac Beare* and similar female figures from the Celtic tradition.

Mary Bryden accounts for Beckett's caustic portrayal of his early female characters in relation to another figure from the Celtic tradition, *Sheela-na-gig*. As the *Cailleac Beare* is grotesque and sexually provocative, Bryden argues that the 'menacing female figure of the *Sheela-na-gig*, with its exaggerated and gaping sex organ, powerfully embodies the overwhelming nature of the female presence for the Beckettian male' (Bryden 1993, 34). In *More Pricks Than Kicks*, Belacqua's numerous partners, the Alba, Ruby, Lucy, Thelma and the Smeraldina[9] are all grotesquely described, and objectified through animal imagery such as 'a kind of duck or a cobra sneer to the nostrils' (*MPTK*, 190), but most of all, they are associated by Belacqua with sexuality. Similarly, Miss Counihan in *Murphy* is presented as a grotesque anthropoid with a large mouth, which suggests a devouring female, emphasizing her sexuality. The narrator comments that 'For an Irish girl Miss Counihan was quite exceptionally anthropoid', and the 'kissing surface was greater than the rosebud's' (*M*, 118). What is highlighted in Beckett's early fiction is not only the satirization and caricatural imagery of the female body, but also an inversion of the male and female roles represented in romantic literary convention. In contrast to passive Belacqua and Murphy, the female characters are threatening figures with an assertive desire to change the male protagonists. According to Bryden, this feature can also be traced to the Celtic legends of Deirdre and Grainne:

> In this connection, it is significant to note that Beckett in his 'Whoroscope' notebook at one point draws attention to enterprising women within Celtic legend, his entry instancing Deirdre and Grainne as examples of two such female initiative-takers. Beckett's interpretation is interesting. There is indeed within these ancient story traditions an element of female assertiveness in the romantic interaction.
>
> (Bryden 1993, 46)

The legends of Deirdre and Grainne are indeed two of the most popular topics picked up by the Celtic twilighters in such works as George Russell (A.E.)'s *Deirdre* (1901), Yeats's *Deirdre* (1906), Synge's *Deirdre of the Sorrows* (1910), James Stephen's *Deirdre* (1923) and Lady Gregory's *Grania* (1910). In the Ulster cycle, the beautiful young Deirdre falls in love with Naoise and elopes with him, escaping from her betrothed, the ageing King Conchubar. Similarly in the Fenian cycle, Grainne evades the unwanted attentions of the hero Finn by falling in love with his nephew Diarmuid, with whom she elopes. In both legends, as Bryden argues, 'the young male partners of these women meet their deaths as a result of complying in the female defiance of the older pursuant' (Bryden 1993, 47). While the young Beckett criticizes the twilighters' recycling of the same theme by commenting, 'Haven't we had enough Deirdreeing' (*DFMW*, 197), he also appropriates the very imagery of Deirdre as 'initiative-taker', emphasizing the threatening and devouring nature of her sexuality while eliminating her legendary physical beauty.

While Belacqua cannot free himself from sexual desire, in *More Pricks Than Kicks* the women are portrayed as compelling the reluctant

Belacqua to sexual encounters with their Deirdre-like 'female assertive-ness'. If Belacqua wants to truly ignore his sexual desire, he should avoid women. On the contrary, however, Belacqua has liaisons with a number of women, and marries three times – with Thelma, Lucy and the Smeraldina. In the story 'Love and Lethe', Belacqua's well-arranged double suicide pact, which might sever his connection with the world, is abandoned owing to Ruby's sexual provocation. Ruby, whose father terms her 'Slut' (*MPTK*, 98), takes off her skirt while climbing a fence, 'looking more bawdy Magdalene than ever' (100–1). Despite Belacqua's appeal to 'put back [her] skirt', Ruby, still insisting 'I prefer it off' (101), manages to arouse him, which leads to 'inevitable nuptial' (105) rather than to the double suicide. In 'Walking Out', Belacqua tries to avoid sexual relations with Lucy, 'urg[ing] her to establish their married life on this solid basis of a cuckoldry' (110–11), with which she refuses to agree. On 'the very eve of their nuptials' (116), Belacqua attempts to escape from Lucy by taking a long walk in 'Croker's Gallops' (109), the suburbs of Dublin. Lucy, however, chases after him and finds him with 'her little manoeuvre' (113). Belacqua, giving various reasons and with much difficulty, manages to push her away. On her way back, Lucy has a terrible accident and becomes 'crippled for life' (118). Since the question of making love no longer arises, Belacqua is later found 'happily married to Lucy' (120).

What is interesting in this pattern – whereby the female characters are described by the narrator as pursuing Belacqua, who resists them yet is unable to be free from them – is that it is in fact Belacqua who projects onto the women his own fear of attachment. When Lucy finds Belacqua 'all alone in the Gallops' (113), for instance, he feels that he 'ha[s] been spied from afar' by Lucy, and 'wonder[s] what the hell she wanted. But it appeared that she did not want anything in particular, she just wanted to be with him' (114). However, in the next line, the narration, which consistently follows Belacqua's point of view, notes that 'This was a falsehood of course, she did want something in particular' (114), as if she intended to demand something from Belacqua. The female gaze mentioned by Belacqua, who thinks that he has been spotted by Lucy, further leads us to consider Deirdre's gaze, which Bryden compares with that of Beckett's early female characters. Bryden argues that 'it is the penetrating female gaze which is decisive, for it is through the stimulus of sight that Deirdre is prompted to approach her quarry' (Bryden 1993, 47). As in the Deirdre story the Celtic twilighters emphasize her gaze and 'initiative-taking when Naoise comes to her attention' (47), so does Beckett. The same kind of female gaze in relation to decisiveness is

presented in the last story of the book, 'Draff', when the narrator introduces the last Mrs Shuah, the Smeraldina:

> This particular Mrs Shuah, as stated thus far at all events, does not
> sound very like Thelma née bboggs, nor [are...] Lucy [...] Ruby [...]
> Winnie [...and] Alba Perdue [...]. Belacqua looked round and the
> Smeraldina was the only sail in sight. In next to no time she had
> made up his mind by not merely loving but wanting him with such
> quasi-Gorgonesque impatience as her letter precited evinces.
>
> *(MPTK, 189)*

It is clear from this passage that the Smeraldina 'had made up his mind'
with her 'quasi-Gorgonesque' manner, and impelled passive Belacqua
into marriage. The Gorgon, like the Medusa, is not only exemplary in
feminist readings as the representation of the male fear of a powerful
female gaze, but also a recurrent image in connection with Beckett's
male protagonists' fear of castration, as Chapter 4 will show.

The role assigned by Beckett to the female characters in *More Pricks
Than Kicks* is to use their sexuality to entrap Belacqua into staying in
the world he is trying to leave. In 'Love and Lethe', as if emphasizing
his wish to escape from Dublin, Belacqua's intended last journey starts
at the heart of the city centre. The narrator describes in detail how
Belacqua drives 'fiercely' (96) and rushes into the Wicklow mountains
to fulfil his wish to die. Yet, as we have observed, Belacqua's plan found-
ers on Ruby's sexuality. Likewise, in 'Walking Out' Belacqua walks out
to the Dublin suburbs in order to achieve privacy, escaping from both
Lucy and the city centre. However, guided by her penetrating gaze,
Lucy chases after him and thus disrupts his solitude. In *More Pricks Than
Kicks*, the female characters are closely linked to Ireland – to Dublin in
particular – in parallel with Belacqua's attempt to be detached from both
women and country/city. It can be argued then that the young Beckett's
desire for exile is represented in Belacqua's resistance to Dublin and
woman-as-Ireland. Moreover, the presentation of women as frightening, clinging, devouring and possessive suggests that the young Beckett
feels Ireland is making demands on him to stay against his will.

'Poets and peasants and politicians': Dublin in the 1930s

Dublin city centre in *More Pricks Than Kicks* embodies the Irish Free State
and is populated with a certain group of people who are closely associated with it. In the story 'A Wet Night', Belacqua makes a detour where
'there was nothing to stop him' in order to avoid encountering 'poets

and peasants and politicians' on a street that the narrator describes as 'a perilous way, beset at this hour with' such people (*MPTK*, 54). Poets, peasants and politicians can indeed be regarded as the representatives of Beckett's hated nationalistic Dublin in the 1930s. Beckett's protagonist, therefore, expresses his abhorrence at being in the centre of Dublin, and tries 'to move constantly from place to place' (39) either to the suburbs or abroad when he can afford to. Belacqua's desire for privacy and 'his solipsism' (39) reflect his discontent with the place where he has his roots, his desires for another world and his search for the self. Whereas Synge attempted to find an ideal world and 'imaginative sense of community in the peasant' (Watson 1994, 40) after his visit to the Aran Islands following Yeats's famous advice of 1896, Beckett seems to believe that no such idealized version of Ireland can exist and it is always sought in vain.

As many critics point out, Synge tried to idealize 'a peasantry untainted by any marks of the "bourgeois", or prosperity' (Watson 1994, 40–1). What Synge praises most highly in the noble peasants and tinkers is particularly characterized as an aloofness from the filthy modern urban setting tainted by prosperity, a distance from modernity valued as wildness. Thus Synge 'asserts again and again the value of the individual who projects himself above and beyond his society' (Watson 1994, 83). It is this image of noble peasantry constructed by Synge that is largely satirized in 'Walking Out'. As Belacqua's escape from Lucy shows, the plot of this story is mainly about achieving privacy. Yet, it is also a parody of idealized peasant nobility and aloofness since the tinker's privacy is violated by Belacqua's dog, which urinates on his trousers: 'This privacy which he had always assumed to be inalienable, this ultimate prerogative of the Christian man, had now been violated by somebody's pet' (*MPTK*, 112). Reflecting the form of pastiche in which the narrator praises the pedlar in 'Ding-Dong', the narrator here caricatures Synge's wildness of the peasantry, eulogizing the tinker's 'most handsome' appearance 'with his thick, if unkempt, black hair and moustache': 'The instinctive nobility of this splendid creature for whom private life, his joys and chagrins at evening under the cart, was not acquired, as Belacqua one day if he were lucky might acquire his' (112).

This search for the 'private life' – by both Belacqua and the tinker – however, is shown to be ridiculous when they actually violate the privacy of others. Belacqua, who becomes furious when he realizes that he has 'been spied from afar' (114) by Lucy, in fact appears himself to spy on the strange German couple (Fräulein and Tanzherr)'s secret 'performance' (119) in 'Tom Wood' (110), a name that clearly suggests a peeping Tom. As a punishment for his hypocritical voyeurism, Belacqua, when discovered, is badly beaten by 'the infuriated Tanzherr' (119). Similarly, if the tinker's own privacy is disturbed by Belacqua and his dog, the tinker is also found to be enjoying spying on Belacqua and Lucy's argument: 'The vagabond could see them between adjoining spokes of his wheel, by moving his head into the right position he was far enough away to frame the whole group in a sector of his wheel' (115). Thus, both Belacqua and the tinker's attempts to achieve a private life are undermined by their own contradictory and hypocritical behaviour. Satirizing Synge's idealization of the peasantry, Beckett exposes the falseness of Synge's construction of the image of peasant nobility through his hyperbolic and contradictory characterization. As the story 'Love and Lethe' shows (in that the name of Synge is invoked to help Belacqua regain his resolve to commit suicide – 'he thought of Synge and recovered his spirits' (100)) the 'private life' both Synge and Beckett seek cannot be found in Ireland, and can only be achieved through the protagonist's death, as happens in the penultimate story, 'Yellow'.

'Wandering to find home'

If *More Pricks Than Kicks* portrays Belacqua's solipsism, his desire for privacy and longing to escape from Dublin through his resistance to the female characters, in *Murphy* the same desire is expressed by the 'seedy solipsist' Murphy himself (*M*, 82). In this novel, Murphy's longing for a private life is described as his desire for the 'little world' that represents his mind, whereas the 'big world' (178) stands for his body, his bodily desire and the material world. The narrator comments, '"I am not of the big world, I am of the little world" was an old refrain with Murphy' (178). Like the women in *More Pricks Than Kicks*, Murphy's partner, Celia, symbolizes his sexual desire, which he tries to resist, as we see in the very beginning of the novel: 'The part of him that he hated craved for Celia, the part that he loved shrivelled up at the thought of her' (8). With her Deirdre-like female gaze and decisiveness, Celia appears to have found Murphy and 'accosted him' (15) while he 'occupied himself with his sheet [his newspaper]' (13) on the street. Celia's sexuality, or rather Murphy's sexual desire for her, instigates his attempts to change himself as Deirdre's sexuality does to Naoise. When Celia insists on his getting a job, showing her 'desire to make a man of Murphy' (65), he tries hard to resist the idea of being changed by insisting, 'Have I wanted to change you? Have I pestered you to begin things that don't belong to you and stop things that do?' (37). When Murphy asks, 'Either I do what you want or you walk out. Is that it?', Celia is persistent, holding her 'position unchanged' (40). She pushes him further to make a decision by making a gesture to leave, and manages to trap him into joining the job market of the big world which he detests.

Later on in this novel, the narrator tells us how Celia was wrong: 'her efforts to make a man of him had made him more than ever Murphy; and how by insisting on trying to change him she had lost him, as he had warned her she would. "You, my body, my mind ... one must go"' (190). While Celia, using *Cailleac Beare* and Deirdre-like sexuality, impels Murphy to attempt to change, neither her love nor their love-making would transform either of them, because Celia is not the queen of the legend and Murphy is not a patriotic male. The following passage, towards the end of the novel, offers another parody of the legend and Yeats's *Cathleen ni Houlihan* as the emphasis on being 'transfigured and transformed' implies:

> Note that of all these reasons love alone did not splutter towards its end. Not because it was Love, but because there were no means at its disposal. When its end had been Murphy transfigured and trans-formed, happily caught up in some salaried routine, means had not been lacking. Now that its end was Murphy at any price, in whatso-ever shape or form, so long as he was lovable, i.e. present in person, means were lacking, as Murphy had warned her they would be.
>
> (*M*, 202)

Here, Celia's 'desire to make a man of Murphy' and to transform him brings about not only the end of their relationship but also his death. Celia and the big world where she belongs are the objects that Murphy attempts to negate and expel in constituting his own self-identity. Whereas the sexually provocative and devouring characteristic of Celia is derived from Murphy's own sexual desire, he cannot pursue his search for the self while he still longs for her body. The tension arising from the contradictory desires – longing for the body and the mind – can be resolved only through his death, by his leaving his body and Celia as well as the big world.

Murphy's resistance to the big world and Celia can be considered as a manifestation of Beckett's own desire for exile. From the beginning of the novel, Murphy expresses his desire to belong to the little world where he can achieve freedom in mind, like 'a mote in the dark of abso-lute freedom' (112). It is implied that this was the reason for moving to London: as he says to Neary, 'wandering to find home' (4), 'Tired. Cork County. Depraved' (6). Emigration to London, however, reinforces Murphy's distaste for the material world, the big world, and reveals that he cannot fit into London life any more than he could fit into life in

Cork. Thus, in *Murphy* the main protagonist attempts to move away from Ireland, and to exile in England, only to fail to find home again. What is intriguing is the fact that although Murphy appears to be in London, woman-as-Ireland – woman taking on the role of Ireland – still exists as threatening and devouring in the novel. For example, sexually-provocative Miss Counihan, representative of Ireland, sends her agents to England in order to bring Murphy back home. Celia, an Irish girl in London, whose face 'combines the colours of the Irish national flag' (Kiberd 1996, 534) – 'Eyes. Green. Complexion. White. Hair. Yellow' (*M*, 10) – as Declan Kiberd points out, appears as a prostitute, and also functions as a devouring provocative female who threatens Murphy. Beckett's intention to portray Celia as woman-as-Ireland becomes clear from a letter to Thomas MacGreevy, written on 8 March 1938. In this letter, Beckett complains of the cover of *Murphy* which was published on the previous day: 'I got some advance copies of <u>Murphy</u>. All green white & yellow. In honour of Celia? They do their best, and not merely with the blurbs, to turn me into an Irishman' (*LSB*, 611).

As we saw in the Introduction, Celia's 'efforts to make a man of him [Murphy]' reiterate 'the exact words that Beckett's mother used' when she is said to be attempting 'to make a man of him' (*DF*, 203). This biographical element shows that the possessiveness of Irish females in *Murphy* is derived from the young Beckett's own conflict between his desire for exile and his ensnarement in Ireland. We see this again in the kite-flying episode that is taken from Beckett's life and used in *Murphy*. His letter to MacGreevy indicates that Beckett always knew that he wanted to use the kite scene for the ending of *Murphy*: 'The book closes with an old man flying his kite' (*LSB*, 274). 'My next old man, or old young man, not of the big world but of the little world, must be a kite-flyer. So absolutely disinterested, like a poem' (274). The role of the kite-flyer in *Murphy* is assigned to Celia's grandfather, Mr Willoughby Kelly. Mr Kelly appears to be the only main character who does not chase after Murphy, but, on the contrary, tells Celia to 'Sever your connexion with this Murphy' (*M*, 24). This advice can be construed as a narrative voice which insinuates Murphy's own desire to achieve detachment from both Celia and the big world. 'So absolutely disinterested' indeed, Mr Kelly's aloofness represents the young Beckett's own desire for detachment from the big world as kite flying symbolizes his wish for escape and exile. However, since the kite will be always bound to the kite-flyer on the ground, this symbol also anticipates Beckett's failure to sever his connection with his country.

The young Beckett's use of hostility as his chosen method of deconstructing the idealized form of woman-as-Ireland simultaneously reveals his ambivalence by presenting both his attack on this naive connection and his engagement with it in parodic but psychologically significant ways. This unresolved conflict in Beckett's early fiction lingers, evolving throughout his works, adding fascinating tensions by revealing repulsion and attachment towards both women and Ireland, and by showing the curious association between the two. In contrast to Beckett's later female characterization, which is broadly in sympathy with feminine style and feminist concerns, his early female characters are grotesques, objectified and remain as 'the other'. Such caustic female representations are largely attributable to Beckett's satirization of the personification of Ireland by the Celtic revivalists, to his resistance to the Irish Free State and to his desire to become a cosmopolitan writer detached from the predominant literary nationalism. Beckett had not yet found his own voice and style when he wrote the early fiction, so that this resistance can be seen as a part of his attempt to apply his artistic theory – defined in his essay *Proust* – that 'the progress of an artist is one of rejection', in which both Ireland and women exist as the other to serve this purpose. In Beckett's later works, however, Ireland and women start to exist as his 'lost others' in relation to which his male characters show symptoms of melancholia. Thus in the next chapter, Beckett's male narrators in his French fiction will be analysed using Sigmund Freud's theory of melancholia. First, however, I will briefly introduce some symptoms, manifested in Beckett's early fiction, that foreshadow the male narrators' melancholia, and also some significant biographical elements that influence his later writing.

IV 'The comic exaggeration of what elsewhere is expressed in elegy'

In a letter to publisher George Reavey written on 13 November 1936, Beckett explains that the 'wild and unreal dialogues' in *Murphy* 'are the comic exaggeration of what elsewhere is expressed in elegy, namely, if you like, the Hermeticism of the spirit' (*D*, 103). In this comment, as the genre, elegy, indicates, one can wonder whether Beckett implies the importance of the theme of loss, the lost 'spirit', represented in *Murphy*, or shows his intention of satirizing elegy in general and the pervasive elegiac tone of Yeats's *Deirdre* and Synge's *Deirdre of the Sorrows* (Deirdre in Irish Gaelic means grief) in particular as, in the Alba's words: 'Haven't we had enough Deirdreeing [...?]' (*DFMW*, 197). While the latter is apparent in both *More Pricks Than Kicks* and *Murphy*, Beckett's own sense of loss is also 'hermetically' presented. Beckett's resistance to the elegiac mode used by the Celtic twilighters is best represented in his treatment of the death of his protagonists. Murphy's last will and testament which 'appears to be addressed to [Celia]' (*M*, 269), for example, is directed to the older generation of Irish writers:

> With regard to the disposal of these my body, mind and soul, I desire that they be burnt and placed in a paper bag and brought to the Abbey Theatre, Lr. Abbey Street, Dublin, and without pause into what the great and good Lord Chesterfield calls the necessary house, where their happiest hours have been spent, on the right as one goes down into the pit, and I desire that the chain be there pulled upon them, if possible during the performance of a piece, the whole to be executed without ceremony or show of grief.
>
> (*M*, 269)

'"Their happiest hours," groaned Miss Counihan' (269) after she hears this will. While 'their' indicates Murphy's own way of seeing himself in the Cartesian mind and body division, it also refers to and parodies Yeats, Synge and Lady Gregory who spent their happiest hours in establishing the Abbey Theatre to 'show that Ireland is not the home of buffoonery [...] but of an ancient idealism'.[10] *Murphy*, however, represents Ireland as just that 'home of buffoonery and easy sentiment' (Harrington 1991, 99), and by directly referring to the Abbey Theatre, Beckett satirizes Yeats and Synge's 'ancient idealism'. By making Murphy address his will to Celia and ask her to execute it 'without ceremony or show of grief', Beckett categorically rejects the excessive elegiac tone of Yeats and Synge's plays about Deirdre, in which Deirdre responds to grief with passionate 'keening', lamenting and wailing after Naoise's death.[11] In Synge's *Deirdre of the Sorrows*, after Naoise's death, Deirdre *'goes up slowly and looks into grave. She crouches down and begins swaying herself backwards and forwards, keening softly'* before *'she presses knife into heart and sinks into the grave'* (Synge 1996, 213, 217). Unlike Deirdre, who kills herself following Naoise's death in both Yeats and Synge's plays, Celia not only refuses to display signs of grief, as Murphy wishes, but also merely 'grasped [the will] to tear it across' (*M*, 269). By satirizing Yeats and Synge's use of the female as a mourner, then, Beckett both appropriates and resists the literary convention of elegy used by his predecessors.

In Beckett's illustration of the practice of mourning in *Murphy*, the novel reveals the socio-historical contexts of mourning as well as the writer's own attitudes towards the social practices involved. As Jahan

Ramazani points out in *Poetry of Mourning: the Modern Elegy from Hardy to Heaney*, from 'the first English cremation in 1882, the numbers rose to ten thousand in 1936', and 'the growing popularity of cremation reflected an ever more scientific, secular, and privatistic attitude toward the dead' (Ramazani 1994, 16). Moreover, as Geoffrey Gorer states, 'cremation is chosen because it is felt to get rid of the dead more completely and finally than does burial' (cited in Ramazani 1994, 16). According to Gorer, the speeding up of the mourning process through cremation reflects the broader tendency of social denial and suppression of grief. The cremation of Murphy coincides with this historical context – the novel, set in London, and completed in 1936. On the one hand, Beckett's choice of the cremation of his protagonist can be seen as his resistance to the cultural codification of mourning such as the wake tradition in Ireland and keening appropriated by the Celtic twilighters. On the other hand, as mentioned in the Introduction, it also suggests Beckett's inclination towards the literary tradition that encourages writers to control and suppress their emotions in talking about their personal experience of the loss of loved ones.

It is important to note that *Murphy* and the stories 'Yellow' and 'Draff' in *More Pricks Than Kicks* that describe Belacqua's death and mourning practices, were written immediately after Beckett's first big losses: the death of his cousin Peggy Sinclair, known to have been his first love, in May 1933, and that of his father in June 1933. Such autobiographical elements feed into Beckett's treatment of the death of the male protagonists and expressions of mourning in his early fiction. As Knowlson remarks, in 'Draff', written later in summer of 1933, 'Belacqua's grave is decorated by his former best man, Hairy, and the Smeraldina. In reality [when his father died], this was done by Beckett in the company of his mother' (*DF*, 166). Furthermore, Belacqua in 'Yellow' dies by accident during the operation for the cyst, 'anthrax', 'on the back of his neck' (*MPTK*, 75, 176). On 3 May 1933, Beckett too had an operation for 'the cyst on his neck', and it was 'as he was lying there, at a low ebb, that he was shocked to learn that his cousin and former love, Peggy, had died of tuberculosis in Bad Wildungen Hospital in the early hours of the day of his operation' (*DF*, 163–4). What is intriguing is Beckett's choice of the Smeraldina as the conductor of the mourning ritual for Belacqua, since, as is well known and confirmed by the author, she is based on Peggy Sinclair: 'She [Peggy]'s the Smeraldina Rima in my work, yes' (cited in Knowlson and Knowlson 2006, 37). In 'Draff' the narrator tells us that among all the female characters, this 'particular Mrs Shua' (*MPTK*, 189), the Smeraldina, is selected for Belacqua's spouse in a story in which the main storyline is about the wife undertaking the mourning process for her husband, as if she is most suitable for the role of his mourner.

'Draff' shows then not only another 'comic exaggeration' of mourning rites that display the social and historical contexts of mourning in Ireland during the 1930s, but also Beckett's attempt to objectify the mourning process by mocking it and displacing its affect. The lengthy illustration of the mourning practices in 'Draff' begins with the Smeraldina reading the obituary of Belacqua and thinking of the mourning procedure she has been through so far:

> SHUAH, BELACQUA, in a Nursing Home.
>
> Though this was stale news to Mrs Shuah, for she had inserted it (by telephone) herself, yet she felt, on reading it in the morning after paper, a little shock of surprise, as on opening telegram confirming advance booking in crowded hotel. Then the thought of friends, their un-assumed grief giving zest to their bacon and eggs, the first phrases of sympathy with her in this great loss modulating from porridge to marmalade, from whispers and gasps to the calm ejaculations of chat, in a dozen households that she could have mentioned, set in a motion throughout her bodily economy, with results that plainly appeared at once on her face, the wheels of mourning. Whereupon she was without thought or feeling, just a slush, a teary coenaes-thesis.
>
> (*MPTK*, 189)

This description of the social customs of the rites of mourning focuses on the hollow practical aspects that lack emotional authenticity. The Smeraldina's 'wheels of mourning' are also merely a gesture of grief 'without thought or feeling'. This is followed by a sequence of mourning processes: the visits of the coffin-maker, the parson and Hairy, and their exchanges of the clichés of sympathy that stand in for grief. When the Smeraldina leads Hairy to the 'death-chamber', she tries to show her grief and produce crocodile tears in front of him, yet fails to do so: 'Shed a tear, damn you, she thought, I can't' (*MPTK*, 194). After the description of the burial scene, Hairy, out of the blue, proposes to the Smeraldina: 'Why not come with me [...] now that all this has happened, and be my love?' (203). As Celia, immediately after Murphy's death, goes back to her work as a prostitute, the Smeraldina accepts the proposal, saying, 'Perhaps after all [...] this is what darling Bel would wish' (203). In the contrast between the prolonged mourning rites and Smeraldina's accepting her late husband's best man's proposal of marriage immediately after the burial, Beckett attacks the inauthenticity of such displays of grief and ostentatious rituals of mourning.

However, in such mockery and displacement of grief, Beckett seems also to be suppressing his own sense of loss and refusing to give way to the grief caused by the loss of his cousin, Peggy. As Gorer points out, when mourners repress grief and ignore the 'complicated psychological and social adjustments' of mourning, they are often left with 'the permanent despair of depression or melancholia' (cited in Ramazani 1994, 16). The death of the male protagonist, Belacqua, instead of the Smeraldina – an inversion of the real event in Beckett's life – can be considered as a manifestation of melancholia. According to Freud, for the patient who suffers from melancholia, the ego often identifies itself with the lost object, 'an object-loss [is] transformed into an ego loss' (Freud 1991, 258). To this end, the following passage, immediately after the burial of Belacqua, offers a telling correspondence to the Freudian concept of the melancholic's identification with the lost object:

> Already Belacqua was not wholly dead, but merely mutilated. The Smeraldina appreciated this without thinking.
>
> As for her, it was almost as though she had suffered the inverse change. She had died in part. She had definitely ceased to exist in that particular part which Belacqua had been at such pains to isolate, the public part so cruelly made private for his convenience, her least clandestine aspect reduced to a radiograph and exploited to ginger his secret occasions. That was down the mine Daddy with the dead Sadomasochist. Her spiritual equivalent, to give it a name, had been measured, coffined and covered by Nick Malacoda. As material for anagogy (Greek g if you don't mind) the worms were welcome to her.
>
> (*MPTK*, 200–1)

In this cryptic text Beckett attempts to record the deaths of Peggy Sinclair and, presumably, also of his father, as is implied by echoes of 'Malacoda', a poem which was provoked by his father's death. Interestingly, the passage insinuates more strongly the death of the Smeraldina than it does that of Belacqua: 'Belacqua was not wholly dead', but 'She had definitely ceased to exist'. It is significant here too that the Smeraldina was the 'particular part which Belacqua had been at such pains to isolate' just as Celia 'was a piece out of' Murphy (*M*, 234). Whereas Murphy and Belacqua reveal their ambivalence towards the female characters by displaying both attachment and resistance to them, the women in

Beckett's early fiction are described as objects that need to be expelled from the male subjects in their search for the self. As 'the inverse change' of the real event implies, the death of Belacqua prefigures Beckett's melancholic male narrators in the French fiction who incorporate the object-loss as their ego loss and the 'spirit' loss mentioned in his letter on *Murphy*.

However, those female characters who are rejected and expelled by the male protagonists as well as ridiculed by the narrators in Beckett's early fiction do not seem simply to 'expire', to borrow the narrator's word in *More Pricks Than Kicks*. Instead, they leave an indelible imprint on the author's mind. Anthony Cronin asserts that the hostile portraits of women in general and the Smeraldina in particular caused 'moral torment' that lasted until Beckett's later life (Cronin 1997, 578). The caustic description of the Smeraldina's appearance in 'Draff', for instance, echoes that of Peggy Sinclair: 'Bodies don't matter but hers went something like this: big enormous breasts, big breech, Botticelli thighs, knock-knees, square ankles, wobbly, popputa, mammose, slobbery-blubbery, bubbub-bubbub, the real button-busting Weib, ripe'[12] (*MPTK*, 189–90). Knowlson also reports that Beckett feared that they [Peggy's parents] would be very upset at the inclusion of 'The Smeraldina's Billet Doux', the love-letter, 'which they would recognize as based on one of Peggy's letters to him' (*DF*, 176) in *More Pricks Than Kicks*. Beckett wrote to Peggy's younger brother, Morris, 'I didn't know what I was undertaking […] peinlich [painful] no matter what angle contemplated' (176). 'Fifty-four years later', Beckett told Knowlson that he 'still regretted it' (176). The following chapters, then, will explore how such a sense of guilt and repressed grief affects the representation of the females in Beckett's later works, and will also argue that Ireland, equally importantly, stands for the place where male characters have left their loved ones behind.

2
Memories and Melancholia in Beckett's Early French Fiction

I Introduction

A three-page story entitled 'F—' by Suzanne Deschevaux-Dumesnil (later Mme Beckett) was published in 1949 in the anglophone, Paris-based review *Transition*, and was reprinted by Ruby Cohn in *Samuel Beckett Today/Aujourd'hui* (Cohn 1998). Although no translator is named, Samuel Beckett told his bibliographers Raymond Federman and John Fletcher that he was '"certain" of having translated it' (ibid., 41). Critics such as Martin Esslin even suspect that Beckett wrote the story, since it resembles his four *Nouvelles/Novellas* (1946) and *Molloy* (1947), in all of which the male narrators obsessively tell a story of setting off on a journey, and of then losing their way. In the 'F—' story, the narrator, whose gender is not identified, mentions an otherwise unnamed 'he' bumping into the narrator from behind. The man claimed that 'he had lost something very important' when they fell down, and the narrator 'found it strange that he should be [so] distressed over a loss' (Cohn 1998, 44–5). They both search for the lost thing in vain, and during the search in the dark, they both lose their way: the narrator is on the way to F—, and the unnamed man is going to a neighbouring area to F—, a region whose name is censored in the story.

If it is Beckett himself who wrote the story under his partner's name, there are intriguing questions as to why he felt he had to borrow a female name and present a male character who is similar and yet different from the male narrators in his other French fiction. Whereas the man in the 'F—' story is 'distressed over a loss' and claims to have 'lost something very important', in the *Novellas* and *Molloy* the male narrators repress their sense of loss, and resist displaying feeling over the memories of separation from home and from the female characters. Does this suggest that Beckett felt free to write in a more open way about such a loss by borrowing Suzanne's name? In addition, why are the names of regions, both F— and the man's destination, censored? The operation of the censor in naming the regions and the characters in the 'F—' story reminds us further of the censorship in the four *Novellas* and *Molloy*.

In contrast to the conspicuously Irish setting of *More Pricks Than Kicks* and *Murphy*, in Beckett's early French fiction, the narrators' remembered landscapes become uncanny, both familiar and alien, and the names of the female characters become equally uncertain. In the *Novellas* and *Molloy*, which were written shortly after Beckett's self-imposed exile to France in 1937 and in French, the language of his exile, a fascinating tension arises from the male narrators' contradictory feelings towards fading yet haunting memories of both Ireland and women: between their attempts to erase the memories and their urge to repeat the stories. This chapter argues that the male narrators' ambivalent attitude towards memories of severance with Ireland and women in general and the mother in particular not only corresponds to Freud's model of melancholia but is also closely related to Beckett's exile. By examining the melancholia of the male narrators, this chapter shows that the 'something very important' that is lost in Beckett's *Novellas* and *Molloy* can be identified as women and Ireland. Beckett, understanding psychoanalytic theories in depth as well as Freud's theory of melancholia, uses such knowledge as a framework within which he can attain the necessary emotional distance for an exploration of his personal experience and the memory of the separation from his homeland and his mother.

II Mourning and melancholia

Freud's 'Mourning and Melancholia'

In his essay 'Mourning and Melancholia' (1915), Freud argues that both mourning and melancholia are 'the reaction to the loss of a loved person, or to the loss of some abstraction which has taken the place of one, such as one's country, liberty, an ideal, and so on' (Freud 1991, 252). Mourning and melancholia share the same symptoms as grief – 'profoundly painful dejection, cessation of interest in the world, loss of the capacity to love, [and] inhibition of all activity' (252). However, Freud distinguishes the loss in melancholia as being of a 'more ideal kind' (252). That is, 'the object has not perhaps actually died but has been lost as an object of love' (252). In other cases, 'the patient cannot consciously perceive what he has lost' or even if knowing '*whom* he has lost', he cannot be aware of '*what* he has lost in him' (253, Freud's italics). As observed in the Introduction, Beckett's transcriptions of Freud's theory of melancholia, taken from Ernest Jones's *Papers on Psycho-Analysis*, focus on the ego's narcissistic identification with a lost loved object as a main cause of melancholia:

> <u>Melancholia</u>: After some deprivation connected with loved object the subject has withdrawn his love from that object, but instead of transferring it to some new one, as the normal person would, or introverting it on to unconscious fantasies, as the neurotic does, or on to the ego, as the paraphrenic does, he replaces it by narcissistic [love] of himself with former object, thereby no doubt regressing to original narcissism of his love-making. Thus the ego becomes split, the conscious part criticising, abusing & hating the unconscious part formed by fusion with idea of object. It is this ability to treat oneself as object that leads to suicide.
>
> (TCD MS10971/8; cited in Tonning 2007, 151)

With the exception of the discussion that Beckett summarized above, Jones does not define a 'normal process' (Jones 1923, 62) of mourning in his book. According to the transcriptions, what makes melancholia distinct from mourning is the ego's inability to withdraw its love from the lost object and to transfer it to a new one. Freud does not fully explain the process of mourning, or what he calls 'the work of mourning' either, yet the underlying difference between mourning and melancholia accords with Beckett's notes. The process of mourning can only take place when one is fully conscious of one's loss. First, 'reality-testing' (Freud 1991, 253) shows that the loved object no longer exists, then the libido is gradually withdrawn from its attachments to that object, and finally the ego becomes once again free and uninhibited and is able to reinvest in a new object of desire; a displacement of the lost object by a new one.

   In the *Novellas* and *Molloy* Beckett attempts to apply his understanding of the Freudian models of mourning and melancholia filtered through Jones's text. In order to imply the male narrators' symptoms of melancholia, for instance, Beckett shows how they refuse an economy of change from the lost object to the new one. Both *First Love* and 'The End' present the narrators' unusual and significantly similar attachment towards a flower: a crocus and a hyacinth bulb respectively. When the plant is dead, a woman – the narrator's first love, Lulu, in *First Love* and a landlady in 'The End' – 'wanted to remove it', and 'wanted to get [him] another'[1] (*CSP*, 42), but in both stories the narrators refuse, using exactly the same words, 'I told her I didn't want another' (42). Instead, the narrators keep the dead plant although it 'smelt foul' (42). Here, we can clearly see that the process of the work of mourning – in this case admitting the loss, severing their attachment from the plant and replacing the loss with a new one – fails.

On the Irish mourning practice: 'Tears and laughter, they are so much Gaelic to me'

In contrast to the male narrators' melancholic attachment to the lost object in the *Novellas*, in *Molloy* Beckett's female character, Lousse, immediately accepts a new object after the loss of a loved one – as Smeraldina does in *More Pricks Than Kicks*. Molloy happens to kill Lousse's dog which leads him to stay at her place since she asks him to help carry the dog and bury it. In the burial scene, what puzzles him is her ability to get over her grief immediately after the ritual:

> But what was my contribution to this burial? It was she dug the hole, put in the dog, filled up the hole. On the whole I was a mere spectator, I contributed my presence. As if it had been my own burial. And it was. [...] When she had finished her grave she handed me the spade and began to muse, or brood. I thought she was going to cry, it was the thing to do, but on the contrary she laughed. It was perhaps her way of crying. Or perhaps I was mistaken and she was really crying, with the noise of laughter. Tears and laughter, they are so much Gaelic to me.
>
> (*T*, 36–7)

Whereas direct references to Ireland are rare in *Molloy*, the most conspicuous being to his vegetable knife which has 'the handle of so-called genuine Irish horn' (45), it is interesting to note that the puzzling nature of Lousse's emotion during the mourning ritual is specifically linked to something 'Gaelic', as if the weeping or crying of the mourner in the Gaelic tradition is something that Molloy finds ludicrous. What Lousse does is to shed crocodile tears in public; Lousse needs Molloy to attend the burial merely as a matter of show. The function of the mourning process described in *Molloy* is limited to helping the mourner to find a new object rather than enabling the expression of genuine grief. Molloy is clearly aware that he is Lousse's new object after her loss of the dog: 'I would as it were take the place of the dog I had killed' (47).

What Beckett criticizes, then, is the lack of authentic emotion and the superficiality of the Irish mourning practice, as is also demonstrated in an episode of 'The Expelled'. In this story, the male narrator, shortly after he is expelled from a house, encounters a policeman. As soon as the narrator is distinguished from the rest of the crowd on the street by a policeman 'as if it was quite obvious that [he] could not be assimilated to that category' (*CSP*, 52), a funeral passes. Witnessing the ritual actions whereby the Catholics showed respect to the funeral, the narrator is scathing:

> There was a great flurry of hats and at the same time a flutter of countless fingers. Personally if I were reduced to making the sign of the cross I would set my heart on doing it right, nose, navel, left nipple, right nipple. But the way they did it, slovenly and wild, he seemed crucified all of a heap, no dignity, his knees under his chin and his hands anyhow.
>
> (*CSP*, 52)

The narrator sets himself apart from the Catholics in Ireland and attacks them for the lack of sincerity in their mourning. Later on, when the narrator looks to a cabman for 'hiring him for the day', the cabman initially refuses, saying he has 'a funeral at three o'clock' (55). However, the cabman easily abandons the funeral when the narrator invites him to eat. The narrator ironically shows his satisfaction at this, observing that, 'He had preferred me to a funeral, this was a fact which would endure forever' (57). Immediately after this sentence, the narrator mentions that the cabman 'sang, *She is far from the land where her young hero*,[2] those are the only words I remember' (57, Beckett's italics). Given that this is a famous song written by an Irish poet, Thomas Moore, and that the subject of the song is Sarah Curran, the fiancée of Irish patriot Robert Emmet, the setting is clearly Ireland.

The practices of mourning in Beckett's *Novellas* and *Molloy* are attributed to the Irishness of the characters, and need to be resisted by the male narrators. As if any expression of grief through the mourning practices is not an authentic and spontaneous response to a loss of the loved one, the male narrators mock the tradition and vehemently refuse to display their emotion. Thus, in *First Love*, while the narrator proclaims that he is talking about 'melancholy matters, on [his] father's death' (*CSP*, 27) following a recent visit to his 'father's grave' (25), what he actually does is to repress his feeling towards his loss. To this end, he mocks female mourners such as Deirdre, who is best represented in Yeats and Synge's plays as a conductor of mourning and keening. Observing 'widows' (27) in the graveyard, the narrator thinks of interment, echoing the actions of Deirdre who '*presses knife into her heart and sinks into the grave*' of Naoise (Synge 1996, 217), as if it is a matter of amusement to him: 'Then with a little luck you hit on a genuine interment, with real live mourners and the odd relict trying to throw herself into the pit' (*CSP*, 26–7). Beckett's resistance to the mourning tradition, however, is not merely limited to the Irish one but also incorporates the literary convention of elegy, as he once again attempts 'the comic exaggeration of what elsewhere is expressed in elegy' (*D*, 103). As William Watkin points out, 'the so-called English "graveyard" poets of the eighteenth century' isolated 'themselves in graveyards, [and] ruined abbeys' in order to 'find the correct external topography to establish sympathy with their internal, emotional landscapes' (Watkin 2004, 27). In *First Love* Beckett satirizes the graveyard poets and their stock allusions by starting the story in the graveyard of the narrator's father and attacking the supposedly emotional landscape. The male narrator points out the futility of having 'Groves' and 'artificial lakes' in the cemetery, commenting that they are intended to 'offer consolation to the inconsolable' (*CSP*, 27). For the narrator, it is difficult to understand how such a public space, which is specifically designed for the display of grief, can console one for bereavement. Thus, instead of showing grief over his father's death, what the narrator does is to eat, sitting on a tomb, 'vomit' (27), and 'piss' holding 'on to the cross, or the stele, or the angel, so as not to fall' (26).

Melancholia and lost objects

The young Beckett's statement in his essay, *Proust* (1931) – 'the dead are only dead in so far as they continue to exist in the heart of the survivor' (*P*, 44) – reveals his idea of authentic grief and his attitude towards a loss of the loved object. Rather than withdrawing attachment from the lost object and replacing it with a new one, Beckett's male narrators in his French fiction show narcissistic identification with the lost object and pathological symptoms of melancholia. While the narrators' melancholic symptoms are evidenced by their responses to the loss of small objects, such as a crocus, what they have actually lost is concealed.[3] Whereas the 'F—' story at least tells us that the male character 'had lost something very important', the male narrators in Beckett's French fiction seem neither to realize nor to be able to admit their loss. As Freud explains, in the process of melancholia, since the lost object is concealed and unconsciously preserved within the ego, the libido withdraws into the ego, and projects resentment and aggression onto the self. This produces the pathological symptom of self-reproach, the subject blaming himself for the loss as if 'he has willed it' (Freud 1991, 260). Freud includes the loss of one's country in the category of loss to which melancholia and mourning respond. In the case of self-imposed exile, such as Beckett's, melancholia reflects the exile's self-reproach and self-blame for the loss, as 'he has willed it'. Moreover, this separation from country goes together with a perhaps more painful separation. Self-imposed exile from Ireland for Beckett also meant separation from his mother, in relation to whom he experienced many emotional difficulties. Or rather, as suggested in Knowlson's *Damned to Fame*, the troublesome relationship with his mother contributed, in part, to his final decision to leave his home country.

It might not merely be a coincidence, then, that the narrators of the four *Novellas* and *Molloy* – all written shortly after Beckett left Ireland – talk compulsively about the memories of their separation from one house and their search for another. The three stories other than *First Love* in the *Novellas* show the anonymous male narrators, who are similar enough to be considered as the same figure, obsessively repeat the story of setting off on a journey after being thrown out of their family house or after being expelled from a refuge or shelter. Similarly, the anonymous narrator of *First Love*, having been banished from his father's house, also looks for a shelter. In *Molloy* not knowing when and why he is lost, Molloy narrates his memories of searching for his mother's house. By investigating the male narrators' ambivalent and melancholic attitudes towards these memories, the lost objects that are concealed in Beckett's early French fiction will be identified as his homeland, Ireland, and women in general and the mother in particular.

'Taboo of names'

The *Novellas* and *Molloy* offer an important way of dealing with haunting memories of lost objects by using a psychoanalytic frame. The strategy is comparable to Freud's work of mourning, which consists in recalling the memories of the lost object 'bit by bit, at great expense of time and cathectic energy'.[4] 'Each single one of the memories and expectations in which the libido is bound to the object is brought up and hypercathected, and detachment of the libido is accomplished in respect of it' (Freud 1991, 253). Similarly, the narrator in 'The Expelled' states:

> Memories are killing. So you must not think of certain things, of those that are dear to you, or rather you must think of them, for if you don't there is the danger of finding them, in your mind, little

by little. That is to say, you must think of them for a while, a good while, every day several times a day, until they sink forever in the mud. That's an order.

(*CSP*, 46–7)

According to the narrator, in order to erase the memories that are evoked involuntarily, he should think of them over and over again until 'they sink forever in the mud'. However, even if this process of recalling memories is similar to that of Freud's work of mourning, the male narrators' melancholic disavowal of what they have lost foretells their failure to free themselves from the memories.

The narrator's dilemma in exorcising the haunting memories of home and the loved ones is resolved in part by censoring the names of both Ireland and women. In order not to be affected by a painful memory of loss, the narrators deliberately repress and avoid the names of the lost objects by not mentioning the name or by changing it in the middle of the story. Jean Laplanche's essay on Freud offers an interesting explanation for this. In his discussion of mourning and the 'taboo of names', Laplanche claims that the 'best way to avoid the temptation of uttering the dead person's name is to change his name [...] so that the use of the former name shall not recall the dead man to memory' (Laplanche 1999, 243). The narrators' changing of female characters' names can be construed in the same vein: in *First Love* Lulu's name changes to Anna, and in *Molloy* Mrs Loy or Sophie becomes Lousse, and Ruth becomes Edith. Beckett was also very familiar with the theory of repression as his detailed summary from Jones's chapter, 'The Repression Theory in its Relation to Memory', shows: '<u>All forgetting due to repression</u>'. Beckett further underlined, '<u>Forgetting material not in itself unpleasant</u>: The affect invensting [sic] painful complexes is in a state of high potential & so tends to radiate on to whatever ideas become associated with it (displacement of affect)' (Beckett's emphasis).[5] That is, it is not the first forgotten material that is unpleasant but the secondary ideas that are associated with it. The taboo treatment of the women's names suggests that those names are related to the narrators' other memories. The reason for this is hinted at in *Molloy*: Molloy states that his 'memory confuses' Lousse and Ruth, and is 'tempted to think of them as one and the same old hag' (*T*, 59). He further confesses, 'And God forgive me, to tell you the horrible truth, my mother's image sometimes mingles with theirs' (59).[6]

What is most 'literally unendurable' (59) to Molloy, then, is the memory of his mother. Molloy calls his mother 'Mag' in order to avoid calling her 'Ma'. He recollects, 'I called her Mag because for me, without my knowing why, the letter g abolished the syllable Ma' (17).[7] This memory immediately reminds him of Ireland, but he refuses to mention its name too: 'And da, in my part of the world, means father' (17). In talking about how he calls his mother 'Mag' and how his mother calls him Dan which was his father's name, it is not necessary to remind the reader of what father is called in Ireland. Although enough information is given for us to identify the place as Ireland, the country is never designated by its name. Instead, the name of Ireland is repressed and displaced as 'Ballyba'. As many critics have pointed out, Ballyba shows specific references to Dublin or *Baile Atha Cliath* – where *baile* means 'town' in Gaelic. Moran, who searches for Molloy in the novel, further brings to mind the etymology of Dublin (*dubh* in Gaelic means black, and *linn*, pool). Moran specifically refers to the 'stagnant' and 'leaden water'[8] of the 'creek of Ballyba' that is reminiscent of the river Liffey, and also describes Dublin mountains, 'the sea' (134) and other features which often appear as identifiable Irish settings in Beckett's other works. Yet, Beckett intentionally avoids the word, Ireland, and instead uses words such as a 'bog-land' (134) and 'the Molloy country' (133). Molloy's association of his mother with Ireland and his taboo treatment of them both further strengthen the link between the mother and Ireland in Molloy's mind; it is this link that leads to taboos on the names of women as well as on Ireland.

Molloy also fails to differentiate between Ruth/Edith when talking of his first sexual experience. Furthermore, as Beckett's early male protagonists blame devouring females for their own sexual desire, Molloy claims that 'it was she who started it' (57), sexually provoking him. Here, Molloy delivers a long and detailed passage about how he made love with Ruth, drawing attention to grotesque features, such as her senile body and her androgynous appearance, in which she is seen to resemble Lousse, whom he describes as 'an androgyne' with a 'hairy face' (56). After offering this anti-romantic version of his experience by focusing on love as a physical act while questioning whether it is 'true love' (57), Molloy rapidly moves to the death of Ruth. However, her death itself is not the major concern in his narration. Rather, as the narrator of *Murphy* consciously raises a moral (sexual) issue for the Irish Free State, Molloy brings our attention to how the Irish community reacts to sexuality. The narrator shows how Ruth's neighbours' self-censorship about 'sexual matters' works: 'the fact of having found a man when they should have found a woman was immediately repressed and forgotten, by the few unfortunate enough to know about it' (58). The name of Ireland is again not uttered, indicating that it is taboo: 'It is true they were extraordinarily reserved, in my part of the world, about everything connected with sexual matters' (58). 'But things have perhaps changed since my time' (58), Molloy adds after the comment. Things might have changed since Molloy (or Beckett) left Ireland, but in his memory, the Irish community still remains extremely conservative especially about 'sexual matters'.

While such 'sexual matters' immediately bring him back to the memory of self-censorship in the Irish community, Molloy's taboo treatment of the names of both women and Ireland implies a psychologically important motivation for concealment. Women and Ireland can be seen as objects that the male narrator had to expel in his search for the self in the *Novellas* and *Molloy*. However, since it is himself who has 'willed' the losses, he shows a disavowal of the losses and presents the pathological symptoms of melancholia.

The next section will continue to show how the female characters and Ireland are bound up with each other in the narrators' memories, and further argues that the narrators' efforts to separate from both women and Ireland echo Belacqua and Murphy's vehement resistance to woman-as-Ireland in Beckett's early fiction.

III Women and Ireland as lost objects

Women and the 'dispeopled kingdom'

In the *Novellas* and *Molloy*, the narrators recall encounters with several women and the separations from them. Even though the female characters are less central than the ones in Beckett's early fiction, they share many features with the early Beckettian females. For example, in the *Novellas* and *Molloy* the role of the female characters is mainly confined to offering a place to the narrators who are looking for a shelter, and in the narrators' memories the women are entirely tied to these places. In Molloy's memory, his mother exists mostly in connection with her house, and Lousse offers him her house to stay in on his journey to his mother. It is also a woman in 'The End' who offers her basement to the narrator after he has been expelled from a charitable institution. Of these works, it is *First Love* in which a female character shares the most striking features in common with Beckett's earlier devouring female.

In *First Love*, the old narrator talks of his young self, at 'about twenty-five at the time of [his] marriage' (*CSP*, 25) with his first love, Lulu, and the consequent separation from her. Having been evicted from his father's house, and 'having nowhere to go' (30), the narrator settles on a bench on the bank of the canal, where he meets Lulu. Lulu resembles Celia in *Murphy* in many aspects. Both of them are prostitutes, and like Celia, who spots Murphy on the street and accosts him, it is Lulu who approaches the narrator, who is sitting on a bench. Like Belacqua in *More Pricks Than Kicks*, who becomes vexed by Lucy's penetrating gaze which magically helps her to locate him in the wide forest, the young narrator in *First Love* is perturbed by Lulu's gaze and expresses unease, saying, 'I felt her eyes on me' (30). For the narrator, 'she [is] a most tenacious woman' who chases after him by visiting his bench 'every evening' (30) even if it is a bench that does not belong to anyone. Later on, she takes the initiative in seducing the narrator by inviting him to her place. As soon as they arrive, she begins to 'undress', taking off 'everything, with a slowness fit to enflame an elephant, except her stocking, calculated presumably to bring my concupiscence to the boil' (39). When Lulu is naked, the female body is ridiculed by the narrator as are the bodies of most women in *More Pricks Than Kicks* and *Murphy*. The young narrator, for instance, emphasizes Lulu's squint eyes in her naked body, describing how she 'gazed at [him] with her big eyes [...] with one big eye rather, for the other seemed riveted on the remains of the hyacinth' (44). We can see that Lulu inherits significant traits from Beckett's early female characters: she is a sexually provocative initiative-taker with a penetrating female gaze.

Moreover, in this story the narrator's desire for Lulu is underplayed, and he, as Murphy does, projects his fear of attachment to Lulu onto her. As Murphy's attempt to expel Celia results from his belief that Celia is an obstacle in his quest for the 'little world' of the mind and the self, so the young narrator also feels Lulu ensnares him in her house by means of sexuality, and threatens his sense of 'self' in a 'dispeopled kingdom' that echoes Murphy's 'little world'. The following passage shows the young narrator's state of mind when he is excited by Lulu:

> What mattered to me in my dispeopled kingdom, that in regard to which the disposition of my carcass was the merest and most futile of accidents, was supineness in the mind, the dulling of the self and of that residue of execrable frippery known as the non-self and even the world, for short. But man is still today, at the age of twenty-five, at the mercy of an erection, physically too, from time to time, it's the common lot, even I was not immune, if that may be called an erection. It did not escape her naturally, women smell a rigid phallus ten miles away and wonder, How on earth did he spot me from there?

One is no longer oneself, on such occasions, and it is painful to be no longer oneself, even more painful if possible than when one is.

(*CSP*, 31)

This passage discloses the narrator's covert way of blaming women for his own sexual desire. Although it is rather the man who first sexually responds to women 'ten miles away' and is aroused, he condemns the sexually provocative female by emphasizing how 'women smell a rigid phallus' and how Lulu did not fail to spot his erection. By stressing the verb, 'smell', women are allocated the active role, whereas his male 'member' is described as if it passively responded. It becomes clear that the characteristic of Lulu as a temptress and a snare derives from the tension felt by the young narrator himself between his desire for her and his resistance to her, which is based on his belief that she pushes him to be his 'non-self'. As Murphy attempts to seek for his self by expelling Celia, who stands for the body, for the young narrator in *First Love* his sexual desire is something that belongs to the 'non-self', something that is dreadful, something that needs to be negated.

Lulu is closely associated with the bench, as the narrator claims, 'her image remains bound, for me, to that of the bench' (31), and he attempts to leave her by 'abandon[ing] the bench' (33). The narrator, however, becomes baffled by the fact that 'She disturbed [him] exceedingly, even absent' (32), and also confused by his 'feeling which gradually assumed, to [his] dismay, the dread name of love' (33). It is at this moment while he tries to define his love for Lulu after abandoning her for the first time that a curious association between Lulu and Ireland arises as Molloy's discussion of 'true love' and 'sexual matters' leads him to talk about self-censorship in the Irish community. Here is a passage where suddenly the criticism of the Irish Free State's policy on contraception and of Irish patriotism interrupts his discussion about love:

It was in this byre, littered with dry and hollow cowclaps subsiding with a sigh at the poke of my finger, that for the first time in my life [...] I had to contend with a feeling which gradually assumed, to my dismay, the dread name of love. What constitutes the charm of our country, apart of course from its scant population, and this without help of the meanest contraceptive, is that all is derelict, with the sole exception of history's ancient faeces. These are ardently sought after, stuffed and carried in procession. Wherever nauseated time has dropped a nice fat turd you will find our patriots, sniffing it up on all fours, their faces on fire. Elysium of the roofless. Hence my

happiness at last. Lie down, all seems to say, lie down and stay down.
I see no connexion between these remarks. But that one exists, and
even more than one, I have little doubt, for my part. But what?
Which? Yes, I loved her, it's the name I gave, still give alas, to what
I was doing then.

(CSP, 33–4)

What is intriguing in this passage is the parallel between the Irish patriots and his young self that is drawn in the narrator's scatological attack
on them. The narrator here criticizes the Irish patriots, the Celtic revivalists in particular, for their attempts to construct a national identity
by reclaiming the past, especially the Gaelic tradition. The tradition,
which had been mostly suppressed during the period of colonization, is
described as 'history's ancient faeces', 'nauseated time' and a 'fat turd',
and the Irish patriots as 'ardently [seeking] after' the turd and 'sniffing it
up'. Immediately after the passage, however, the narrator also presents
an excremental vision by recalling his young self as having inscribed
'the letter of Lulu' in old cowshit 'with [his] devil's finger into the
bargain, which [he] then sucked' (34). While the narrator struggles to
define his love for Lulu after having left her, he emphasizes three times
that he has written Lulu's name in cowshit. In his use of scatology in
both contexts, what is common is conception of past time as excrement: 'history's ancient faeces', 'old heifer pat' 'old cowshit' (34) and
'time's forgotten cowpats' (35).[9]

'What goes by the name of love is banishment'

The fact that the scatological attack on the past is directed towards both
the Irish patriots and his young self shows that the narrator has the
same sentimental attachment to the past as the Irish patriots. Indeed, if
'history's ancient faeces' are 'ardently sought after, stuffed and carried in
procession' by the patriots, what is also persistently 'sought after' – all
the way through the narrator's story – is his own memory. The narrator's
scatological assault on himself when he was trying to separate from
Lulu can be examined using Kristeva's concept of abjection. Excrement,
in Kristeva's theory, is one of the 'objects generating abjection', an
'improper' and 'unclean' object that is expelled from one's body, and 'the
disorderly elements of its corporeal existence' must be 'separated from
its clean and proper self' in order for the infant to form its sense of the
self (Gross 1990, 86–8). As Beckett transcribed from Karin Stephen's *The
Wish to Fall Ill*, the 'Overwhelming quality of infantile excretory processes' is 'that they are both dreaded & desired by the subject', causing

the infant's ambivalent emotion and 'melancholia' (TCD MS10971/7/2; cited in Feldman 2006, 100). By indicating that the young male narrator is contaminated by excrement when trying to define his love for Lulu, Beckett suggests the narrator's melancholic state of mind during the separation process from her. His 'inscribing the letters of Lulu' and 'tracing her name in old cowshit' (*CSP*, 34) implies the narrator's identification of Lulu with the excrement. While such identification shows that he defines her as an object that needs to be abjected from him, 'the dread name of love' also reveals his simultaneous contradictory attachment to and detachment from Lulu – the abject entity. Despite the narrator's vehement refusal to explain the 'connexion between these remarks' on Lulu and his homeland, Ireland, the only answer he gives us – 'Yes, I loved her' (34) – hints at the association between them.

In *First Love*, the narrator attempts to portray the moment when his young self sought for self-identity by abjecting Lulu and by leaving his 'country'. As the narrator's resistance to Lulu and his 'country' shows, they are both defined as objects that he had to negate in the quest for his self. The connection between his love and his homeland in relation to his search for the self is further strengthened when we look at the statement that immediately follows the quoted passage above: 'What goes by the name of love is banishment, with now and then a post-card from the homeland, such is my considered opinion, this evening' (31). Given that this statement is written in the present tense – unlike his remembered story, which is described in the past tense – it can be seen as the narrator's diagnosis of his young self in regard to what love brought to him at that time. As David Lloyd asserts, the narrator's statement is ambiguous: 'we are left in the dark as to whether banishment is the condition of love, or love that of banishment' (Lloyd 1993, 42). Yet, what is important in reading the statement is how the narrator combines the ideas of love, banishment and homeland.

Lloyd, for example, reads the narrator's statement as a remark that 'scrupulously disdains a Western tradition from the *Odyssey* to *Ulysses* where love is the figure simultaneously for homecoming and for truth' (42). The statement, however, does not simply reject such a tradition, but rather reveals Beckett's complex way of exploiting home in a metaphorical connection with love, here ironically in an antithetical connection with the idea, as James Joyce adds complexity to Homer's *Odyssey* by portraying Molly, who is hardly a faithful Penelope, in *Ulysses*. In *First Love*, home is also closely associated with his wife (or the woman he claims to be married to) and love – particularly the love standing for his bodily desire which made him 'no longer [him]self' (31).

The narrator takes a different course from Odysseus, however, in banishing himself from his wife and his homeland. Despite the narrator's distance from them, in his memory his wife and his homeland are constantly bound up with one another, reminding him of each other.

Thus, when portraying the homecoming of male characters in his other works, we see that Beckett often uses ideas reminiscent of Odysseus' return to his waiting wife, Penelope. For example, in *All That Fall* (1956) Mrs Rooney is anxiously waiting for her husband's homecoming in the railway station. Among these works, *The Unnamable*, the third of the *Three Novels*, tells us the 'fable', which best exemplifies Beckett's convoluted way of using the idea of love, wife and homecoming, while also hinting at a psychologically significant way of dealing with the 'nature of emotion' (*T*, 406) when talking about such a matter:

> They love each other, marry, in order to love each other better, more conveniently, he goes to the wars, he dies at the wars, she weeps, with emotion, at having loved him, at having lost him, yep, marries again, in order to love again, more conveniently again, they love each other, you love as many times as necessary, as necessary in order to be happy, he comes back, the other comes back, from the wars, he didn't die at the wars after all, she goes to the station, to meet him, he dies in the train, of emotion, at the thought of seeing her again, having her again, she weeps, weeps again, with emotion again, at having lost him again, yep, goes back to the house, he's dead, the other is dead, the mother-in-law takes him down, he hanged himself, with emotion, at the thought of losing her, she weeps, weeps louder, at having loved him, at having lost him, there's a story for you, that was to teach me the nature of emotion, that's called emotion, what emotion can do [...]
>
> (*T*, 406)

After this passage, Beckett summarizes the story, highlighting the close relationship between homecoming, love and emotion: 'so that's emotion, that's love, and trains, the nature of trains, and the meaning of your back to the engine, and guards, stations, platforms, wars, love, heart-rending cries' (406).[10] Beckett here emphasizes the wife's emotion and her display of grief over her loss of her husband while questioning the authenticity of her feeling as she replaces her loss with a new husband. In order to avoid emotional engagement, the narrator quickly moves his topic to an investigation of whether the woman who takes the man down is his mother or mother-in-law, and states that what matters in the story is 'how I reason to be sure this evening, it was to teach me how to reason' (407). The way in which the narrator ends the story, however, significantly echoes the melancholic denial of loss by the narrator of *First Love*: 'there's a story for you, I thought they were over, perhaps it's a new one, lepping fresh, is it the return to the world of fable, no, just a reminder, to make me regret what I have lost, long to be again in the place I was banished from, unfortunately it doesn't remind me of anything' (*T*, 407). The narrator claims that the fable neither makes him 'regret what [he has] lost' nor yearn for the place he 'was banished from'. Yet, just like the narrator of *First Love*, the story of love and loss does remind him of his departure from his own homeland. As the following chapters will further demonstrate, the loved one and the homeland from which Beckett is separated are connected in his mind and continue to exist as lost objects in his oeuvre.

The Unnamable's melancholic disavowal of his loss (of his loved one and place) represents a common theme in Beckett's early French fiction. The next section will further link this sense of loss to Beckett's separation from his mother and Ireland. The psychoanalytic theories that Beckett studied through his attentive reading of psychoanalytic texts during his psychotherapy sessions from early 1934 to late 1935 seem to offer him not only an understanding of his symptoms but also useful material and a framework for writing about his own separation from the mother with some emotional detachment. Beckett's transcriptions from Otto Rank's *The Trauma of Birth* (1929) in the 'Psychology Notes' indicate that his early French fiction is his attempt to accomplish mastery of the severance with his mother, which he felt was incomplete:

> Analysis the belated accomplishment of incomplete mastery of birth trauma.
> Analytic situation identified with intrauterine one, patient back in position of unborn.
> Just as all anxiety goes back to anxiety at birth (dyspnoea), so every pleasure has as its final aim the reestablishment of the primal intrauterine pleasure.
> (TCD MS 10971/8/34; cited in Feldman 2006, 107)

The following sections, therefore, are going to explore how Beckett's psychotherapy, his study of psychoanalysis and his self-imposed exile add a new angle to his writing of the mother figure as well as his use of the womb metaphor. Less than a year after he left Ireland, in a letter to Thomas MacGreevy on 26 May 1938, Beckett wrote, 'I feel sorry for her often to the point of tears. That is the part that was not analysed away, I suppose' (*LSB*, 625). As scholars such as H.P. Abbott and, here, Matthew Feldman claim, Beckett's 'self-writing' in his early French fiction written some time after his psychotherapy and exile, 'appears in large part an attempt, via psychology, to make "mental reality" bearable again' (Feldman 2006, 84), and I would add, to 'analyse away' the part that the author felt was left out during the therapy sessions.

IV Analysing away

The mother

In contrast to the relative absence of a mother figure in Beckett's early English fiction, a mother or a maternal surrogate starts to emerge early in his writing in French. In *Murphy*, both Murphy and Celia appear as parentless, and the word 'mother' appears only once, when Murphy 'tried to get a picture of [...] his mother' (*M*, 251) in his mind shortly before the accident that causes his death, but fails to do so. It seems that Beckett actually intended to avoid the mother figure in *More Pricks Than Kicks* by assigning the typical role of the mother to someone else. In 'Dante and the Lobster', it is Belacqua's aunt who asks him the favour of buying a lobster and later on cooks it for him. As Knowlson highlights, Beckett feared that his family members and friends in Dublin would recognize themselves as unsympathetically portrayed and caricatured in *More Pricks Than Kicks* when it was first published, and, most of all, he was worried about his mother's response to the book (*DF*, 176). Evidently the young Beckett was highly aware of and concerned about his mother as a reader of his work. Excluding the protagonist's mother from his fictions must have been a solution to the perennial problem of auto-biographical interpretation; it would also prevent him from the danger of unconsciously alluding to his own mother in depicting the fictional mother. Despite the hazards of bringing autobiographical elements into the analysis of an author's writing, there are several significant aspects of Beckett's life that shed light on changing features in the representation of the female in his works. Before analysing Beckett's early French fiction using a psychoanalytic framework, such aspects will be introduced.

Beckett's psychotherapy sessions and his intensive study of psycho-analysis can be regarded as one of the elements that affected his writing. As Knowlson's *Damned to Fame* remarks, the sessions facilitated Beckett's understanding of himself and made him realize that his anxiety was largely rooted in his uneasy relationship with his mother. Beckett's own recollection of his therapy strongly supports this point:

> I used to lie down on the couch and try to go back in my past. I think it probably did help. I think it helped me perhaps to control the panic. I certainly came up with some extraordinary memories of being in the womb. Intrauterine memories. I remember feeling trapped, of being imprisoned and unable to escape, of crying to be let out but no one could hear, no one was listening. I remember being in pain but being unable to do anything about it.
>
> (Cited in *DF*, 171)

Whether Beckett truly remembered the extraordinary 'intrauterine memories', which echo his transcriptions from Rank's book quoted earlier, or whether those 'memories' were triggered by his study of *The Trauma of Birth*, this account significantly discloses what the young Beckett felt towards his mother. Beckett's anxiety is represented as 'feeling trapped and imprisoned' in the womb, and desiring 'to escape' from it. It is hard to ignore the correlation between the womb and the mother, and certainly his analyst, Wilfred Bion, was unlikely to fail to read such an account as revealing that Beckett's anxiety stemmed from his relationship with his mother. Whether influenced by Bion's suggestion of separation from an 'umbilical dependence' (*DF*, 172) on his mother or not, it seems that the therapy sessions prompted Beckett to delve into psychoanalytic ideas concerning the womb, birth and severance from the mother.

In this regard, Beckett's 'Psychology Notes' provide a helpful way of tracing his investigation into psychology in relation to the mother's womb. His transcriptions from Rank's *The Trauma of Birth* state: 'Anxiety of child left alone in dark room due to his unconscious being reminded (*er-innert*) of intrauterine situation, terminated by frightening severance from mother' (TCD MS10971/8/34; cited in *DF*, 172). Echoing Beckett's own account of his intrauterine memories, this note indicates that he felt this specific psychoanalytic theory useful in understanding his own anxiety in relation to his mother. Indeed, Rank's theory of the severance from the mother's womb as the prototype for all later anxieties offers an insight into the narrators' anxieties as well as the womb motifs in Beckett's works. Rank's anatomical emphasis on the womb and the physical severance with it as a root of major anxiety must have offered Beckett a safe emotional distance when using the womb metaphor in his writing. Beckett could feel that rather than treating of his actual mother, it is the womb more generally with which he is concerned, regardless of his initial psychological motivation.

There is also another important recurring birth motif – 'not having been born properly' – in Beckett's oeuvre, and the original source of this psychoanalytic idea can be traced to an encounter during the period of his therapy. It is a well-known anecdote that in 1935 Beckett, together with Bion, attended a lecture given by C.G. Jung at the Institute of Psychological Medicine at the Tavistock Clinic. The lecture, as Knowlson states, stayed in Beckett's mind for many years and he remarks his impression of it in *All That Fall* through the character of Mrs Rooney: 'The trouble with her was she had never really been born!' (*CDW*, 196). All of this reveals Beckett's interest in and understanding of psychoanalytic theories in relation to expulsion from the womb and severance from the mother, and shows that his attention to this motif stemmed from his own personal experience, such as 'memories of being in the womb' excavated during psychotherapy.

'Anglo-Irish exuberance and automatism'

Why, then, despite an interest dating from 1935, did it take more than ten years for Beckett to start using this motif of rebirth with a more specific allusion to severance with the mother? Further, why does this motif become such a strong repetitive pattern particularly in works written shortly after his exile? This phase of Beckett's life is considered as a significant turning point in his writing in many respects. First of all, before permanently settling in Paris, Beckett experienced a vision in 1945 in his mother's room in Dublin, which helped him to transform his approaches to his own writing. According to Beckett's own account of this revelation, the *Novellas* and *Molloy* are the very products of the vision. Beckett remarked, '*Molloy* and the others came to me the day I became aware of my own folly. Only then did I begin to write the things I feel' (cited in *DF*, 319). While many critics have discussed Beckett's recognition of his 'folly' as a pivotal moment in establishing his own artistic style as distinct from James Joyce's – that is, 'working with impotence, ignorance' instead of 'tending towards omniscience'[11] like Joyce – I would like to draw attention to the fact that this vision also helped Beckett to write about his own emotions and therefore, to turn towards the inner material of feeling, a change that bears a psychological significance. The change from English to French and his self-imposed exile also contributed to Beckett's moving away from Joycean allusions and from what he called 'Anglo-Irish exuberance and automatism' (cited in Lake 1984, 49), and to his gaining a sense of distance from Anglo-Irish and English literary memory.

Equally importantly, whereas the perturbed relationship with his mother and his anxiety caused by it might have hindered Beckett from writing about any mother figure and from using the womb motif had he stayed in Ireland and continued to write in English, geographical distance, and perhaps more specifically freedom from his mother's critical influence gained by writing in French, would have made it easier for him to include the mother figure and the womb motif in his French work. As Beckett's own term, 'automatism', implies in relation to English, writing in the language of his exile offered him a new kind of control over his own emotion in writing about 'the things' he 'felt' – among them the womb motif – together with enough distance to have the strength to talk about them.

As quoted in the Introduction in relation to the ways in which language is closely bound up with emotion and memory, James Olney claims, 'Beckett decided, when memory became in all ways central to his work, to write in French' (Olney 1998, 347). This statement is disputable since Beckett's later works, written in English, also concentrate on memory. *Krapp's Last Tape* (1958), for example, is mainly about Krapp listening to his recorded memories, and *All That Fall* overflows with Beckett's own memories of Ireland, probably triggered by the 'automatism' of his mother tongue. Olney's reading, however, becomes very persuasive when applied to Beckett's French works. Even if Beckett did not 'wish to indulge in memory', Olney argues, 'he had no choice but to take it on as subject along with the self' (347) when creating the French fiction. By writing fiction in French, in the language of exile rather than in 'the language of memory' (347), which is his mother tongue, Beckett seemed to attempt to achieve some emotional distance from the memories about which he was writing. It can be then argued that writing the *Novellas* and *Molloy* in French was an inevitable decision, enabling Beckett to write the things he felt to be closely related to his memories. When considering 'the positive frenzy of writing' or the 'torrent of work' that Beckett 'produced in the four years immediately following the war', and that 'never failed to surprise even Beckett himself' (*DF*, 322), we can assume an important inner urge to write at the moment of composing the *Novellas* and *Molloy*. Significantly, the new element that Beckett desired to express, and which recurs throughout his works after his vision, is the memory of separation from the womb-like shelter. That this memory is written in French implies the need to gain control over his feelings.

In contrast to the emotional control in Beckett's early French fiction, in his short story, *From an Abandoned Work* (1954–55),[12] the first work written in English since *Watt* (1948), we find a narrator who is so emotionally agitated that he often fails to manage to control his narration.

The text is full of his unreasoning hostility towards 'moving things', and filled with the his violent feelings and 'sudden rages', which 'made [his] life a misery' (*CSP*, 157). Although these 'sudden rages' come to the narrator 'like a great wind suddenly rising in [him]' (157), he cannot describe them. The narrator is also disturbed by the frequent appearance of the word, 'white' saying, 'there is that word white again' (161) as if the narration is not under his control. Of course, the *Novellas* and *Molloy* also often give us the impression that the narrative voice is not the narrator's own. Moran, for instance, states that he follows 'an ambiguous voice' (*T*, 132) within him. Notably, while Moran talks about obeying the order from the voice, he suddenly questions whether he 'shall one day be banished from [his] house', and abruptly stops talking about this topic saying, 'I am too old to lose all this, and begin again, I am too old! Quiet, Moran, quiet. No emotion, please' (*T*, 132) as if attempting to prevent himself from becoming emotional. What distinguishes *From an Abandoned Work* from the *Novellas* and *Molloy*, however, is that the narrator of the former more openly expresses his emotion, and furthermore, that his hostility and rages are clearly traced to his separation from his mother. A close reading of the text reveals that his 'savage rages' and 'violence', provoked while watching the white horse, are impelled by the association between the word white and his mother. However, as the narrator of *First Love* denies the 'connexion between' homeland and Lulu, so the narrator of *From an Abandoned Work* also claims, 'the white horse and then the rage, no connexion I suppose' (*CSP*, 158) while inferring the connection later on: 'the white horse and white mother in the window' (160–1).

Like the *Novellas* and *Molloy*, *From an Abandoned Work* starts with the narrator's setting off on his journey. Yet, even though presenting a very similar pattern of departure to the previous ones, by specifying that it is his mother's room that he has left behind, *From an Abandoned Work* helps us to open the possibilities that link the other narrators' separation to the metaphor of severance with the mother:

UP BRIGHT AND EARLY that day, I was young then, feeling awful, and out, mother hanging out of the window in her nightdress weeping and waving. Nice fresh morning, bright too early as so often. Feeling really awful, very violent. [...] Then I raised my eyes and saw my mother still in the window waving, waving me back or on I don't know, or just waving, in sad helpless love, and I heard faintly her cries. The window-frame was green, pale, the house-wall grey and my mother white and so thin I could see past her (piercing sight I had then) into the dark of the room, [...] I remember it [...]

(CSP, 155–6)

The narrator's comment on 'the dark of the room' reminds us of Beckett's notes from Rank's book regarding the association between the dark room and the womb. Moreover, after talking about his 'savage rages' and 'violence' accompanied by his separation from his mother, the narrator confides, 'vent the pent, that was one of those things I used to say, over and over, as I went along, vent the pent, vent the pent' (158). As if outpouring his imprisoned emotion and memory, the narrator describes the moment of severance from the mother.

As the discussion about *From an Abandoned Work* has offered us a useful link to connect the narrators' departure specifically with the separation from the mother, the next section will further unravel the coded metaphor of rebirth and severance from the mother's womb in the *Novellas* and *Molloy*.

'Room for womb or for woman'

Love is home-sickness.

(Freud 1985, 368)

What goes by the name of love is banishment, with now and then a postcard from the homeland, such is my considered opinion, this evening.

(CSP, 31)

Phil Baker begins his insightful analysis of the womb motif in Beckett's texts with the epigraph 'Love is home-sickness', quoted from Freud's essay, 'The "Uncanny"' (1985; first published in 1919), and uses Freud's idea of longing for the intrauterine home or the 'Lost Paradise' (Baker 1997, 65) in his discussion. I would also like to mobilize the idea of love as homesickness, but approach it from a different angle by juxtaposing it with the seemingly contrary statement in *First Love* (quoted above) in discussing the narrators' simultaneous attachment to and wish for detachment from the intrauterine home in Beckett's French fiction. There is, of course, the metaphor of heading towards the womb in Beckett's *Novellas* and *Molloy*, but the narrators' courses of action can be seen as derived from the inevitable need for the womb in order to be properly born, and thus to master severance with the mother rather than from longing for the 'Lost Paradise' as Baker claims. This section is further intended to show how Beckett, using his psychoanalytic knowledge, attempts to 'analyse away' and to try a 'belated accomplishment of incomplete mastery of birth trauma' in his early French fiction.

Beckett's use of a room and a woman to symbolize the womb in the *Novellas* and *Molloy* can be traced back to his 'Psychology Notes'. His transcriptions, as mentioned earlier, reflect his particular interests and were expanded upon in his personal notes. For example, Ernest Jones, in 'The Theory of Symbolism' from *Papers on Psycho-Analysis*, writes that 'a room is a regular unconscious symbol for woman' (Jones 1923, 167). In his notes, however, Beckett comments in parentheses, '(as room for womb or for woman)', adding 'womb', as if pointing out a crucial link that Jones misses out (TCD MS 10971/8/12, Beckett's emphasis). His transcriptions from Rank's text also confirm the connection between woman and place in Beckett's works: 'Town as mother symbol' (10971/8/35; cited in Feldman 2006, 31). It is difficult to ignore the significance of the first line of *Molloy*, 'I am in my mother's room' (*T*, 7), which is resonant with the womb.[13] A few pages later, however, Molloy suddenly appears to be lost, and sets off on a journey to find his mother. Likewise, in the *Novellas*, even though the narrators' mother is mentioned much less than in *Molloy*, we find other female characters serving as mother surrogates, offering their rooms/wombs. In spite of Beckett's famous claim, 'no symbols where none intended' (*W*, 255) in *Watt*, the symbols used in psychoanalysis offered Beckett a useful tool for analysing the raw material of his personal experience and transforming it – at an increased emotional distance – into his writing.

The Greek or Turkish woman in 'The End', Lulu in *First Love*, and Lousse in *Molloy* all appear as mother surrogates who nurture the narrators by bringing them meals at appointed hours and emptying their chamber-pots.[14] However, their central role is to offer a womb-like room to the narrators, evicted from their houses and looking for shelter. As Baker usefully details, the *Novellas* 'concentrate on their womb theme' presenting a 'relatively coherent treatment of birth trauma and re-birthing' (Baker 1997, 74) allowing the narrators to be properly born again. In *First Love*, when the narrator enters the room offered by Lulu for the first time, he 'survey[s] the room with horror', and recalls 'Not a doubt, I must have seen that room somewhere' (*CSP*, 39). The allusion to the previously-known room/womb becomes fully apparent in the following sentence: 'As I was taking them down, strange memory, I heard the word fibrome, or brone, I don't know which, never knew, never knew what it meant and never had the curiosity to find out. The things one recalls!' (40).

Baker rightly relates 'fibrome' to 'fibroma', which refers to 'a benign tumour of the wall of the uterus' (Baker 1997, 95), confirming that the room unmistakably implies the womb. What is also notable in this story is the narrator's reluctance to leave Lulu's house despite several earlier claims to be leaving her. In her house, 'Gradually [he] settled down' (42), and was 'united' with her by what he refers as his 'marriage' (25). He states, however, 'What finished their relationship was the birth' (44) of their child. As if suggesting he had to stay in Lulu's room/womb for as long as the nine-month period of pregnancy in order to be born properly, the narrator procrastinates until the day of the child's birth.

Similarly, in 'The Expelled' the moment of the narrator's expulsion from his house is recalled as the 'scene of my birth' (*CSP*, 49). After being forcibly ejected, the narrator meets a cabman who with his wife functions as a surrogate parent. The cabman invites the narrator to his house, and with his wife's support, the narrator stays a night in a cab in which he 'lie[s] well back' with a foetus-like position in the womb 'with [his] feet higher than [his] head on the other seat' (59). Baker claims that at the end of the story, when the dawn breaks, the narrator is 'impelled to leave his refuge in a re-birth fantasy' to 'be "properly born" a second time' (Baker 1997, 82), and this time the action is voluntary unlike the birth by expulsion at the beginning of the story.

Freud's *fort-da* game

If the narrator has finally been born properly through a voluntary birth, as Baker infers, then how should we understand Beckett's compulsion to repeat more or less the same sequence of events in the subsequent stories of the *Novellas*, in which the narrators are similar enough to be considered as the same person?[15] One way is to consider that the narrators' impulse to reiterate the same story indicates that what they reveal is not just a fantasy of rebirth, of being properly born, but the moment of severance of the umbilical cord from the mother. The theme is emphasized in the *Novellas* and *Molloy* through Beckett's repeated use of the image of a string or lace by which the narrators' hats are attached to their 'buttonhole[s]' (*CSP*, 69, 89, 99). It is given along with the narrators' hats when they set off on their journeys. While all the narrators are unwilling to take off their hats, the female characters are keen on their removal, hinting at their wish for giving birth. The return of a hat, still attached to the buttonhole by the string, however, shows unsuccessful severance of the umbilical cord.

If what the narrators are talking about is merely, as Baker claims, Freudian nostalgia for a return to the womb as the lost paradise, or a longing to die as proposed by the Freudian death drive, it seems evident that they would prefer to stay in their womb-like shelters.[16] But almost none of the narrators in the *Novellas* are still in their shelters at the end of the story; instead they have embarked upon other journeys.[17] Molloy's narration concludes with the resumption of his search for his mother, although he contrives for himself an apologetic and self-defensive excuse: 'I longed to go back into the forest. Oh not a real longing. Molloy could stay, where he happened to be' (*T*, 91). In spite of all these internal conflicts, there is a strong urge to repeat the journey over and over again, and the reason for this repetition is given at the beginning of the novel:

> I resolved to go and see my mother. I needed, before I could resolve to go and see that woman, reasons of an urgent nature, and with such reasons, since I did not know what to do, or where to go, it was child's play for me, the play of an only child, to fill my mind until it was rid of all other preoccupation and I seized with a trembling at the mere idea of being hindered from going there, I mean to my mother, there and then.
>
> (*T*, 15)

For Molloy, his quest for the mother is 'child's play', which is comparable to Freud's *fort-da* game. In *Beyond the Pleasure Principle* (1920), Freud describes his grandson's *fort-da* game in response to the pain he feels during the absence of his mother. In this game, the child repeatedly experiences the disappearance and return of the lost object by throwing a reel away saying '*fort* (gone)' and retrieving it on a string saying '*da*' (there) (Freud 2003, 53). As Daniel Katz remarks, Freud claims that the essential aim of the game is to experience the distressing moment of separation rather than the 'staging of the pleasurable return of the mother through her surrogate, the wooden reel' (Katz 2003, 255). Several rooms, which Molloy encounters and leaves during his search for the mother, can also be considered as involved in his game of separation.

Similarly in *First Love*, as several critics have pointed out,[18] we find the young narrator repeating the separation with Lulu as if playing the game of *fort-da*. Lulu's song is for him the symbol and surrogate of the wooden reel. When the narrator encounters Lulu after having abandoned the bench for the first time, he asks her to sing. With this song, the narrator plays a game as if trying to practise his abandoning of her. He leaves her, walking away as the song becomes fainter and fainter and finally does not reach him any more, then he retraces his steps until he hears the song again. He repeats this leaving and returning to the bench until the song has surely ceased. Later on, when he leaves Lulu for good at the moment of her giving birth, he once again 'began playing with the cries' of her during her labour, 'in the same way' as he 'had played with the song, on, back, on, back' (45). At the end, the young narrator does succeed in leaving Lulu. The cries, however, do not cease and the story concludes with his confession: 'For years I thought they [the cries] would cease. Now I don't think so any more' (45). Although it was the narrator's young self who left Lulu, although he tried to master the separation by playing with the song and cries just as in the *fort-da* game, still the separation is painful to him. As the ceaseless cries imply, the memory haunts him: 'all that matters is that it [the cry] should cease' (45).

What is urgent in *Molloy* and the *Novellas* is then to speak of the very act of separation in order to fill their mind and to ease and master the painful memory of the severance. The narrator of 'The Calmative', therefore, states at the outset, 'So I'll tell myself a story, I'll try and tell myself another story, to try and calm myself', claiming he has 'come back to life, after [his] death' (*CSP*, 61), thus, after having been born again. The narrators' melancholic attitudes towards the separation, and their contradictory attachment and detachment to the severed object – the female and the mother in particular – only make sense when we consider the rebirth as mastering the separation and loss rather than simply as longing for the lost paradise.

Geulincx

Since Molloy is unable to free his mind of his mother, he repeats the memory of the severance over and over again, as does the narrator of 'The Expelled'. Whereas the narrator of *First Love* is bewildered by the driving force towards Lulu and haunted by the memory of her cries, Molloy seems to be free of the force, rather admitting his urge to continue his quest. Before resuming his search for his mother, Molloy asks, 'Now as to telling you why I stayed a good while with Lousse, no, I cannot. That is to say I could I suppose, if I took the trouble. But why should I?' (*T*, 50). The answer he offers us is elusive yet not impossible to decipher: 'I who had loved the image of old Geulincx, dead young, who left me free, on the black boat of Ulysses, to crawl towards the East, along the deck. [...] Which, as it bears me from no fatherland away, bears me onward to no shipwreck' (*T*, 51). This undoubtedly refers to Arnold Geulincx's statement, 'while the ship moves westward carrying its passenger to his destination, nothing prevents this passenger from walking eastward on the deck' (cited in Federman 1965, 78).

According to Raymond Federman, Geulincx believed that as long as one relies on divine intervention, there is no longer any need to make a conscious effort to understand the action of the body. We can see that Molloy compares himself to a passenger on a ship which carries him westward but does not distance him from no fatherland. Molloy's 'crawl[ing] towards the East along the deck' refers to his staying in Lousse's house and 'in several rooms one after the other' (*T*, 51).[19] A few pages later Molloy wonders 'Could a woman have stopped me as I swept towards mother?' (*T*, 56), thus it is clear that the mother is the destination towards which the ship is carrying him. Molloy's reference to Geulincx can be construed as his recognition that despite his persistent efforts to go – or 'crawl to the East along the deck' – in the opposite direction from the mother, in the end the ship carries him towards 'no fatherland', that is, to the motherland. Although Molloy's recurrent journeys seem to take different courses, they are all eventually leading to the mother. Molloy's remark on Geulincx, however, also reveals the inevitable nature of heading to the mother and the impossibility of severing the connection with the mother at this stage despite ceaseless attempts to do so.

In Molloy's reference to Geulincx, the movement of the ship from east to west is coincident with the actual geographical course from France to Ireland, as if Beckett's own imaginative journey from France to Ireland is implicated in his writing of *Molloy*, and as if in spite of his exile Beckett's mind is inevitably directed back towards Ireland. What is interesting in *Molloy* and the *Novellas*, then, is the contradiction between the narrators' wish to obliterate their memories of homeland and women and their attachment to them. Since the narrators are not aware of the significance of their separation from women and home and fail to recognize them as their lost objects, they can only demonstrate unfocused feelings of loss and the symptoms of melancholia. The abject entity, the object that has been expelled from the subject, as Kristeva's theory shows, can never be fully eradicated but lingers at the border of the subject's identity, 'threatening apparent unities and stabilities with disruption' and recurs in those events which Freud described as the 'return of the repressed' (Gross 1990, 87). The narrators' uncanny feelings of familiarity and alienation towards their surroundings are responses to the repressed memories come to mind.[20] Equally, the male narrator of *First Love*, confides 'Indeed she still disturbs me' (*CSP*, 32), and ends his narration, 'For years I thought [the cries of Lulu he heard during her labour] would cease. Now I don't think so any more' (45).

So in Beckett's French fictions written shortly after his exile, the work of mourning is endlessly deferred. If the narrators obsessively evoke the act of severance from the womb in order to master the separation, there is also the author himself who persistently considers the same story of the severance in his writing shortly after he had achieved geographical distance from his mother through exile. The failed severance with the mother, therefore, is represented as the ceaseless repetition of the act of severance, which fails again and again, in the *Novellas* and *Molloy*. Molloy's comment long after his journey echoes this predicament: 'if I should soon find my mother and settle the matter between us. [...] For it was no small matter and I was bent on it. All my life, I think I had been bent on [...] settling this matter between my mother and me, but had not succeeded' (*T*, 64–5). The memories of severance haunt the narrators of the *Novellas* and *Molloy*, and they talk compulsively about their memories 'until they sink forever in the mud' (*CSP*, 47). Those memories seem to sink for a short while in Beckett's French plays of the 1950s; *En attendant Godot* (1952) for instance occupies a non-specific setting and notably contains not one female character. However, in his works written in his mother tongue almost ten years after Beckett first ceased writing in English, we can expect to come upon what Freud describes as the return of the repressed, the return of the memories of women and Ireland.

3
The Gendering of Mourning and Melancholia in Beckett's Early Drama

I Introduction

'Mother at rest at last....' (*CDW*, 217), reads Krapp from his ledger for the tape which is later played on stage. As James Knowlson points out in his biography of Beckett, *Krapp's Last Tape* (1958) is Beckett's first work to reveal the autobiographical details of his mother's death: May Beckett died in August 1950 and it took Beckett more than seven years to achieve 'enough control over his emotions to draw on elements of his mother's death' (*DF*, 347) in his work. Such a control over one's emotions is, of course, an important feature in aesthetic practice in general and in Beckett's in particular. For instance, Knowlson reports that Beckett told him around 1980, 'You have to bring Yeats' "cold eye" to bear on anything you write', 'to bear on a personal experience before it could be used in a work of art.'[1] Beckett's comment on Yeats's epitaph, 'Cast a cold eye on life', reveals that he shares this artistic tendency with Yeats and also that he made life-long efforts to achieve emotional distance in writing about personal experience in his texts. Beckett's emphasis on the 'cold eye', however, also implies the struggle he had in controlling his feelings while writing about his personal memories. Throughout Beckett's oeuvre, certain memories, including those of home, Ireland, and his mother persist, and resist the 'cold eye' upon them.

Beckett's English plays from *All That Fall* (1956) onwards are distinct from his earlier French fiction and plays in many respects, and specifically in maintaining a 'cold eye' on his memories in his works. In contrast to the male narrators' melancholic disavowal of the memories of home in Beckett's French fiction, in *All That Fall* Beckett's memories of his home town and childhood are narrated through the voice of Maddy

Rooney, which is coloured by emotion. Similarly, both Winnie in *Happy Days* (1961) and Ada in *Embers* (1959) are nostalgic for the 'good old days' (*CDW*, 256). Beckett seems to find it easier to imbue these female voices with longing for the past. They also allow Beckett to develop alternative ways of using memories by letting the female characters mourn openly for their lost objects rather than being trapped in melancholia by the disavowal of their loss and failure to move on to the work of mourning as the male characters do. Although in Beckett's early English drama of the 1950s and 1960s women still appear in relation to their husbands or lovers, they are no longer ridiculed and silenced by the male narrators as they are in his early English and French fiction. If his early fiction focuses on Ulysses-like male characters 'wandering to find home' (*M*, 4), in these later English plays Beckett started to pay attention to Penelope-like females who are waiting for their husbands at home, and to give them different voices from those of the men.

In Beckett's English plays, the attitudes of male characters towards separation from home and their lovers are different from those of the male narrators in the French fiction. Whereas the narrators in the French fiction deny what they have lost, and thus show melancholic reactions towards 'a loss of a more ideal kind' (Freud 1991, 252), in the English plays, written after the deaths of his mother and brother, an acute sense of real loss starts to dominate the characters' memories. As Freud claims, the consciousness of loss differentiates mourning from melancholia, and in the English drama the male characters' awareness of their loss shows the first step towards the work of mourning. In contrast to the French fiction in which the work of mourning is endlessly deferred, it can be argued that in *Krapp's Last Tape, Embers* and *Eh Joe* (1965), the male characters start the process not of normal but of 'melancholic mourning'. The term, 'melancholic mourning' is adapted by Jahan Ramazani from Freud to 'distinguish mourning that is unresolved, violent, and ambivalent' (Ramazani 1994, 4). The male characters in Beckett's English drama display the melancholic mourning that Ramazani describes. Krapp, for example, attempts to recall the memories of separation from his loved ones, in a process that can be compared to Freud's work of mourning, but his response to the loss – his refusal to express grief and purge sorrow, and his failure to admit the significance of the loss – makes him remain as a melancholic.

Mourning and melancholia in Beckett's English plays written in the 1950s and 1960s, then, take gendered forms: while his male characters still attempt to cast a 'cold eye' on their memories of the lost loved one and repress their emotion, showing symptoms of melancholia, his female characters mourn openly for their loss and express their grief through other kinds of pathological symptoms such as hysteria and mania. Beckett's characters' reactions to the memories of the loss of loved ones no longer fit the Freudian binary distinction of mourning and melancholia, and thus, a reassessment of the theory of mourning and melancholia is necessary.

Re-reading Freud's 'Mourning and Melancholia'

Juliana Schiesari in her book, *The Gendering of Melancholia*, re-examines the 'conceptual limits' of Freud's 'Mourning and Melancholia', and re-evaluates melancholia as 'a specific cultural as well as pathological phenomenon', by tracking its 'historical indebtedness' to the Renaissance discourse on melancholia (Schiesari 1992, 18, 21). According to Schiesari, melancholia has been associated with a 'specific representational form for male creativity, one whose practice converted the feeling of disempowerment into a privileged artifact' (8). Melancholia has also been legitimated as a part of male literary practice whereas mourning has been allocated to the female domain. This male melancholic tradition has developed from the fifteenth-century philosophy of Marsilio Ficino, through the poetry of Torquato Tasso, and reaches its high point with the publication in 1621 of Robert Burton's monumental *Anatomy of Melancholy* (2). As mentioned earlier, Beckett not only extensively quotes Burton's book in his early English fiction, but also acknowledges its influence on his writing, as we see in his asking Duncan Scott whether he 'had ever detected the influence of Burton's *Anatomy of Melancholy* in his own works' (cited in Knowlson and Knowlson 2006, 217).

On the one hand, such a cultural tradition has granted melancholia a privileged representation and made it the creative condition of an intellectual male affliction, while women have been eliminated from the tradition, which either devalues female melancholia as 'prosaic', connecting it with the 'unprestigious term "depression"' or dismisses mourning practice as an undesirable 'collective women's ritual' (Schiesari 1992, 4, 18). On the other hand, such a cultural codification of mourning has made it difficult for males to express their loss or grief. As Ramazani argues in *Poetry of Mourning*, since mourning in public is 'marked as unavailable and alien' to men, the genre of elegy functioned to afford 'male poets the exploration of feelings publicly', and permit the 'social mask of the griefless male to slip a little' (Ramazani 1994, 20). According to Ramazani, while working in the elegy tradition of Milton, Shelley and Tennyson, male writers could perform psychological work that 'might have been more dangerously feminizing' (20) outside of literary practice. Expressing grief in their work, however, is still an uneasy practice for male elegists since, as Ramazani points out, traditional male elegists 'guardedly associated their laments with nymphs and muses', and likewise 'modern poets sometimes overtly link femininity with mourning in their elegies' (20). In Yeats's 'Easter 1916', for example, 'the male speaker even undergoes a momentary disturbance of gender, switching from male to female' (20) when the speaker murmurs over the names of the dead 'As a mother names her child' (Yeats 1996, 288). Borrowing a female voice, then, seems to be an inevitable choice for some male writers in order to assuage their anxiety over expressing their grief and over transgressing the social and cultural codification of mourning.

To some extent, as in the case of some elegists and modern poets, Beckett's feminization of mourning shows his discomfort in writing about his loss and grief. His use of female voices in mourning, however, is by no means a devaluation of female mourning practices; rather it is an alternative way of expressing his loss of Ireland as well as his lost (m)other when memories – which had been repressed for a long time – start to return. By borrowing female voices Beckett started to experiment with varieties of work on grief, and to move away from the earlier dominant melancholic male voice. In expressing the female characters' loss, Beckett uses 'hysterical' (*CDW*, 174) or manic voices, which are symptoms traditionally associated with female maladies. Yet, Beckett's sympathy with his female characters suggests that he is both appropriating and resisting the social codification of mourning and the traditional psychology that is seen to accompany it. For instance in *All That Fall*, Mrs Rooney's shrill outcry, 'What kind of a country is this where a woman can't weep her heart out on the highways and byways' (176), can be read as Beckett's critical comment on the social and cultural mode in which mourning in public is not tolerated. Below we will see how Beckett, using Mrs Rooney's voice, protests against the social and cultural codification of mourning and, at the same time, temporarily allows himself to display grief and longing for his homeland, Ireland.

II Alternation between mourning and melancholia in *All That Fall*

'All came over me again, like a flood'

Beckett's decision to write *All That Fall* in English, after having abandoned the language for nearly ten years (with the exception of the short prose piece *From an Abandoned Work*), could be seen as predetermined since it was written in response to an invitation from the BBC to write a radio play. As if triggered by his mother tongue, Beckett's childhood memories of his home town, Foxrock, in Ireland, which are absent from his earlier French plays, 'all came over' him 'again, like a flood' (*CDW*, 176), like the return of the repressed in *All That Fall*. A letter to Aidan Higgins shows that Beckett had this particular Irish setting and these memories in mind for the radio play from the beginning of his writing, suggesting the link between the language choice, his 'boyhood memories' and the setting:

> Have been asked to write a radio play for the 3rd [the BBC Third Programme] and am tempted, feet dragging and breath short and cartwheels and imprecations from the Brighton Rd to Foxrock station and back, insentient old mares in foal being welted by the cottagers and the Devil tottered in the ditch – boyhood memories.
>
> (Cited in *DF*, 385)

The final version of the play also begins with the sound of dragging feet and the breathing of Mrs Rooney who starts her journey from her house to Boghill railway station, which closely resembles Foxrock. The details of Mrs Rooney's route echo the route between Beckett's family home, Cooldrinagh, and Foxrock station, and as Knowlson's *Damned to Fame* reveals, the names used in the play are those of local people, whom Beckett knew in his childhood, or are those names slightly changed (*DF*, 385).

What is intriguing, then, is the connection between Beckett's first full exploration of his memories of Ireland after he settled in France and the emergence of his first female leading character. It can be argued that the main female role in *All That Fall* was Beckett's inevitable choice in order to alleviate his discomfort in expressing grief. Beckett seems to find it easier to display grief and homesickness when writing of memories of home and its landscape using the female voice. When Mrs Rooney arrives at the Boghill station accompanied by the 'dark Miss Fitt' (*CDW*, 184), and is left out of the other characters' conversation, she talks about the 'entire scene' of Boghill with its specific resonances of Beckett's home town, Foxrock and the Leopardstown Racecourse near the railway station:

MRS ROONEY: Do not flatter yourselves for one moment, because I hold aloof, that my sufferings have ceased. No. The entire scene, the hills, the plain, the racecourse with its miles and miles of white rails and three red stands, the pretty little wayside station, even you yourselves, yes, I mean it, and over all the clouding blue, I see it all, I stand here and see it all with eyes ... [*The voice breaks.*] ... through eyes ... oh if you had my eyes ... you would understand ... the things they have seen ... and not looked away ... this is nothing ... nothing ... what did I do with the handkerchief? ... [*Mrs Rooney blows her nose violently and long.*]

(CDW, 185)

This passage, which does not seem to correspond to the other characters' conversation, can be seen as being directed towards the audience. Instead of asking us to cast a 'cold eye' on 'the entire scene', Mrs Rooney's speech invites us, who cannot see the scenery, to imagine it in our mind's eye, and implores us to be sympathetic to her nostalgia, as she says 'oh if you had my eyes ... you would understand'. Furthermore, Mrs Rooney's asking her interlocutor not to assume that her 'sufferings have ceased' since she holds 'aloof', and her breakdown while describing the landscape, both suggest Beckett's own difficulty in talking about the memory of his home town without giving way to his feelings. Here, Mrs Rooney directly speaks for Beckett whose own aloofness is in hiding his 'sufferings' and longing for home.

A close analysis of the moment of Mrs Rooney's breakdown further helps decipher Beckett's own sense of loss, which is encoded in a similar mode to Belacqua's funeral scene in *More Pricks Than Kicks*, as observed in Chapter 1. Prior to Mrs Rooney's breakdown, we hear that Miss Fitt has come to the station looking for her mother. During the usual chaotic greetings and chatter of the busy railway station, the thread of conversation about Miss Fitt's mother persists, and the words 'mother' and 'Mamma' (CDW, 184) constantly recur. Mr Tyler, for example, asks Miss Fitt, 'You have lost your mother, Miss Fitt?' (185), which is repeated twice immediately before Mrs Rooney's long speech, quoted above. Although *All That Fall* is Beckett's first English play written after both his mother's and brother's deaths, he does not directly speak about this experience. Instead, we see that Beckett insinuates his sense of loss and 'sufferings' into Mrs Rooney's effort to join the conversation about Miss Fitt's search for her mother and the emotional breakdown which is triggered by this conversation. While on the surface Mrs Rooney explicitly describes only the landscape of Beckett's home town, her breakdown is also closely linked to her own sense of loss and her compassion for Miss Fitt, as her following words suggest: 'I am sorry for all this ramdam,

Miss Fitt, had I known you were looking for your mother I should not have importuned you, I know what it is' (185). As Mrs Rooney's sympathetic words are not acknowledged by the other characters and thus she is deprived of her chance to express her own sense of loss, so the theme of Miss Fitt and her mother is also discontinued after Mr Rooney's arrival. It remains uncertain in the end whether or not Miss Fitt has found her mother. However, the importance of the theme is confirmed when it returns in Beckett's later play *Footfalls* (1975). Miss Fitt's story reappears in *Footfalls*, and as Mary Doll rightly points out, May's sequel in the play is 'a literary sequel of another crisis-crossed Mother-daughter pairing' like that presented in *All that Fall* (Doll 1989, 117). Until Beckett achieves enough emotional distance to write about his own lost loved ones, he settles for focusing on the physical setting of his own home town in *All That Fall*.

'It is suicide to be abroad'

It can be argued that Maddy Rooney not only functions to express Beckett's own homesickness by articulating his memories of his home town, but that she is also closely associated with the idea of home itself. Beckett's wish to achieve detachment from home and Ireland, however, is represented through her husband, Dan Rooney.

The play is loosely divided into three parts: Mrs Rooney's journey to the railway station, her waiting in the station, and her way back home with her husband. Mrs Rooney's main concern in this play is to bring her husband back home safely as she tells him, 'Now we are in safety and a straight run home' (*CDW*, 190). Her wish to tie her husband to their house is symbolically presented in 'a tie' which she gave to Dan as a birthday present in the morning, wishing him 'happy returns' (188). Like the string or lace which is used as an umbilical symbol in the *Novellas* and *Molloy*, and which is given to the narrators with their hats when they set off on their journeys, the tie is given to Dan, and his wife makes sure he '[has] it on' (188) when he returns. In *Watt*, the homecoming of the signal-man, Mr Case, is persistently linked to his 'lonely' and 'unquiet wife' (*W*, 230) who is, like Penelope, anxiously waiting for her husband; in *All That Fall* we find Mrs Rooney nervously doing the same.

However, in contrast to Mr Case's wife, who is silenced and never introduced in the novel, in *All That Fall* Beckett starts to turn his attention to this Penelope-like wife, Mrs Rooney, and to give her a voice and a more active role, so that instead of waiting passively for her husband to come home, she goes to the railway station to assist his homecoming.

All the way to the station and while waiting for the train, Mrs Rooney expresses her apprehension – over whether she will get to the station in time and over the delay of the train. To get to the station is not easy for Mrs Rooney: she is physically decrepit and fat, and she fears the dangers of the world outside her home. After she has been nearly run over by 'Connolly's van' she resents the idea of leaving home, exclaiming, 'It is suicide to be abroad' (*CDW*, 175). While in *Watt* Mr Case's wish to 'go [back] home, to his lonely wife' is represented by showing his reading George Russell's '[*Homeward*] *Songs by the Way*' (*W*, 227),[2] Mrs Rooney, as if expressing her difficulties in getting to the station and her wish to go back home, sings a hymn, 'Lead, Kindly Light', specifically the part which echoes her situation: 'The night is dark and I am far from ho-ome, tum tum –' (*CDW*, 184). Though hindered by her own failing body as she heads towards the station, Mrs Rooney is determined to bring her husband safe back home.

'I dream of other roads, in other lands. Of another home'

It becomes clear from Dan Rooney's statement, 'I dream of other roads, in other lands. Of another home, another – [*He hesitates.*] – another home' (192) that home in this play has a wider meaning than that of home in an essentially domestic context. While his comment on 'the horrors of home life' (193) and the long list of the household things that he detests demonstrates his refusal of a domestic way of life, it also expresses his resistance to the land to which he belongs (that is to say, Ireland). In his account of arriving at the station, Mr Rooney says: 'And the next thing was Barrell bawling the abhorred name. I got down and Jerry led me to the men's, or Fir as they call it now, from Vir Viris I suppose, the V becoming F, in accordance with Grimm's Law' (195). To Mr Rooney Boghill is an 'abhorred name'; he recalls Barrell's signalling arrival of the train by '*shouting "Boghill!"*' (187). Even though the name of Beckett's home town Foxrock has changed to 'Boghill' – which is already recognizably an Irish name – as if the name is taboo as in his French fiction, Mr Rooney refuses to utter it. In so doing he is reflecting Freud's model of melancholia in which a patient deliberately represses and avoids the name of the lost object by not mentioning it by name or by referring to it in some other way in order not to be reminded of it. As if the name of Ireland reminds him of what has been lost, Beckett avoids naming it directly. Also, as if attempting to reverse Maddy Rooney's strong feelings towards Boghill, Beckett returns to a melancholic man whose attitude is similar to that of the male narrators in his French fiction in order to display his own resistance to home, Ireland.

In *All That Fall* Beckett's cultural memory of Ireland is frozen at the moment at which the Catholic state sought national identity by following the Gaelic tradition. As the young Beckett criticized the Irish Free State's pervasive nationalism and policy against contraception, Dan Rooney also makes critical comments about the country. In the passage quoted above, as Nicholas Grene claims, by saying 'as *they* call it now', Dan distances himself from 'the Catholic nationalists, who are now in control of the state, and who have decreed that all public signs such as that for the men's toilet should appear in the first national language as "FIR" not "MEN"' (Grene 1999, 181). This remark comes shortly after Maddy Rooney's, 'it will be dead in time, just like our own poor dear Gaelic' (*CDW*, 194). Whereas Maddy's remark – her *'our* own poor dear Gaelic' – is clearly sympathetic to the fact that Gaelic language is 'dead', Dan's focus is on the futility of the nationalists' attempt to revive it and on marking his own separation from this tendency. Dan's criticism becomes more significant when we consider it as a recapitulation of Beckett's early material where the male characters resist the Irish Free State and its dominant nationalism, which in part impelled the young Beckett to exile. In contrast to Maddy's cry 'It is suicide to be abroad' and her mournful reaction to her home town, what Dan offers is a melancholic refusal of home and his (and Beckett's) justification of exile.

Mourning practice in the Anglo-Irish Protestant community

Whereas both Mr and Mrs Rooney's melancholic and nostalgic reactions towards the same object, Beckett's home town, indicates Ireland as a Freudian lost object, the play does not reveal the reason behind Maddy's emotional and 'hysterical' (174) response nor Dan's abrupt 'crying' (197) at the end of the play. Instead, while suggesting that Maddy is mourning the loss of her daughter, Minnie, *All That Fall* focuses on the response of the Anglo-Irish Protestant community towards Maddy's expressions of grief and loss. Ireland had been considered as 'Western Europe's last national enclave for [the] traditional mourning ritual' (Ramazani 1994, 23), and as observed in Chapters 1 and 2 Beckett is critical of Irish Catholic mourning practices and literary representations of mourning as manifested in Yeats and Synge's plays on the legend of Deirdre. However, as Ramazani states, even in Ireland, between 1880 and the early twentieth century, traditional mourning practices such as wakes and keening had largely died out. Since the Great War, the Western world has experienced shifts in mourning practices: social practices of mourning have diminished, and have been reduced to the private sphere; rational men and women are supposed to keep their mourning private and under complete control by strength of will 'so as not to offend others' (15). Also, 'denial of mourning' had become prevalent in 'English-speaking countries with a Protestant tradition' (15). Although Catholics are in the majority in Ireland, as many critics point out, the setting of *All That Fall* is Boghill/Foxrock, a community of Anglo-Irish Protestants, the religion of the Rooneys.[3]

Privatization of the work of mourning in the Irish Protestant community is explained by Mrs Rooney. When she starts her journey to the railway station, we hear Schubert's 'Death and the Maiden' coming from a woman's house, and Mrs Rooney's explanation: 'Poor woman. All alone in that ruinous old house' (*CDW*, 172). And again at the end of the play, Mrs Rooney comments, 'All day the same old record. All alone in that great empty house. She must be a very old woman now' (197). This not only suggests the old woman's Anglo-Irish background in her inhabiting the 'Big House', but also implies that she has been confined in her house, grieving alone for a long period of time.[4] Mrs Rooney shows her sympathy for the old woman, and joins her in her grief by 'murmur[ing] [the] melody' (172).

Furthermore, in *All That Fall* Mrs Rooney brings to the minds of other characters scenes of illness, dying and death, and appeals to them to express their loss and grief. Apart from Miss Fitt – who as Grene comments, is closely linked to the Church of Ireland through her emphasis on the 'Protestant thing to do' (183) (Grene 1999, 180), but who fails to show any true compassion to Mrs Rooney – all the characters whom Mrs Rooney encounters on the way to the railway station are male. Mrs Rooney's first greeting to the male characters is invariably to ask after their sick family members. To Christy, she asks, 'How is your poor wife? [...] And your daughter then?' (*CDW*, 172); to Mr Tyler, 'What news of your poor daughter?' (174); and to Mr Slocum, 'How is your poor mother?' (177). She reminds Mr Barrell of his dead 'father' (181). However, unlike Mrs Rooney, who displays evident sympathy towards the sick and dying, the male characters remain distant and conceal their emotions, cutting the conversation short and answering briefly, 'No better', 'No worse' (172), or 'Fair, fair' (174). The male characters also refuse to express their compassion for Mrs Rooney in her lament for the loss of her daughter many years before. When she tells Mr Barrell that she 'was so plunged in sorrow', for instance, he '*turns to go*' (181) without making any comment, even before she finishes speaking. When Mr Barrell leaves her, she breaks down, crying, 'I estrange them all. They come towards me, uninvited, [...] anxious to help ... [*The voice breaks.*] ... genuinely pleased ... to see me again ... looking so well ... [*Handkerchief.*] A few simple words ... from my heart ... and I am all alone ... once more' (182). This significantly suggests people's reaction to loss in the Irish community as well as Mrs Rooney's awareness of it. As if her 'words from her heart' offended the men she encountered, they leave her 'all alone', refusing to join her work of mourning or to expose their feelings. Echoing her own comment on the poor woman, who is 'All alone in that ruinous old house' (172), Mrs Rooney is also left 'all alone', and forced to carry on her work of mourning in private.

In a society where the expression of grief is not welcome perhaps the only way of discharging emotions is to borrow a hysterical voice. At the railway station when Mrs Rooney learns that the train is delayed, she not only reveals her 'anxiety' about Dan's possible accident, but also criticizes Mr Barrell who reports the situation:

> MR BARRELL: I know nothing. All I know is there has been a hitch. All traffic is retarded.
> MRS ROONEY: [*Derisively.*] Retarded! A hitch! Ah these celibates! Here we are eating our hearts out with anxiety for our loved ones and he calls that a hitch!
>
> (*CDW*, 187)

While Mrs Rooney's expression, 'eating our hearts out', could be seen as rather excessive in this circumstance, unlike Beckett's male characters, she is not afraid of expressing her apprehension over losing her loved one. Furthermore, she criticizes Mr Barrell's aloofness and unsympathetic reaction. She '*derisively*' comments on his lack of emotion by comparing him to 'celibates!' As the plural form of the word, 'celibates' indicates, her criticism is directed to the collective of males who are emotionally deprived, and who with the absence of a loved object do not have the ability to love or to express sympathy.

We see something similar when Mrs Rooney laments the loss of her daughter, Minnie. Mr Tyler tries to calm her down, but she exclaims, as quoted earlier, 'What kind of a country is this where a woman can't weep her heart out on the highways and byways without being tormented by retired bill-brokers!' (176). Mrs Rooney's condemnation here is directed not only towards Mr Tyler, but also towards Ireland. It is true that Mrs Rooney is unnecessarily emotional both about the delay of the train and in relation to Mr Tyler's gesture to calm her down and indeed, her reaction can be perceived as hysterical. However, Beckett's use of hysteria in this play is far from the stereotypical representation of hysterical females in the male literary canon, in which women such as

Ophelia in *Hamlet* are silenced and end up committing suicide. Rather, Mrs Rooney raises her 'hysterical' (174) voice in order to protest against the society in which expressing grief in public is to be avoided. It is also important to note Mrs Rooney's self-awareness of her hysterical voice. As Grene states, a 'whole style of life, a whole social milieu is summed up brilliantly in Maddy Rooney's self-pitying self description' (Grene 1999, 180):

> Oh I am just a hysterical old hag I know, destroyed with sorrow and pining and gentility and church-going and fat and rheumatism and childlessness. [*Pause. Brokenly.*] Minnie! Little Minnie! [*Pause.*] Love, that is all I asked, a little love, daily, twice daily, fifty years of twice daily love like a Paris horse-butcher's regular, what normal woman wants affection? A peck on the jaw at morning, near the ear, and another at evening, peck, peck, till you grow whiskers on you.
>
> (*CDW*, 174)

As we see, the description 'a hysterical old hag' is provided not by any other character in the play, but by herself. Moreover, given that she immediately connects the comment with her plea for 'love' and 'affection' from her husband, she is using a 'hysterical' voice to resist social restrictions about displaying emotions. By allowing her to criticize this social tendency while prohibiting any comment on her hysterical reaction from other characters, Beckett suggests sympathy towards Mrs Rooney's 'hysterical' voice.

Beckett's use of a 'hysterical' voice, then, can be seen as an attempt by him to express his own grief, to move on to the work of mourning, while at the same time revealing his unease in transgressing the social and cultural codification of mourning. Hysteria is also a reaction to the loss of a loved one, and closely connected to the work of mourning. As Schiesari asserts, 'it was in his case study of hysteric Elisabeth von R. that Freud first discovered the work of mourning' (Schiesari 1992, 62). Freud's description of Elisabeth von R. whose 'character bears evidence of hysteria' is strikingly similar to Mrs Rooney's actions in the play: Elisabeth von R. undergoes the work of mourning by recollecting her memories obsessively 'br[inging] up before her eyes the scenes of illness and death. Every day she would go through each impression once more, would weep over it and console herself' (Freud 1955a, 162). Likewise, Mrs Rooney endeavours to console herself by weeping over the loss of her daughter who died a long time ago, 'remembering ... [*The voice breaks.*] ... all the silly unhappiness' (*CDW*, 181) and mourning her loss as well as invoking the scenes of illness and death to the other characters and to the audience.

Homecoming, the train and the womb metaphor

While the first two parts of *All That Fall* centre on Mrs Rooney's mournful voice and her appeals to the other characters to join her work of mourning, the last part of the play focuses more on conversations between Mr and Mrs Rooney. In contrast to Maddy who encounters numerous people and seeks attention from them, as soon as Dan appears all the other characters vanish apart from the boy, Jerry, whose role is to guide Dan from the railway station to home, and also, like a messenger in the Greek play, to reveal the truth of the delay of the train – 'a little child fell out of the carriage' (199). Their only encounter with people from then on is with the Lynch twins, who are 'jeering at' (191) them in the same way as Watt and Molloy are bullied by local people. Implying that this happens often, Dan asks Maddy, 'Will they pelt us with mud today, do you suppose?' (191). What is interesting is the sudden change of the tone of the play after Dan Rooney's appearance, from Mrs Rooney's nostalgia to Mr Rooney's hostility towards Beckett's home town and its people: the play develops towards a more solipsistic view of the world by leaving the pair alone in silence. As if attempting to counterbalance Mrs Rooney's emotion, and also as if suggesting Beckett's own uneasiness in expressing his homesickness, in the later part of the play he introduces a male character who restrains his emotions, and reins back the nostalgic atmosphere created by Mrs Rooney.

In many aspects, Mr Rooney represents the opposite pole from Mrs Rooney, and instead shares characteristics in common with the male narrators in Beckett's French fiction. As the passage above shows, Mrs Rooney's complaint about lack of 'affection' centres on her husband, and it is he who resists expressing emotion in public. After the train arrives and when they finally meet each other, Mrs Rooney asks for a kiss. Mr Rooney's response to her appeal for 'affection' is that of a *rational* man who withholds emotion: 'Kiss you? In public? On the platform? Before the boy? Have you taken leave of your senses?' (188). While this indicates Mr Rooney's general repression of emotion in 'public', it is his resistance to home – in his words, 'the horrors of home life' (*CDW*, 193) – and his homeland that most particularly echoes that of the melancholic male narrators in Beckett's French fiction.

Furthermore, Mr Rooney's 'horrors of home life' are connected to a womb metaphor like that used in Beckett's French fiction. In order to lead us to the mental world of Mr Rooney, Beckett first of all casts off the other characters, and leaves the Rooneys alone in the play. Immediately after they scare the Lynch twins away, Mrs Rooney makes an incantatory speech about shutting themselves into their own world leaving 'No living soul' around them:

> MRS ROONEY: All is still. No living soul in sight. There is no one to ask. The world is feeding. The wind – [*Brief wind.*] – scarcely stirs the leaves and the birds – [*Brief chirp.*] – are tired singing. The cows – [*Brief moo.*] – and sheep – [*Brief baa.*] – ruminate in silence. The dogs – [*Brief bark.*] – are hushed and the hens – [*Brief cackle.*] – sprawl torpid in the dust. We are alone. There is no one to ask. [*Silence.*]
>
> (*CDW*, 192)

Following Maddy's spell, even the animals disappear after brief cries, leaving the pair in absolute silence. Immediately afterwards, Dan, who has been refusing to explain what had happened in the train during the delay, begins to speak. What we hear, however, is not an explanation for the delay, but rather what was going through his mind at the time: 'Alone in the compartment my mind began to work, as so often after office hours, on the way home, in the train' (193). Not only does this speech recall *The Unnamable*'s fable of homecoming and 'the nature of trains' (*T*, 406) in relation to birth trauma, but also significantly Dan attempts to describe his anxiety of being in the womb-like compartment in the train, not being able to get out of it: 'Then gradually a – how shall I say – a growing desire to – er – you know welled up within me. Nervous probably. In fact now I am sure. You know, the feeling of being confined' (*CDW*, 195).

There is a literal reading of this passage that sees it as describing Dan's desire to urinate and the anxiety attendant on his being unable to leave the carriage. The delay of the train and his fear of confinement, however, also reveal a different type of anxiety. Trains in Beckett's works are often associated with homecoming and also, as he noted in his 'Psychology Notes', 'the departure as meaning <u>separation from the mother</u>' (TCD MS 10971/8/35; cited in Feldman 2006, 31, Beckett's emphasis). Whereas in Beckett's French fiction the narrators' main concern is to repeat the separation from the womb-like room without explicitly spelling out their anxiety, in *All That Fall* Dan Rooney's anxiety is not only specifically connected to his being confined in the womb-like train,[5] but also echoes Beckett's own description of his 'extraordinary memories of being in the womb' and his anxiety at 'feeling trapped' and 'imprisoned' (*DF*, 171). Thus, Beckett still does not seem to believe that he has managed to sever the umbilical cord with his mother and his homeland.

The womb metaphor that Beckett uses in *All That Fall* is even more complex than that used in his French fiction since his voice may arguably be heard in the words of two main characters, Mr and Mrs Rooney. When Dan describes his anxiety at being confined in the train, Maddy, as if attempting to offer him and the audience an explanation for the anxiety, talks about the lecture of a 'new mind doctor' (*CDW*, 195) she attended. As often cited by critics, here Beckett uses C.G. Jung's lecture he heard at the Tavistock Clinic in 1935, the story of a little girl, who 'had never really been born!' (196), hinting that Dan's feeling of being confined is related to the failure to be born properly. After uttering these words, Maddy unexpectedly '*weeps*', and states 'There is nothing to be done for those people!' (196). Even if Maddy's sympathy here is addressed to the little girl and the people who share 'the troubled mind' (195) with the girl, her excessive emotion, which otherwise seems to be out of context, can be explained when considering it as related to Dan's unsuccessful separation from the mother. Maddy here not only understands Dan's anxiety, but also weeps for Dan's trouble and speaks for Beckett.

This section has explored the ways in which Beckett oscillates between female mourning and male melancholia in *All That Fall*. Even if Beckett conceals what the real lost object is in the play, Mr and Mrs Rooney's opposing reactions to the same matter, home and Ireland, as well as to the metaphor of birth, hint at Beckett's ambivalent feelings towards his own country and the memories of home. To a degree, as in the case of some elegists and modern poets, Beckett's feminization of mourning reveals his discomfort in writing about his own loss and grief. His use of Mrs Rooney's voice, however, needs to be seen not as devaluing female mourning practices, but as enabling an alternative way to express his loss of Ireland and the lost loved objects. Moreover, unlike the male narrators in Beckett's French fiction, who attempt to suppress the memories of home, in *All That Fall*, in spite of Dan's wish for 'another home' (192), the pair manage to head homewards as Beckett manages to delve into his repressed memories of Ireland.

III   Farewell to Love: *Krapp's Last Tape*

'Retrospective loss and mourning'

If in *All That Fall* Beckett rather unexpectedly experiences an overflow of his memories of childhood and homeland and expresses his sorrows by borrowing Mrs Rooney's voice, in *Krapp's Last Tape* (1958) – his second play written in English – he attempts to write about his personal experience in a more controlled male voice. However, as if suggesting that talking about the memories of the lost loved ones is still not easy for him, in this play Beckett creates a clever device through which to channel and control his emotion. Instead of sixty-nine-year old Krapp directly recalling for the audience the moment of his mother's death, he plays a tape which was recorded shortly after her death thirty years earlier, so that his present feelings about the subject do not have to be verbally expressed. Krapp at thirty-nine briefly describes the moment of his mother's death, repressing his emotion in a way that is reminiscent of the melancholic male narrators in Beckett's French fiction. On the surface the melancholic voice seems to be pervasive because the main action of the play is the old Krapp listening to the voice from the tape.

The last words of the play from Krapp at thirty-nine – 'I wouldn't want them [my best years] back' (*CDW*, 223) – also increase the melancholic tone of the play. Beckett's intention of ending the play with the younger Krapp's vehement refusal of his recent past can be understood in the same vein as the change of tone in *All That Fall* from Mrs Rooney's mourning voice to Mr Rooney's melancholic one. Even though the old Krapp's last speech – 'Be again, be again' (223) – shows a nostalgic longing for the past, by ending the play with the younger Krapp's disavowal of the past Beckett manages to prevent the old Krapp from developing a more sentimental voice, and reins in his emotions after some telling slippages.

On stage, however, we see not the younger melancholic Krapp, but the old Krapp's immediate ambivalent reactions when the memories are vividly recollected. Unlike fiction, in which language is the only medium, theatre offers Beckett room to express his repressed feelings and conflicts by using gestures which can be used to contradict the words that the audience hear. The tension and rupture arising from the gap between what Krapp at thirty-nine says and how Krapp at sixty-nine behaves not only indicate the significance of what has been repressed for thirty years, but also invite us to map out the psychological journey that Krapp has been through. Like the male narrators of Beckett's French fiction, the younger Krapp has tried to obliterate his memories by repressing them. Having missed out on a chance to undertake the work of mourning by failing to realize the significance of the separation from his loved ones, Krapp has not properly severed his attachment with the lost objects. *Krapp's Last Tape*, then, presents the moment when the old Krapp finally endeavours to expose himself to the painful memory of the separation and to take the first step towards the work of mourning. What he experiences by listening to his old tape is comparable to what Beckett calls 'retrospective loss and mourning' (*P*, 50).

This 'retrospective loss and mourning' is mentioned in Beckett's essay, *Proust* (1931), in order to diagnose Marcel's delayed response to his grandmother's death in Marcel Proust's *À la recherche du temps perdu*. As the loss of his grandmother only starts to mean much to Marcel a year after her burial,[6] so Krapp reassesses the loss of his loved one thirty years after the separation and mourns for the loss. In contrast to Krapp at thirty-nine and the male narrators in Beckett's French fiction, the old Krapp begins to gain a conscious awareness of what has been lost, and to proceed with the work of mourning, or rather, what Ramazani terms the work of 'melancholic mourning' – in which although one mourns a 'specific death, not the vague or unconscious losses of melancholia', the mourner displays intense 'self-criticism' (Ramazani 1994, 4). It is not only melancholic mourning, since Krapp still refuses to fully express his grief and purge his sorrow, but it is also a privatization of the work of mourning; unlike Mrs Rooney, Krapp only can undertake his work of mourning in private. We will now identify Krapp's significant loss as the separation from his loved one, and show that his act of listening to the tape is his work of melancholic mourning.

Krapp at twenty-nine

It has been said that Beckett was inspired by the 'cracked quality of [the actor Patrick] Magee's distinctively Irish voice' (*DF*, 398) to write a piece which was provisionally titled as 'Magee Monologue' and that became *Krapp's Last Tape*. Whether the Irish voice triggered Beckett's memories or not, *Krapp's Last Tape*, like the overflowing memories of his home town in *All That Fall*, contains many personal elements, such as the 'illness of his father' (*CDW*, 218) and the death of his mother, together with a Dublin landscape. By making Krapp at sixty-nine listen to the tape in which Krapp at thirty-nine also recalls a tape made 'ten or twelve years ago' (218), the play portrays Krapp over a span of forty years. Notably, the stories, which are told through the voices from the different stages of Krapp's life, echo Beckett's personal memories as well as his own literary works. The stories of Krapp's relationships with women, for instance, correspond to Beckett's early fiction, *More Pricks Than Kicks* and *Murphy*. In the early manuscripts the woman with whom the young Krapp 'liv[ed] on and off' (218) is 'first Belacqua's Alba, then Murphy's Celia'.[7] Also in a letter to Rick Cluchey, dated 17 July 1977, Beckett notes characteristics of Krapp which resonate with Belacqua and Murphy, who believe that women entrap them by means of sexuality.

In explaining how Cluchey is to play the part, Beckett wrote, 'make the thing your own in terms of incarceration, for example. Incarceration in self. He escapes from the trap of the other only to be trapped in self' (cited in Knowlson 1980, 127). In *Krapp's Last Tape* Beckett portrays a male protagonist who has managed to expel the women in search of his self and is confined in the 'little world' of his own that Belacqua and Murphy desire.

Beckett's comment above is strikingly similar to Victor Krap's confession at the end of his first play *Eleutheria*:

> VICTOR: I have always wanted to be free. [...] That's all I desire. At first I was a prisoner of other people. So I left them. Then I was a prisoner of myself. That was worse. So I left myself.
>
> (*E*, 147)

Beckett's *Eleutheria*[8] – the Greek word for freedom – was written in French fairly quickly in 1947. Since the male protagonist, Victor Krap, resembles the young Krapp as well as (more or less) sharing his name, further discussion of *Eleutheria* will be used to shed light on Krapp's past. Throughout his lifetime, Beckett adamantly refused to have this play published,[9] possibly because, as Knowlson states, 'autobiographical tensions and reminiscences seemed insufficiently distanced or inadequately integrated into the play' (*DF*, 328). As the title of the play and what Victor says above indicate, the autobiographical elements, on which Beckett failed to cast a cold eye, can be argued to concern the separation from his loved ones, who in this play are represented as Victor's mother, Mme Krap and his fiancée, Mlle Skunk. Similar to Celia's 'desire to make a man of Murphy' (*M*, 65), Mme Krap's determined efforts to make Victor a man of 'gainful employment, love, [and] marriage' are particularly close to 'what his own mother had attempted to do with [Beckett] in the 1930s' (*DF*, 329). As Victor's conflicts mainly derive from his resistance to his mother and fiancée's fanatical attempt to bring him back home, it is these women who, he believes, imprisoned him. In contrast to Victor's father's emotional detachment from Victor's absence, Mme Krap is 'terribly worried' (*E*, 55) about Victor, and 'begged', 'shouted' and 'wept' (56) in front of Victor to try to persuade him back home.

Similarly, at the end of the play Mlle Skunk also visits Victor to plead with him to come back home:

> MLLE SKUNK: [*taking Victor by the arm*] Come away! [...]
> VICTOR: 'Come away'? Where?

MLLE SKUNK: [*in exultation*] With me! Towards life! Hand in hand! Dawn is breaking!

(*E*, 163–4)

While this passage parodies Yeats's poem, 'The Stolen Child' echoing 'Come away, O human child! [...] With a faery, hand in hand' (Yeats 1996, 53), unlike the fairy in Yeats's poem who seduces a child to take him to the fairy land, in *Eleutheria* Mlle Skunk endeavours to bring Victor back to her mundane world, 'Towards life'. Just as Miss Counihan, a devouring female who tries to bring Murphy back to Ireland, is closely associated with Yeats's Cathleen ni Houlihan, so Mlle Skunk's desire to entice Krap is the feature inherited from Yeats's fairy of the Celtic twilight. While Belacqua and Murphy passively achieve distance from their female partners only through their deaths, Victor more emphatically resists his fiancée and mother. Despite Mlle Skunk and Mme Krap's plea, Victor rejects them, and the play ends with Victor lying on his bed alone in his room at the boarding house '*turning his emaciated back on humanity*' (*E*, 170), suggesting his refusal of his fiancée and his mother as well as his parents' home.

Eleutheria, written immediately after Beckett finished the *Novellas* and before starting to write *Molloy*, shares much in common with the French fiction, particularly in the male protagonist's refusal to express his feelings. When hearing that his mother has a 'broken heart' and Mlle Skunk 'is sick with grief' (*E*, 76), he [Victor] declines to show any emotion towards them replying that he has 'no more feeling for her', 'Nor for anyone' (76). However, whereas in the French fiction the importance of the male narrators' separation from home and women is underplayed as a result of the narrators' failure to be consciously aware of what they have lost, in *Eleutheria* Victor's conflicts and troubles are evidently linked to the separation from his mother and fiancée. Such a link was perhaps too 'autobiographical' and 'insufficiently distanced' for Beckett to want to publish it.

Krapp at thirty-nine

This close association between Victor's desire for isolation and his choice to leave his loved ones – despite Beckett's wish to suppress *Eleutheria* as something unworthy – not only confirms the correlation between the early devouring females and the male protagonists' desire for leaving Ireland, but also leads us to see the significance of the separation as a central loss for the male characters in other plays. *Krapp's Last Tape*, written more than ten years after *Eleutheria*, presents a man who invokes the moment of abandoning his love in order to seek for freedom, and stays in his own solipsistic world, the little world, where he might compose an 'opus...magnum' (*CDW*, 218). Krapp, trapped in himself as Victor Krap, is a man, according to Beckett's own explanation, caught in loneliness, and has spoken monologues to himself throughout his entire life: 'this is what marks the character of his voice' (cited in Knowlson 1992, 127). Thirty years after he had chosen to be isolated from other people, Krapp revisits the moment of his decision.

The tape, which is played on stage, includes three important incidents which significantly coincided in the same year: 'Mother at rest at last' which refers to his mother's death, 'Memorable equinox' which records his moment of vision in his artistic approach – echoing Beckett's own experience as discussed in the previous chapter – and 'Farewell to [...] love' (*CDW*, 217). As Beckett's 'Production Notebook' for *Das lezte Band* at the Schiller-Theatre Werkstatt, Berlin (dated 5 October 1969) states, the tape is selected as Krapp's 'choice and not [by] chance' (cited in Knowlson 1992, 49). In this notebook Beckett remarks, 'At curtain up he is thinking of the story of the boat and trying to remember which year it was (how old he was)' (49). At the opening of the play, all Krapp's activities, brooding in silence, *'pacing to and fro'* and sometimes remaining *'motionless'* (*CDW*, 216), are all related to remembering the year of the boat scene in order to locate the tape and hear the story. As the length of time Krapp takes to remember his age when he recorded the tape indicates, he has not listened to it for a long while, and has forgotten most of the details of the story. When *'Finally he has an idea'* (216), he brings an old ledger 'that will allow him to identify box and tape' (cited in Knowlson 1992, 49). After locating and loading the tape, Krapp winds it forward and backward, until he locates the boat scene, his moment of 'Farewell to – [*he turns the page*] – love' (*CDW*, 217). The old Krapp's intention of listening to the tape, then, is to rummage through the memories that are stored on the tape in order to recall the particular moment of his separation from his loved one.

Recollecting the forgotten memories by means of the tape-recorder is an act of 'retrospective' mourning for his lost love. What Freud calls the work of mourning consists in recalling the memories of the lost object bit by bit, at great expense of time and cathectic energy: 'Each single one of the memories and expectations in which the libido is bound to the object is brought up and hypercathected, and detachment of the libido is accomplished in respect of it' (Freud 1991, 253). Since the younger Krapp has failed to notice the separation as his significant loss, the work of mourning has been deferred for a long time. Thirty years after his farewell to love, the old Krapp finally realizes the importance of the loss of his loved one, and starts the work of mourning by recalling the memory of the separation. The boat scene in the tape describes how Krapp initiated the separation by saying good-bye to his lover: 'I said again I thought it was hopeless and no good going on, and she agreed, without opening her eyes' (*CDW*, 223). Hinting at the relation between Krapp's decision to separate from his loved one and his 'vision' for his new artistic search, 'Farewell to […] love' follows 'Memorable equinox' in the tape. Since the moment of the separation is described by Krapp at thirty-nine when he had recently experienced the separation, the memory that is retrieved is vivid, and like the male narrators of the *Novellas*, he shows melancholic negation of and resistance to the loss: 'Here I end this reel. Box – [*Pause.*] – three, spool – [*Pause.*] – five. [*Pause.*] Perhaps my best years are gone. When there was a chance of happiness. But I wouldn't want them back. Not with the fire in me now. No, I wouldn't want them back' (*CDW*, 223).

The younger Krapp vaguely senses the possible significance of the moment, and that it was his 'chance of happiness', which the old Krapp later on admits as the 'Happiest moment of the past half million' (222). However, Krapp at thirty-nine attempts to defend his decision to isolate himself from the world for his 'opus … magnum' by making a melancholic disavowal of the lost happy moments, claiming, 'No, I wouldn't want them back.'

Krapp at sixty-nine

The old Krapp's immediate reactions towards the same memories, however, are much more ambivalent than those of his younger selves, and a melancholic resistance coexists with longing for the past. At the beginning of the play, when the old Krapp comes across the words, 'Memorable equinox', he is puzzled – not because he does not understand the words but because 'he cannot remember what made it memorable' (Knowlson 1992, 20) – as Beckett explained to Knowlson. When Krapp realizes that the 'Memorable equinox' is about the revelation which has led to his isolation from others, he can no longer bear to listen to it, and thus '*impatiently, winds tape forward*' (*CDW*, 220). The memory is unbearable for the old Krapp since his solitude has not helped him to achieve anything; he comments scornfully, 'Seventeen copies sold' (222), referring to his own book. He adds another remark, 'drowned in dreams', which supposedly refers to the young Krapp's 'aspirations' (218) and visions. After these comments, the old Krapp resists the memories saying, 'Last fancies. [*Vehemently.*] Keep 'em under!' (222). In contrast to his melancholic refusal of the memory of the 'Memorable equinox', how-ever, the old Krapp's very last words disclose his yearning for the past: 'Be again on Croghan on a Sunday morning, in the haze, with the bitch, stop and listen to the bells. [*Pause.*] And so on. [*Pause.*] Be again, be again. [*Pause.*] All that old misery. [*Pause.*] Once wasn't enough for you. [*Pause.*] Lie down across her' (*CDW*, 223).

Contrary to the younger Krapp's last words, 'No, I wouldn't want them back' which are uttered in order to reassure himself about his choice, the old Krapp's act of repeating the words 'Be again' reveals his nostalgic longing for past moments. Krapp at thirty-nine has failed to notice the significance of his lost love, and has repressed the memory of the separation ever since, but the sudden realization of the loss of his loved one is poignant to the old Krapp.

It is this unexpected awareness, which leads the old Krapp to be 'sen-timental',[10] as Beckett puts it, which is rare among his male characters. This passage is also exceptional among representations of male longing for Beckett's home in referring to a specific Irish region, Croghan – one of the Wicklow mountains near Dublin where Beckett used to take long walks with his father. Beckett, admitting that the play is 'nicely sad and sentimental', wrote to Jacoba van Velde, 'People will say: good gracious, there is blood circulating in the man's veins after all, one would never have believed it; he must be getting old' (cited in *DF*, 399). These 'sen-timental' and autobiographical elements in the play might have made Beckett feel uneasy as the letter to Barney Rosset shows: 'I feel as clucky and beady and one-legged and bare-footed about this little text as an old hen with her last chick' (399). After the old Krapp briefly expresses his sentiment towards his homeland and lost love, when he finishes recording the tape, he once more loads the same tape which he has just finished listening to, and searches for the boat scene. As if having listened to it once 'wasn't enough' for him, he plays it again, and the memory of the loss of his loved one is brought up and hypercathected again in order to enact the belated work of mourning.

IV 'All the others … Throttling the dead in his head': *Embers* and *Eh Joe*

'Mental thuggee'

As in *Krapp's Last Tape*, in *Embers* (1959) and *Eh Joe* (1965) the act of listening plays a crucial role in evoking the male characters' once for-gotten and repressed memories. As Krapp is confined in his little world with 'Not a soul' (*CDW*, 217) around him, in *Embers* Henry's alienation from other people is underlined using the words, 'Not a living soul' (*CDW*, 261), and in *Eh Joe*, the female voice assures Joe of his solitude saying, 'No one can see you now … No one can get at you now' (*CDW*, 362). Like Krapp, isolated for a long time and having no one to talk to, Henry and Joe cling to their memories and examine their relationships with their lost loved ones in retrospect. What the male protagonists do in *Embers* and *Eh Joe*, however, is not merely to recollect the memories of the lost loved objects. They also attempt to establish the relationship with these lost psychic others through imaginary conversations.

Krapp's last words, 'Once wasn't enough for you', and his repeated listening to the old tape prefigure Henry and Joe's endeavour to listen to the voice of the lost others. Krapp's words particularly echo Estragon and Vladimir's conversation in *Waiting for Godot*: 'All the dead voices. […] They talk about their lives. To have lived is not enough for them. They have to talk about it' (*CDW*, 58). While this comment is rather casually made when Estragon and Vladimir try to speak in order to avoid silence and thus without any connection with a specific death, Henry and Joe's listening to the voices of the lost objects is closely related to their wish to understand the dead. As Jean Laplanche states, for the person in mourning, the message of the other 'has never been adequately understood', and never been 'listened to enough' (Laplanche 1999, 254). What Henry and Joe realize, then, is that they cannot be free from the memory of the lost loved objects by repressing the memory; instead they need to resolve the unfinished business with the lost others by listening to what they want, by attempting to understand them. Henry and Joe's regret at not having been able to sufficiently appreciate the lost others leads them to self-reproach and presents them with important self-reflexive questions.

Beckett's second radio play, *Embers*, like the previous English plays *All That Fall* and *Krapp's Last Tape*, resonates with his childhood memories of Dublin; of learning to swim in the sea and his father inviting him to dive from the rocks of the Forty-Foot at Sandycove, a memory that also recurs in other texts, such as *Eleutheria* and *Company* (1979). Among the memories, what occupies Henry's mind is that of his father's death. Henry imagines 'My father, back from the dead, to be with me' (*CDW*, 253), and as if his father hears him, he keeps talking to him. The fact that his father's body was never found provides the conditions for a pathological symptom of melancholia in Henry since it has given him a good reason to deny the loss of his father. Henry remarks, 'they said there was nothing to prove you hadn't run away from us all and alive and well under a false name in the Argentine, for example, that grieved mother greatly' (254). Henry's fixation on the memory of his father's death and his struggle to get away from the sea where his father was supposedly drowned further indicate the pathological nature of his melancholia.

Whereas Henry's past resembles the male melancholic narrators' behaviour in Beckett's French fiction, his present symptoms are distinct from those of the narrators. As the narrator of *First Love* is puzzled by the cries that haunt him forever, Henry expresses his ambivalent feelings towards the sound of the sea that he can neither 'stay away from' (254) nor stand. Henry, like the narrator of *First Love*, has endeavoured to keep away from the sound by leaving his home. However, as the narrator fails to halt the cries, Henry also fails, as we hear he complains 'I once went to Switzerland to get away from the cursed thing and [it] never stopped all the time I was there' (254). In *First Love*, when the narrator talks about his father's death and his experience of visiting his tomb, he abruptly changes the subject, disclosing nothing about his father's death and hiding his emotion. However, unlike the narrator's melancholic repression of his father's death, Henry is aware that the haunting sea sound is closely related to the loss of his father by drowning. Henry also hints that his attachment to the sea is related to the loss of a loved one as he asks himself why he lives 'on the brink of [the sea]!': 'Some old grave I cannot tear myself away from?' (*CDW*, 258). Being aware of this connection, what Henry attempts to do is to undertake the belated work of mourning by recalling the moment he lost his father.

Henry, first, tries to summon his father's voice, but after failing to do so, he calls upon his wife Ada who immediately responds to his call. Ada's voice, although present, is suggested as a ghostly voice and also as a creation of Henry's imagination; '*No sound as she sits*' (257) is emphasized in the radio play direction. Through the help of Ada's voice, or rather, his own inner voice, Henry recollects in imagination the moment of his father's death. The belated work of mourning seems to intensify his self-reproach regarding his father's death, and as he goes along with reconstructing the memory, his self-criticism is exacerbated. In the following passage, Henry's inner voice, Ada, reveals the last moment when she saw his father:

ADA: You weren't there. [...] None of them knew where you were. Your bed had not been slept in. They were all shouting at one another. Your sister said she would throw herself off the cliff. Your father got up and went out, slamming the door. I left soon afterwards and passed him on the road. He did not see me. He was sitting on a rock looking out to sea. I never forgot his posture. And yet it was a common one. You used to have it sometimes.

(*CDW*, 262)

From this, it can be assumed that Henry has upset his family, and his father's reaction is related to this. Since Ada's voice comes from his imagination, it is not certain whether Henry is implicated in his father's death. Yet, it is apparent that Henry missed the events on the day of his father's death, as Ada asserts, 'You weren't there' (262). Not having been able to understand his lost others and having refused to listen to them while they were alive, Henry endeavours to hear their dead voices and to comprehend the unresolved trouble between himself and the others by imagining what they would have said to him.

While Henry's fixation on his long-dead father shows the pathological symptoms of melancholia, his failure to evoke his father's voice also indicates the possibility of completing the work of mourning. He used to be able to bring his father's voice to mind, as he does with Ada's, but Ada's response, 'I suppose you have worn him out', when Henry complains that his father 'doesn't answer anymore' (262), hints at a process that Henry has already been through. Ada's expression, 'wearing him out dead' (262), for instance, is comparable to Freud's term 'hypercathected'. As Freud explains, it is only when the memory of the lost object is brought up and hypercathected at great expense of time that the detachment of the libido is accomplished (Freud 1991, 253). Henry's failure to conjure up his dead father, then, suggests that he has achieved some libidinal detachment from him.

A similar procedure is introduced in Beckett's television play, *Eh Joe*. Parallel to Ada's remark that Henry's father is no longer evoked because he has 'worn him out', in *Eh Joe* 'Mental thuggee', a process of eliminating the dead voices, is explained through the ghostly female voice at the beginning of the play:

You know that penny farthing hell you call your mind ... That's where you think this is coming from, don't you? ... That's where you heard your father ... Isn't that what you told me? ... Started in on you one June night and went on for years ... On and off ... Behind the eyes ... That's how you were able to throttle him in the end ... Mental thuggee you called it ... One of your happiest fancies ... Mental thuggee ... Otherwise he'd be plaguing you yet ... Then your mother when her hour came ... 'Look up, Joe, look up, we're watching you' ... Weaker and weaker till you laid her too ... Others ... All the others ... Such love he got ... God knows why ... Pitying love ... None to touch it ... And look at him now ... Throttling the dead in his head.

(*CDW*, 362–3)

Like Ada's voice in *Embers*, Joe is aware that the relentless female voice is actually his own inner voice, coming from his mind, from the 'penny farthing hell'. As the ghastly voice tells us, 'Mental thuggee' is a procedure of abolishing the 'plaguing voice' in Joe's mind. The voice suggests that Joe succeeded in stopping his parents' haunting voices by 'Throttling the dead in his head' until they became 'Weaker and weaker' and died out. This process echoes the procedure which the narrator of 'The Expelled' describes: in order to obliterate memories 'you must think of them for a while, a good while, every day, several times a day until they sink forever in the mud. That's an order' (*CSP*, 46–7). While 'The Expelled' does not reveal that the memories that the narrator wishes to erase are those of the loss of the loved objects, Joe not only explicitly mentions the objects but also manages to achieve some distance from certain memories, starting from that of his father, and then his mother, and 'All the others'. The voice he has failed to 'throttle' and is attempting to do so 'now', however, is that of the female we hear in the play.

'Green one'

As in *Eh Joe*, it is the female voice which refuses to disappear in *Embers*. Although it seems to be the memory of his father that dominates Henry's mind, his wife Ada (whose voice still haunts him) bears more psychological significance in his present state than the dead father who is no longer conjured. Just as Henry asks Ada about the moment when his father went missing, he also asks his dead father whether he has met her, and also 'What turned her against me' (*CDW*, 256), implying Henry has lost his wife too in some sense. Since the father, who no longer replies, does not answer Henry's question, and nor does Henry directly ask Ada, it is difficult to determine how he has lost her. The unanswered question, the censored element in the play, indicates that the separation with Ada is still too painful to admit. Yet, even though Henry's yearning for his lost wife is concealed on the surface, his 'melancholic mourning' is implied. At the beginning of the play, Henry tells us a story about 'an old fellow called Bolton' and a doctor called 'Holloway' (254). The autobiographical elements of this are indicated later as Ada suggests Henry consult 'Holloway' (261) about his hearing of sounds and voices. While telling the story, Henry abruptly inserts lines 'Vega in the Lyre very green. [*Pause.*] Vega in the Lyre very green' (255). The star, Vega, in the constellation Lyra, the lyre or harp, is the fifth brightest star in the sky, best seen between June and October in the Northern Hemisphere and, therefore, hard to locate on a 'winter's night' (254). Given the autobiographical aspect of the story, for Henry, seeing the star in his mind's eye in winter implies his identification with the musician, Orpheus.[11] The myth of Orpheus is permeated by the loss of a loved one. Orpheus loses his wife Eurydice not once but twice, failing to bring her back from Hades. Beckett's letter to Barbara Bray, the drama script editor at the BBC, also suggests the significance of the lines. In this letter Beckett asks for a line about Vega that he had previously cut to be reinstated.[12]

This process of censoring and restoring the lines hints at Beckett's ambivalent feelings towards the meaning attached to Vega. Vega also features in *Dream of Fair to Middling Women*, Beckett's first novel, which he refused to release until he died. Just as the lines repeated twice above, the reference to Vega appears twice in the novel, when the narrator describes what 'occupied [Belacqua's] fetid head' and 'gravid heart' – the Smeraldina-Rima: Belacqua in the 'sharp October night', 'his head cocked up uncomfortably at the starfield', is 'looking for Vega', 'green, bright in the Lyre' (*DFMW*, 16–17). As John Pilling points out, 'with a greenish appearance', Vega is 'a very appropriate emblem of the Smeraldina', and Beckett also 'seems to associate the colour green with life and [...] with Ireland' (Pilling 2003, 45, 47). Together with Beckett's attempt to delete and restore it, the intertextual element further illuminates the significance of the seemingly random remark on the star in *Embers*. Immediately before the scene in which Belacqua looks for Vega, the narrator describes Smeraldina's appearance, which reappears in *More Pricks Than Kicks*: 'her body was all wrong [...]. Poppata, big breech, Botticelli thighs, knock-knees, ankles all fat nodules, wobbly, mammose, slobbery-blubbery, bubbubbubbub, a real button-bursting Weib, ripe' (*DFMW*, 15). As mentioned in Chapter 1, this description is based on Beckett's first love, Peggy Sinclair, who died a year after the novel was written, and in later life he told Knowlson how he 'still regretted it' (*DF*, 176). Beckett's deletion of the reference to Vega and its subsequent restoration not only suggests the emotionally charged nature of the emblem, but also shows how the loss in his own life affects the representation of the lost loved one in his work. Furthermore, in spite of Beckett's earlier gesture of censorship, his final decision to reinstate the line about Vega anticipates his later texts in which he endeavours to recuperate the lost objects. This will be discussed more fully in Chapter 4 using Melanie Klein's theory of artistic creation.

The theme of loss and mourning, which involves creativity and imagination, is presented in *Embers* through further parallels to the myth of Orpheus. In this myth, after Eurydice's accidental death, Orpheus is grief-stricken and decides to seek for his wife in the underworld where he meets Pluto and Persephone. Orpheus manages to charm them with his music, and is permitted to take Eurydice back to the land of the living under one condition: he must not look back to see if she is following him until they reach the gate to the land of living. Orpheus, full of doubt since he does not hear any footfall behind him, looks back and loses her forever. As if reminding us of this myth, whereas the sound of Henry's dragging feet, '*Boots on shingle*' (253) is exaggerated, '*No sound as she sits*' is emphasized in the radio play direction addressed to Ada. In both the Orpheus myth and *Embers*, sound in general and footfalls in particular are used in order to distinguish between the dead and the living. As Beckett in *Proust* mentions Eurydice to say that Marcel's grandmother is 'as irretrievably lost as Eurydice among the shades' (*P*, 27), so, even if Ada is still alive in Henry's mind, she is lost to him as irretrievably as Eurydice to Orpheus. Henry can only evoke his lost wife Ada through imagining her voice, and express his sense of loss by cryptically inserting Vega, the symbol of his loss, into his story, as Beckett himself does elsewhere.

Henry, like other male characters in Beckett, did not seem to appreciate his wife when she was still around: as he says to his imaginary father, 'conversation with her, that was something, that's what hell will be like' (*CDW*, 256). After having refused to listen to her while she was still alive, what he does now is to seek desperately for conversation with her. As if longing for her care, and as if endeavouring to restore her as a good internalized object, Henry imagines that she is worrying about his health and taking care of him, asking him to sit on her 'shawl' and to 'put on [his] jaegers' (257). Such an attempt to restore a lost object as a good object can be seen as an important step in enacting the work of mourning in Klein's theory. As we see from these examples, Henry's concern is not merely limited to Freud's concept of mourning, the severance of the ego from the dead, but as Klein emphasizes, it is also to establish the lost person as a good object within himself.

Unlike Henry, Joe in *Eh Joe* fails to recall his lost loved objects as good ones, but instead exacerbates his sense of loss, and displays self-reproach and paranoia, symptoms which are going to be discussed in detail as other reactions to the loss of loved ones in the next chapter.

(Indeed, written in a different decade from *Krapp* and *Embers*, Joe shows more various responses to his loss than simply melancholic symptoms.) Just as Henry's present life is governed by his relationship with psychic others, so is Joe haunted by the voice of the lost loved one, exhibiting a paranoid perception of the voice and the gaze. From the beginning of the television play, Joe is repeatedly 'looking out, closing door, locking door' and checking everywhere in the room such as 'cupboard', and 'under bed' (*CDW*, 361). As if mocking Joe's behaviour, the inexorable female voice comments, 'There might be a louse watching you' (362). Joe's melancholic self-reproach and the paranoiac nature of the haunting voice are the result of the fact that, like Krapp, he has willed the loss of his loved ones. Joe's internalized voice, like that of Henry, invokes the specific moments of his severance from two women: the owner of the ghostly voice and the 'green one' with the 'pale eyes' (*CDW*, 365) even though the similarity between their separation stories implies that they are the same woman.

By recalling the moment of loss and by attempting to throttle the dead through repetition, Joe tries to undertake the work of melancholic mourning. First, the voice reminds Joe of happy days, like those summer evenings in St Stephen's 'Green' in Dublin where they spent their 'idyll', 'Holding hands exchanging vows', describing how he 'admired [her] elocution! ... Among other charms' (363). However, the voice tells us how Joe had coaxed her to leave him, 'Hurrying [her] into [her] coat' to depart, while assuring that the 'best's to come' (362), never to return to her again. The voice then tells Joe about how he separated from the 'green one': once again he fled from his lover promising that the 'best's to come' while 'Bundling her into her Avoca sack' (365). The 'Ticket in [his] pocket for the first morning flight' (365) indicates that he intended to leave her and fly far away. As if Joe does not 'Ever know what happened' (365) afterwards, the relentless female voice further intensifies Joe's sense of guilt by accusing him of the 'green one's' suicide as a consequence of the separation and his betrayal, and by describing the moment of the 'green one' committing suicide in detail. First, she tried to drown herself in the sea, but it did not work. Then she tried to cut her wrist with the 'Gillette' razor which he 'recommended for her body hair' (366), and it did not work either, due to her dread of pain. The next decision, which eventually put an end to her life, was to combine sleeping pills with drowning. With the acute descriptions of the last moment of her life, the voice cruelly calls his mind to picture it: 'Imagine what in her mind to make her do that ... Imagine ... Trailing her feet in the water like a child ...' (366). After this, the female voice harps on Joe's lost chance of love and happiness by repeating 'There was love for you' (365–7) like a refrain.

Echoing the old Krapp's 'my best years are gone. When there was a chance of happiness' (*CDW*, 223), the present state of Joe's loneliness and emotional destitution is implied by the fact that there is no one to visit him apart from 'that slut that comes on Saturday' (*CDW*, 363) whom he pays for her service, just as does Krapp's 'Bony old ghost of a whore' (*CDW*, 222). Joe's melancholic and paranoiac symptoms can be seen as a consequence of the loss of his beloved ones. Unlike the male narrators, who conceal their loss in Beckett's French fiction, Joe is keenly aware of the importance of the loss of the loved objects, and how the loss impacts on his present psychic state, producing self-reproach by positioning him in the role of persecutor who has abandoned his lovers and producing paranoia as a result of the fear of their revenge.

As Ackerley and Gontarski explain, in Beckett's texts the images of Peggy Sinclair, are 'invariably associated with green eyes or a green coat' (Ackerley and Gontarski 2004, 528-9). In *Krapp's Last Tape*, it is suggested that the girl to whom Krapp bids farewell is also reminiscent of Peggy: Krapp at thirty-nine recalls 'A girl in a shabby green coat, on a railway-station platform' (*CDW*, 218). Krapp describes how '[her eyes] opened' after he bid farewell to her, telling her 'it was hopeless and no good going on' (223). In *Eh Joe*, as in *Krapp's Last Tape*, the female voice tells Joe the 'way [the eyes] opened after …' (*CDW*, 365), here, censoring the words that describe the moment. The voice, however, significantly adds that the 'green one' committed suicide after he said good-bye to her. It is intriguing to see how the 'green one' appears again and again as a lost object in Beckett's works written after his exile as well as after Peggy Sinclair's death. While the focus of *Krapp's Last Tape*, *Embers* and *Eh Joe* is not on identifying and recuperating the 'green one' herself, from his English drama onwards Beckett starts to experiment with male protagonists' different emotional reactions to their memory of the loss of the 'green one', from melancholic repression, to melancholic mourning and to paranoia. The recurrence of the 'green one' as the emblem of the lost loved object throughout Beckett's oeuvre allows us to explore his male protagonists' changed attitudes towards their lost others and the revision process as an important part of his artistic practice.

Up to now, we have observed that Beckett in *Krapp's Last Tape*, *Embers* and *Eh Joe* shows the ways in which the male protagonists retrospectively trace the particular moment of the separation from their loved ones, and more importantly how this loss rules their present lives. If Belacqua and Murphy are in flight from the female characters, fearing that women will entrap them in the world that they resist, in the English drama discussed in this section the male protagonist 'escapes from the trap of the other only to be trapped in self'.[13] The self depicted in Beckett's drama, however, in spite of being confined in its own 'little world', is shown not to be free from lost loved ones. As the internalized voice of *Embers* and *Eh Joe* suggests, the male protagonists start to build a relationship with the lost others who they have internalized. Having fled from their female partners seems ironically to help the male protagonists move away from their narcissistic concentration on the self and turn towards consideration of the lost psychic others. Beckett in his drama of the late 1950s and 1960s onwards, then, attempts to understand these lost others and also to focus on establishing the relationship between them and the self. The next chapter will explore the ways in which Beckett tries to recuperate the lost others as well as the female subject that has been silenced in his early fiction.

4
Beyond Mourning and Melancholia: Kleinian Approaches

I Introduction

When Beckett was asked by Linda Ben-Zvi 'which piece of writing he would choose to include in a book on women in his writing' (Ben-Zvi 1990, 249), he suggested the following passage from his radio play, *Words and Music* (1961): '[...] She comes in the ashes | Who loved could not be won | Or won not loved | Comes in the ashes | Like in that old light | The face in the ashes [...]' (*CDW*, 291). This passage, which is reminiscent of W.B. Yeats's 'The Tower', contemplates old age and haunting memories of the lost loved one, particularly echoing Yeats's words, 'Does the imagination dwell the most | Upon a woman won or woman lost?' (Yeats 1996, 305). Despite the fact that there is no female character in this radio play, Beckett's choice of the passage in preference to one from a play which does have a female protagonist suggests the significance of 'woman lost' in Beckett's works. In most of Beckett's drama written before *All That Fall*, women are absent, as in *Waiting for Godot*, or when present, as in Beckett's early fiction, they are vehemently resisted by the male protagonists. Unlike Beckett's fiction and French plays, however, in his English drama from *All That Fall* onwards, not only does his imagination more conspicuously start to dwell upon the 'woman lost' by presenting male protagonists who are haunted by the memories of their lost loved ones, but also his 'woman lost' begins to speak out in her own voice.

Women in Beckett's *Happy Days* (1961) and *Play* (1962) still appear in relation to husbands or lovers, and are closely associated with the idea of home, as are women in his early fiction. The relationship between male and female characters in the plays is also similar to that of Beckett's early fiction in that the woman is either abandoned by her male partner or fears the impending loss of him. Notably, however, it is the female voices on which the plays centre. As if attempting to recuperate the female voices which have been silenced by the male narrators in his early fiction, in *Happy Days* and *Play* Beckett gives a voice to women who appear to be neglected by their men. Beckett deliberately juxtaposes his female character with a melancholic man who is so absorbed in his own misery that he is unable to see the other's suffering or to acknowledge his contribution to this suffering. In these plays, men consciously or unconsciously play the role of persecutors who abandon their female partners, and who do not realize the importance of the separation with the loved ones.

In May 1963, three months after finishing *Film* (1963), Beckett started work on a female monologue, 'Kilcool', which was abandoned at this stage but developed into *Not I* (1972) nine years later. This manuscript reinforces the idea of the existence in Beckett in the early 1960s of a general interest and intention in recuperating the once-silenced female voice. In 'Kilcool', the female speaker, who lost her parents when she was young, and who shows 'her conflicts in response to loss' (Gontarski 1985, 139), constantly claims 'I am not talking to myself' (cited in Pountney 1988, 97), as if expressing her wish to be heard. Similarly, as we see that three of the eight 'Themes' which Beckett outlined in this manuscript are '4. Lover. 5. Age. 6. Never properly [tell or seen], heard',[1] it is not just retrieving the formerly-silenced female voice that is essential in this piece. The female speaker also has a strong desire to talk about her sense of loss and an urge to be properly heard – just as Winnie in *Happy Days* desperately demands a listener.

Why Klein?

It can be argued that in his drama of the early 1960s Beckett makes a significant turn towards lost others and away from his earlier Freudian focus on the narcissistic self. If Freud's stress on 'the severance of the ego' from the lost loved object provides a useful link in understanding the male narrators' melancholic disavowal of their lost loved objects, Melanie Klein's emphasis on 'the complexity of the inner world' (Mitchell 1986, 146) of the ego in relation to lost objects offers a starting point in discussing Beckett's move towards these lost others. In his essay 'Mourning and Melancholia' (1915), Freud claims that the work of mourning is completed when the libido is withdrawn from its attachments to the lost object through 'reality-testing' (Freud 1991, 253). The reality-testing shows that 'the loved object no longer exists', and 'it proceeds to demand that all libido shall be withdrawn from its attachments to that object' until 'the ego becomes free and uninhibited again' (253).

While focusing on the importance of the libidinal detachment from the object through the reality-testing, Freud's work of mourning does not leave room to discuss the ego's ongoing relationship to the lost object. Moreover, with Freud's binary distinction between mourning and melancholia, it is difficult to explain the characters' other reactions towards their loss of the loved object in Beckett's later works. For instance, we have observed that Joe in *Eh Joe* cannot release the lost object even though the loss happened a long time ago, and his present mental state is affected by the persecutory voice of the 'woman lost'. Freud's essay, with its excessive emphasis on melancholia, also overlooks the importance of the work of mourning as re-establishing the ego's relationship with the lost object, and fails to explain other symptoms, such as mania, which often occur after the loss.

In her two related essays 'A Contribution to the Psychogenesis of Manic-Depressive States' (1935) and 'Mourning and its Relation to Manic-Depressive States' (1940), Klein moves away from Freud's narcissistic model and addresses the aspects overlooked in his essay. The work of mourning for Klein, in contrast to Freud's libidinal detachment from the lost object, involves what she calls 'reparation', the process of restoring the lost loved one inside oneself as a 'good object' through increasing love and regaining trust in the lost object by recalling happy experiences. What is important in Klein's work of mourning is to establish a healthy relationship with lost psychic others within the ego; failure to restore the lost object as a good object produces symptoms such as melancholia, paranoia and mania. According to Klein, in experiencing the loss of the loved one, we experience fluctuations between the depressive state (melancholia) and temporary relief through either returning to the 'paranoid-schizoid position',[2] or through flight into the manic state. Klein's extended analysis of mourning and melancholia sheds light on the representations of the lost loved ones in Beckett's drama of the early 1960s, representations unlike – and more various than – those in his early French fiction.

In light of these essays of Klein's, as well as her theory more generally, the paranoid perception of the gaze displayed by characters in *Play* and *Film* and Winnie's 'manic'[3] voice – according to Beckett's own comment – in *Happy Days* will be discussed as specific reactions to the loss of the loved object. With her emphasis on object-relations theory, Klein's two essays also provide considerable resources for a critical investigation of Beckett's works in which the question of how to re-establish the ego's ambivalent feelings and the relationship to the lost object is central. Beckett's English drama is different from those works already considered, which dwell on how to sever this object properly. Using Klein, then, this chapter will contend that Beckett's works of the early 1960s reconstruct his male characters' relationships with women by making the male characters recall the memory of the 'woman lost', and by giving voices to the female characters who have been abandoned or are about to be abandoned. Furthermore, while using a female voice and also attempting to see from a female perspective, Beckett finds an alternative way to express his own sense of loss and anxiety as well as trying to make reparation to the 'woman lost'.

What makes Klein such a key figure in this investigation is that for her, as Esther Sánchez-Pardo claims, 'mourning is fundamental for keeping our psychological integrity', and loss is 'so profoundly inscribed in our psyches that it is always already there' (Sánchez-Pardo 2003, 54). If the loss seems to have always already taken place in Beckett's works, potential explanations can be found in Klein's theory, which claims that the very early psychic and emotional development of the infant and the experience of the loss of the first love-object continuously affect the adult's psychic processes. Beckett, familiar with such psychoanalytical theories, deliberately uses them in exploring the relationship between the self and psychic others. In *Happy Days* and *Film*, for example, Beckett hints that the characters' symptoms of mania and paranoia stem from their infant psychic development, dating back to their experience of being 'four or five' (*CDW*, 163) and as an 'infant [of] 6 months' (*CDW*, 333) respectively. It seems essential, therefore, to explain the psychologically complex development of the infant in detail, a process governed by the mechanism of introjection and projection.

Beckett made notes from his reading of Karin Stephen's *Psychoanalysis and Medicine: a Study of the Wish to Fall Ill* (1933) that explain how, in Klein's theory 'the breast [is the infant's] first love-object' (TCD MS 10971/7/2), and is installed as polarized objects: as a 'good object' when the infant obtains it, and as a 'bad' one when it fails to do so.[4] Klein claims that at around six months of age the infant comes to perceive its internalized and fragmented good and bad objects as a whole object. It is during this period – when introjection of the complete object begins – that what Klein calls the 'depressive position' arises. (The depressive position, according to Klein, is 'a melancholia in *status nascendi*' (*LGR*, 345), and is comparable to the adult's melancholia.) The crucial loss of the loved object is the baby's experience of losing the perfect and ideal object (the mother) when it discovers her imperfection. In other words, the depressive position stems from the infant's ambivalence towards its first love-object: the good mother, who tenderly meets its needs and feeds it, is also the bad mother who frustrates it and makes it wait. Such ambivalent feelings of love and hatred towards the love-object generate a particularly 'poignant sadness that Klein called depressive anxiety' (Hinshelwood 1989, 138).

Paranoia and mania

According to Klein, one of the defensive reactions to the depressive position is a retreat to the earlier 'straightforward paranoid forms' (Hinshelwood 1989, 147). This paranoid defence responds to certain persecutory fears. As Beckett remarks in his 'Psychology Notes', the infant projects its own 'anger', derived from the frustration and 'forcible separation from nipple' (TCD MS 10971/7/3), onto the bad mother (her breasts in particular), or, as Klein puts it, 'bad objects'. The infant 'conceives of them as actually dangerous' persecutors who 'will devour' and 'poison it' (*LGR*, 262). Furthermore, the infant's own 'aggression' results in the 'fear of explosion of anger (suffocation) or of retaliation' (TCD MS 10971/7/2) from the bad objects. The fear of internalized persecutors that cannot be overcome by projection forms the basis of paranoia. For Klein splitting an object into good and bad objects is one of the infant's earliest methods of defence in dealing with anxiety and the fear of loss of its good object. In doing so, at least a part of the object is accepted to protect its ego. One of the results of this paranoid-schizoid position is 'a conception of extremely bad and *extremely perfect* objects' that contribute to form the super-ego, objects which are 'intensely moral', exacting and divine on the one hand, but severe, cruel, relentless and persecutory on the other (*LGR*, 268, Klein's italics).

It is notable that as Klein emphasizes the connection between the super-ego, the depressive position, and paranoiac and persecutory fears, so too Beckett pays particular attention to these links in his 'Psychology Notes':

Acute case of over-severity of super-ego towards ego appears in the melancholic attack. (TCD MS 10971/7/6)

Excessive self-control, resulting from excessive parental control of excretory functions, tends to inhibit aggression & produce loss of initiation & power to stand up to circumstances, as well as to turn the aggression in upon the subject & produce melancholia. (10971/7/2)

Fears of genital attack from parent of same sex (rival). Introjection of parent, producing internal conflict, self-hatred, -love, -denial, -fear, & perhaps melancholia & suicide. (10971/7/3)

In this summary, Beckett remarks the relation between melancholia and an 'over-severity of [the] super-ego' derived from 'excessive parental control', as well as the ego's fears of the 'attack from parent'. Melancholia, according to these notes, as in Klein's theory, is produced when – in an example of paranoid defence – the infant turns its aggression and fears upon itself rather than projecting its fears onto the parent. It is also important to note that it is not only the real parent but also the 'introjected' parent that contributes to the formation of the severe super-ego. Immediately after the summary, Beckett expands the concept of introjected parent: 'Parent Imagos, fantastic creations reflecting the child's own intentions. Thus the Imagos of an aggressive self-assertive child are terrifyingly primitive no matter how mild the real parents' (10971/7/4). In works such as *Film* and *Company* (1979) the mother figure appears to be stern, imposing prohibition and punishment. As Beckett's notes suggest, the stern mother figure in those works needs to be considered as the representation of the introjected mother who treats the infant with 'far more severity and cruelty than the real one had ever done' (Klein 1975, 6). However, the severity of Beckett's own mother towards him, as his biographers point out, must also have contributed to forming the stern introjected mother and the harsh super-ego, and, more importantly, must have influenced his representation of the mother in his works. These Kleinian concepts are essential in explaining O's paranoiac and persecutory fear and his relationship with the introjected mother – not just with the real one – in *Film*, since the film reveals at the end that the persecutory gaze is nothing but his own.

In order to discuss Winnie and E/O's sense of loss using Klein's theory, it is also important to explain how the depressive position can arise not only when the ego encounters the loss of the loved object but also as a result of the 'impending loss' (*LGR*, 345) of it. According to Klein, the infant's depressive feelings reach 'a climax just before, during and after weaning' (345) when the baby experiences the impending loss of the breast. The baby mourns for the mother's breast and all that the breast and the milk represent in the infant's mind: namely, love, goodness and security. Klein claims that all these good objects are felt by the baby to be lost, and that the loss is a consequence of its 'own uncontrollable greedy and destructive phantasies and impulses against [its] mother's breasts' (345). Further distress about the impending loss strengthens the persecutory fear of the bad object which gives rise to feelings of guilt as well as the fear of losing the good object, all of which constitute the depressive position. The infant's first experience of loss is, then, a gradual process as it repeats the loss of its first object, the mother's breast, over and over, particularly during the weaning period. Although Winnie has not yet lost her husband, given that the depressive position arises in response to the object-to-be-lost as well as the lost object, her 'manic' position in *Happy Days* can be interpreted as being reinforced by her fear of the impending loss of him, particularly in view of his earlier abandonment.

Klein's manic position is helpful not only in explaining Winnie's manic voice in relation to the loss of the loved object, but also in clarifying the 'regular alternation of melancholic and manic phases' (Freud 1991, 263) that Freud failed to explain in 'Mourning and Melancholia'. For Klein, both paranoia and mania are defence mechanisms against the depressive position. To explain the process, when distress about the impending loss arises, the baby, in order to overcome its depressive anxiety, needs to go through the testing of reality, which helps to assure that 'the loved object inside as well as outside is not injured, and is not turned into a vengeful person' (*LGR*, 347). What is essential in this reality-testing is to increase love and trust towards the loved objects and to diminish the fear of the bad objects in order to overcome depression and feelings of loss step by step. Until the loved objects are finally and safely preserved as good objects inside the ego, however, the tension between the good and bad objects remains, and the baby experiences fluctuations between the depressive and manic positions. When the depressive position arises, Klein emphasizes, the ego is forced to develop methods – manic defences – which are essentially directed 'against the "pining" for the loved object' (348). Klein further argues that 'in mania the ego seeks refuge not only from melancholia but also from a paranoiac condition which it is unable to master' (277). Mania here is regarded as another defence mechanism constructed as a reaction to the loss of the loved object. Using the characterization of mania by Klein, Winnie's 'manic' symptoms will be fully discussed below. In *Film* and *Happy Days*, while the impending loss of the characters' loved ones activates defence mechanisms such as paranoia and mania respectively, their fear of being destroyed by internal persecutors also plays a significant role in reinforcing these symptoms, and in preventing the depressive position arising.

Guilt and reparation

In addition to the infant's fears and its aggression towards the persecutory internal objects, in her theory of the depressive position Klein also emphasizes the infant's concern, guilt and remorse regarding the fate of those whom it has annihilated in phantasy. Out of guilt and remorse, the baby attempts to resolve its depressive anxiety through restoring the mother, who has been harmed or destroyed, through 'reparation'. This comes out of real concern for the loved object, and a pining for it. It is, as C. Fred Alford points out, the depressive position that is 'the foundation of the morality' (Alford 1990, 172). For Klein, reparation is the strongest element of the constructive and creative urges. Together with the ethical aspect of the depressive position, Klein's theory of artistic creation suggests the legitimacy of discussing Beckett's writing of the 1960s as an act of recuperating the voice of the lost others. The creative impulse, for Klein, is closely associated with the child's early aggressive wishes and 'a destructive attack on or by persecutors – its introjected parents – in phantasy', and its effort and 'subsequent attempt to restore the damage to objects' (Hinshelwood 1989, 263) through the process of reparation. From the beginning of her psychoanalytic career, it was always surprising for Klein to observe that the moment after a child showed aggressive and sadistic impulses (which she believes are instinctual) towards an object, it also showed the capacity for pity and the wish to restore what it had destroyed, as well as the wish to love and be loved.

Notably, Anthony Cronin links Beckett's 'moral torment' not only to his relationship with the 'woman lost' but also to his 'portrait of' women in his early fiction (Cronin 1997, 578). Anne Madden in Cronin's biography of Beckett describes an occasion in May 1984: Beckett 'seemed downcast and, after telling them of his insomnia and night fears which still assailed him, he spoke of being "tormented by what he called his cruelty to people"' (578). Regarding this account, Cronin assumes that 'these people to whom [Beckett] thought he had been so cruel' could be his mother, his wife Suzanne and also Peggy Sinclair, particularly in relation to the 'portrait of Peggy he had drawn in *More Pricks Than Kicks*' (578). Cronin further connects a 'reason for guilt in 1986' to his 'reneging on the permission' to publish *Eleutheria* (578). Cronin reports that Beckett read it again 'with loathing' (578) and had to withdraw his permission. As observed earlier, one of the reasons for Beckett's 'adamant' refusal to have *Eleutheria* published can be found in the 'autobiographical tensions and reminiscences' (*DF*, 328) in the play, including the hostile representations of Victor's mother and fiancée as well as Victor's desire to escape from them.

Born of this sense of guilt, in his drama from *Happy Days* onwards Beckett attempts to recuperate the 'woman lost' that was ridiculed, silenced and perceived as menacing in his early works. In *Happy Days* and *Play*, Beckett's creative impulse focuses on repairing and reconstructing the female subject. This is done by allowing the female characters to speak out in their own voice while at the same time criticizing the male characters by juxtaposing both sexes on stage and exhibiting males who are so self-absorbed by their own suffering that they neglect their women. It is this concern on Beckett's part for the lost others – the reparation of the women who have been ridiculed and harmed in his early works as well as his desire to re-discover those who have been lost actually or in his feelings – that makes it possible to read his drama using Klein's theory.

II Recuperating the female voice in *Happy Days*

In Paris in 1962, during the rehearsal period of *Happy Days*, Beckett 'confided to the actress [Brenda Bruce]', who was playing Winnie, the conception of the play:

> 'There'd be no shade, nothing, and that bell wakes you up all the time and all you've got is a little parcel of things to see you through life.' [Beckett] was talking about a woman's life, let's face it. Then he said: 'And I thought who would cope with that and go down singing, only a woman.'
>
> (*DF*, 447)

According to this, in *Happy Days* Beckett's intention of borrowing a female voice was clear from the outset, although this is not immediately apparent from the context of the play. Generally speaking, in Beckett's works the situations confronted by his male and female characters are similar and the metaphysical human condition he portrays is non-gender-specific. *Happy Days*, for example, is not the only play set in a desert, under '*Blazing light*' (*CDW*, 138). Beckett's French plays, *Actes sans paroles I* and *II* (1956) share a similar setting: 'Desert. Dazzling light' (*CDW*, 203). Just as Winnie is tormented by an invisible bell, the male character in *Actes sans paroles I* is also controlled by an unseen whistle, which provokes him to react to the appearance and disappearance of a certain object. As Winnie has 'a little parcel of things' such as a mirror and a toothbrush in her 'capacious black bag' (*CDW*, 138) in order to keep her busy by bringing out the objects to 'help [her] through the day' (154), so the male characters in *Actes sans paroles II* also have a few items – objects similar to Winnie's – with which they are able to busy themselves. However, while the miserable situation and condition that Beckett's characters face in *Happy Days* and *Actes sans paroles I* and *II* are the same, he thought it was 'only a woman', who could 'go down sing-ing', instead of acting without words as the male characters do in the French plays. Beckett's use of the female voice in *Happy Days*, then, is a deliberate and meaningful decision.

This play thus inaugurates a new set of interesting gender dynamics in Beckett's works. Although some of Winnie and Willie's characteristics are similar to those of characters in Beckett's early fiction, a very impor-tant change is observed in *Happy Days*. Like women in Beckett's earlier fiction, Winnie is also associated with the idea of home. Although unlike his early female characters Winnie does not appear to be com-pletely abandoned, in Act 2 we see that she too has been neglected by Willie for 'a long time' (*CDW*, 160) and her apprehension of losing her husband is pervasive as she keeps asking him 'You *are* going, Willie, aren't you? [*Pause. Louder.*] You *will* be going soon, Willie, won't you?' (148, Beckett's italics). However, in contrast to the females silenced by the male narrators in the early fiction it is Winnie in *Happy Days* to whom Beckett gives a prominent voice while Willie is decentralized at the back of a mound and mainly exists as a listener. As a result of the centrality of the female character, and the fact that she does not serve as an object of male desire, *Happy Days* has been celebrated by feminist critics as a piece that challenges gender stereotypes. Willie has, however, been overlooked in such studies of the play. While agreeing with such feminist readings of *Happy Days*, in this section I am going to argue that Willie's role as a listener is also crucial in understanding the gender dynamics in Beckett's oeuvre, as it significantly reflects the author's own wish for the once ignored and silenced female voice in his previous works to be listened to. By shifting his speaking subject from male to female, in *Happy Days* Beckett reconfigures the male and female relationship, and reconstructs the female subject.

Considering that the voice was predominantly male in the works written before *Happy Days*, such a shift is very important, and worthy of particular attention. On the one hand, Beckett's desire to recover the female subject that was damaged in his early fiction and his attempt to recall the 'woman lost' can be compared to Melanie Klein's process of 'reparation', which is grounded in repairing the harmed lost object in phantasy. On the other hand, by using a female voice and endeav-ouring to see from a female perspective, Beckett seems to find another way to express his own sense of loss and anxiety, and to move away from the prevalent melancholic male voice of his previous works. For instance, Winnie's excessively happy voice, or rather, in Beckett's words, her 'manic' voice, can be analysed in line with his ongoing theme of the loss of loved ones. Klein's manic-depressive position is particularly helpful in analysing Winnie's manic symptoms as defence mechanisms, which are reinforced by her impending loss of her husband and also as a manifestation of her infantile depressive position. In order to substantiate the claim that in *Happy Days* Beckett attempts to recuperate the female voices that were once silenced in his early works, I will first locate the traits in Winnie and Willie that are consistent with the female and male representations in Beckett's early works before engaging with Klein's theory.

Remnants of woman-as-Ireland

Winnie and Willie's relationship echoes that of man and woman in Beckett's earlier fiction in which a female character is closely linked to the idea of home, and clings to a male character while he maintains an emotional distance from her. Winnie is tied to the earth, literally '*Embedded up to above her waist*' (*CDW*, 138) in the centre of a mound that she calls 'home' (158). When Willie tries to come out from his hole and to crawl '*towards her*', Winnie encourages him saying, 'Another foot, Willie, and you're home' (158). Willie also shares some features with Beckett's early male protagonists by having 'no zest for anything no interest in life' (139), which is a typical characteristic of a depressive person. Like the early male characters' narcissistic preoccupation with themselves, Willie is so engrossed with his own misery that he fails to perceive the suffering of Winnie, who exists within a harsher reality than his, at least in terms of her physical condition. This is illustrated in Winnie's insinuation that Willie has attempted to commit suicide with 'Brownie', the revolver, which she keeps: 'Remember how you used to keep on at me to take it away from you? Take it away, Winnie, take it away, before I put myself out of my misery' (151). After quoting Willie's words, Winnie remarks, '[*Derisive.*] Your misery!' (151) as if trying to scorn him and make him notice her own misery.

Just like Beckett's other early male protagonists, Willie also has 'an anthrax' (166) on his neck: Belacqua, for instance, has an 'anthrax that he always wore just above his collar' (*MPTK*, 75), and dies while having an operation to get rid of it. (As observed in Chapter 1, this particular literary memory bears an autobiographical significance: the young Beckett, after his operation for the cyst on his neck, was informed of the death of his first love, Peggy Sinclair, and this experience of loss is encoded in the story 'Draff'.) When tracing the early manuscripts of *Happy Days*, more similarities between the couple in *Happy Days* and Beckett's earlier characters can be found. In the first draft of *Happy Days*, at the rise of the curtain Willie appears asleep in a foetal position with 'his arms on his knees and his head on his arms' (cited in Gontarski 1985, 84), the famous embryonic posture of Dante's Belacqua which is adopted by Beckett's early male protagonists such as Murphy and Molloy and later characters like Estragon. While the deleting of this detail in the final version could be seen as part of Beckett's general strategy of what Gontarski terms the process of 'undoing' and 'vaguening'[5] autobiographical elements in order to create universal art, what has been eliminated in *Happy Days* also suggests a psychological motivation behind this process.

As if implying that certain details – which echo his early fiction and his young self – disturb him, Beckett makes those details less obvious as the following examples show. Notably, among the 'vaguened' details, most of the elements that are censored in the final version of *Happy Days* are references to Ireland and to Winnie's sexuality, the features which Beckett's early male protagonists vehemently resist. In the final version of *Happy Days*, '*Reynolds' News*'[6] (*CDW*, 167), briefly mentioned by Winnie, is the only reference to Ireland, and when Willie reads aloud from the paper there are no Irish references in what he chooses. In the early manuscript, however, Willie, called 'B' at that point, reads 'Aberrant rocket strikes Erin, eighty-three priests survive' (cited in Gontarski 1985, 80), and includes a satirical comment on the Irish Catholic Church. Regarding Winnie's final song, Gontarski reports that Beckett was undecided between 'When Irish Eyes are Smiling' and the less geographically specific, 'I Love You So', waltz duet from 'Franz Lehár's *Merry Widow*' (Gontarski 1977, 13). However, the latter was chosen at Alan Schneider's suggestion. As the setting of Ireland is erased, so too is Winnie's sexual nature – evocative as it is of the women who are described as sexually provocative and demanding in Beckett's early fiction. The following was eliminated from the early manuscript:

> There was a time, do you remember, when once a month was enough for me ... Don't you remember? ... Once a month! ... Then once a fortnight ... The tally-sticks, don't you remember the tally-sticks, Edward, they must be lying about somewhere still, every thirtieth notch, then every fifteenth. (*Pause.*) Then weekly. I would wake up as usual, refreshed for the day and without a care ... Then finally daily ... One just wakes up and finds out ... This irritates you I know ... but it simplifies life for you in a way too at the same time, no more scorekeeping, that is what you should bear in mind when you refuse to satisfy me.
>
> (Cited in Gontarski 1985, 82)

As Gontarski observes, this passage – particularly the last sentence – conveys 'heavy sexual overtones' (83), and as Rosemary Pountney notes, 'a reference to "tally-sticks" suggests that Winnie is making sexual demands on her husband' (Pountney 1988, 147). Unlike Beckett's earlier French plays, as the examples observed above show, *Happy Days* contains the remnants of the characterization of Beckett's early males and females.

Even though Beckett attempted to censor specific details that resembled his early works, 'Some remains' (*CDW*, 161); as Winnie claims, 'One loses one's classics. Oh not all. A part. A part remains' (164). One of the reasons why Winnie is buried on the mound and Willie does not dig her out can be found by examining Beckett's own classics. One function of the mound is to make Willie stay near Winnie, so that he can listen to her. As Belacqua in *More Pricks Than Kicks* is only 'happily married to Lucy' (*MPTK*, 120) when the question of making love does not arise due to 'her being crippled for life' (118), in order to keep Willie next to Winnie she needs to be buried on the mound so that the question of making love does not arise between them. As Belacqua, who feels that Lucy is sexually provocative, can only feel satisfaction through voyeurism, so Willie indulges himself in looking at a pornographic postcard, which pre-empts his need to dig Winnie out. All the 'vaguened' details and the parts that remain indicate that Willie and Winnie are in some ways reminiscent of Beckett's early male and female characters. Yet, unlike Belacqua and Murphy, Willie stays near Winnie, listening to her. Given this, it can be further argued that Beckett in *Happy Days* not only reconfigures the male and female relationship, but also recuperates the voice of the female who was formerly ignored and ridiculed by his male narrators.

Reparation of the woman lost

What Beckett attempts in *Happy Days* is comparable to what Klein calls the reparation of the lost object which is damaged in one's phantasy. Beckett's creative impulse in *Happy Days* can be seen as emanating from his desire to recover and rediscover the 'woman lost' in his early works. In Klein's theory reparation is a process of recalling the lost object and restoring it as a good object. During this process, the ego confirms to itself that the lost object, which was attacked and harmed in phantasy, is not going to turn into a persecutory bad object. Unlike the female characters in Beckett's early fiction, Winnie is not perceived by Willie as a menacing figure. Nor does Beckett allow Winnie to be resentful towards Willie because of his neglect of her. As he commented in rehearsal, Beckett makes Winnie largely 'unaware' of her sad realities to keep her happy (cited in Knowlson 1985, 17). In contrast to the persecutory and ghostly female voice, which is Joe's own inner voice in *Eh Joe*, in *Happy Days* and *Play* Beckett portrays the female characters as victims rather than persecutors, while significantly putting them alongside the male characters who have deserted them. In Klein's theory, during the reparation process the subject also takes the responsibility for the loss and feels a sense of guilt and remorse, rather than denying the loss and repressing those feelings. Arising from a similar sense of guilt, Beckett recuperates the female who was formerly silenced, ridiculed and abjected.

By centring on Winnie and giving a voice to her, then, Beckett significantly turns towards the 'woman lost' by imagining what she could have said, and shows his desire for making reparation of the lost object. Since Beckett made his earlier male protagonists and narrators silence women, in his reparation process Willie's role in *Happy Days* needs to be that of a listener. Or rather, as Winnie states at the beginning of Act 2, for her Willie exists in order to listen to her:

> WINNIE: I say I used to think that I would learn to talk alone. [*Pause.*] By that I mean to myself, the wilderness. [*Smile.*] But no. [*Smile broader.*] No no. [*Smile off.*] Ergo you are there. [*Pause.*] Oh no doubt you are dead, like the others, no doubt you have died, or gone away and left me, like the others, it doesn't matter, you are there.
>
> (*CDW*, 160)

As many critics have pointed out, in this passage Winnie has rewritten the Cartesian formula, *cogito ergo sum*. Rather than seeing that Winnie, as Knowlson argues, touches on the general Cartesian split between body and mind,[7] as the circumstances tell us this should be considered as a statement which specifies her relationship with Willie: I speak, therefore you exist in order to listen to me.

Using Winnie's voice in *Happy Days*, Beckett endeavours to find an alternative way of expressing his own sense of loss and anxiety, and of making reparation to the lost object. While it is the 'woman lost' that Beckett recuperates in *Happy Days*, by writing from a female perspective, he is also able to talk about the female experience of loss. The passage above, for instance, displays many other symptoms which are important in Klein's theory of loss. According to Klein, the depressive position can arise when one experiences the impending loss of the loved object as well as in the event of its actual loss. As Winnie's, 'no doubt you are dead, like the others' shows, she has not only already experienced the loss of 'the others', but also fears the impending loss of her husband, Willie. Winnie's apprehension about losing Willie is crucial in understanding the play and her manic voice. Winnie's fear of losing her husband is also represented in her first quotation, 'woe woe is me [...] to see what I see' (140). According to Knowlson, all the quotations that Winnie borrows from the literary canon are carefully chosen by Beckett with 'concern for their relationship with important themes of the play' (Knowlson 1985, 144). Beckett himself identifies the citation in his early manuscript of *Happy Days*: it is from *Hamlet*, from Ophelia's speech immediately following Hamlet's abandonment of her, saying he neither loves her nor intends to marry her.

Rather than retreating into madness and suicide, as Ophelia does, Winnie's response to her loss is to activate a manic defence. As we see from the passage above, Winnie almost believes that Willie has already left her since she has not seen him for 'a long time' (*CDW*, 160). However, immediately after she expresses her apprehension that Willie has left her, she denies the loss saying, 'it doesn't matter, you are there' (160). The denial of internal and external realities is the primary manic defence in Klein's manic-depressive position. Using Klein's theory, Winnie's excessively happy voice and her manic symptoms can be seen as a specific defence mechanism against the impending loss of her husband. Furthermore, as Klein's theory suggests, the impending loss has also reinstated Winnie's infantile paranoiac and persecutory fear of being punished by bad objects.

In order to identify Winnie's hidden but underlying anxieties, her story about Mildred – which reveals her castration anxiety – is going to be analysed using 'Rita's case' by Klein. Rita's case shows a striking similarity with the Mildred story. The next section, therefore, will demonstrate how Winnie 'in mania', borrowing Klein's words, 'seeks refuge not only from melancholia but also from a paranoiac condition which [she] is unable to master' (*LGR*, 277).

III   Mania and the female castration anxiety in *Happy Days*

Manic defences

Beckett explained Winnie's excessively happy voice at rehearsal using a psychological term: 'She's a bit mad. Manic is not wrong, but too big' (cited in Knowlson 1985, 16), and indeed Winnie's symptoms of mania are pervasive in *Happy Days*. Before examining Winnie's mania as a defence mechanism activated against her depressive position as well as the impending loss of her husband, we will look at her general manic symptoms. According to Klein, mania is a defence mechanism to stop the depressive position arising. Beckett hints at Winnie's depressive state by revealing that she has been under medication. At the beginning of the play, Winnie *'brings out'* a *'medicine'* bottle, which reads 'Loss of spirits … lack of keenness … want of appetite' (*CDW*, 141), the typical symptoms of a depressive person. The following characteristics of the manic defence by Klein and Winnicott are particularly close to Winnie's symptoms. In his essay, 'The Manic Defence' (1935) – based on 'Mrs Klein's concept' (Winnicott 1975, 129) – Winnicott explains that the manic defence is based on 'denial of inner reality' in general and 'denial of *sensations* of depression' (132, Winnicott's italics) in particular. Winnicott uses the word 'ascensive' in describing how his manic patients employed opposite sensations such as 'happiness', 'light' and 'rising' in order to deny feelings of depression such as 'despair', 'gravity' and a 'sinking feeling' (134–5). He further explains how 'balloons, aeroplanes and magic carpets' in children's play bear 'a manic defence significance', and claims that 'light-headedness is a common symptom of an impending depressive phase' (134). As a defence against heaviness and depression, the head 'as if filled with gas' tends to 'raise the patient above his trouble' (134).

In order to find an example in Winnie – who is, as Beckett puts it, 'a weightless being' (cited in Knowlson 1985, 16) – we only need to examine a speech in which, in feeling 'gravity', she claims, 'if I were not held – [*gesture*] – in this way, I would simply float up into the blue […] like gossamer' (*CDW*, 151–2). Instead of complaining that she is sinking into the mound, Winnie claims that without 'gravity' she would be 'sucked up' into the air because 'the pull is so great' (151–2). Immediately after this speech, however, Winnie experiences a state that Beckett calls 'Défaillances' (failures) (cited in Knowlson 1985, 45), which describes the eight moments of her breakdown, saying 'Forgive me, Willie, sorrow keeps breaking in' (*CDW*, 152). While Winnie keeps trying to deny her sadness and the miserable situation of being half-buried in the mound, occasionally we observe a moment when her manic defence fails.

Winnie's breakdown is probably the result of Willie's negligence: he could have rescued her from her miserable situation. When telling the Mr 'Shower – or Cooker' (156) story, Winnie tries to suggest that Willie should dig her out. She quotes from the conversation between Mr Shower – or Cooker and his wife or fiancée: 'Why doesn't he dig her out? he says – referring to you my dear […] I'd dig her out with my bare hands, he says' (157). Gontarski also points out that twice in his manuscript 'Beckett noted the possibility that Winnie believes that Willie may "Come to dig me out?"' (Gontarski 1985, 77). Winnie's manic defence, then, can be seen as being activated by the impending loss of her husband, Willie, and also her feeling that Willie has forsaken her. Rather than begging him to dig her out, however, what Winnie keeps doing is trying to master and control Willie. As Klein explains, the manic 'endeavours ceaselessly to master and control all [his or her] objects, and the evidence of this effort is [his or her] hyperactivity' (*LGR*, 277). Winnie's hyperactivity – keeping herself continuously busy and controlling all her objects by putting them in order – displays her manic tendency in general, and her attempt to disguise her dependence on Willie indicates her particular dread of losing him. Rather than showing her need for him and asking for his help, Winnie prefers to have control over him. This tendency is exemplified when she instructs him about how to get out of his hole. She even expresses her contempt when he fails to follow her direction: 'The knees! The knees! [*Pause.*] What a curse, mobility!' (*CDW*, 158). As Klein's theory explains, here Winnie attempts to detach herself from her loved one by '*denying the importance*' of him, and by mastering and controlling him so that her loss will not be experienced as important (*LGR*, 277, Klein's italics).

However, underneath Winnie's manic defences and her denial of the importance of her loved object, Willie, are her failure to give him up and her desire to keep him. As in *All That Fall* where Beckett's contradictory feelings of simultaneous attachment to and detachment from home and Ireland are divided between the characters of Mrs Rooney and Mr Rooney respectively, by using Winnie's manic voice Beckett also finds another way to reveal his own sense of loss, previously expressed through his melancholic male voices. Whereas in melancholia the ego denies the loss of the loved objects and the lost objects are concealed, in mania the conflict arises because, as Klein claims, 'the ego is unwilling and unable to renounce its good internal objects and yet endeavours to escape from the perils of dependence on them as well as from its bad objects' (*LGR*, 277). In Klein's theory, splitting a loved object into good and bad objects is one of the infant's earliest methods of defence in dealing with the fear of losing its internal good objects, and we see that despite her claim of 'admiring' Willie, Winnie also feels that he is 'cruel' (*CDW*, 158, 163). By splitting her loved object, Willie, into good and bad objects, and by activating manic defences such as omnipotent control over him and denial of his importance, Winnie attempts to detach herself from him without completely renouncing him.

This process of splitting into good and bad objects needs more explanation in order to discuss Winnie's persecutory fears in relation to her infantile depressive position. To reiterate Klein's theory, when distress about the impending loss arises, in order to overcome its depressive anxiety, the baby needs to go through the process which is comparable to the work of mourning in the adult – testing of reality and the reparation which is the process of restoring the lost object as a good internal object. Until the loved objects are safely preserved as good objects inside the ego, the baby experiences oscillations between the depressive and manic positions. Klein emphasizes that the 'fundamental difference between normal mourning on the one hand, and abnormal mourning and manic-depressive state on the other' is that the latter 'have been unable in early childhood to establish their internal "good" objects and to feel secure in their inner world' (*LGR*, 369). That is, they 'have never really overcome the infantile depressive position' (369). It is also important to note that in Klein's theory the manic defences are activated against not only the depressive position, but also a paranoiac condition. Although it is mania that is pervasive throughout *Happy Days*, Winnie nonetheless suffers from internalized persecutors. For example, she has the 'Strange feeling that someone is looking at [her]' (*CDW*, 155), and this gaze controls her sleeping by ringing a bell loudly whenever she closes her eyes. Even though the audience also hears this piercing alarm, given that Willie does not respond to the bell and it does not control his sleeping, Winnie's perception of the gaze and the sound of the bell is a manifestation of her internalized persecutors.

The Mildred story

The poignancy of the impending loss of her husband has also reinstated Winnie's infantile paranoid fear of being punished by internalized persecutors. While Winnie's perception of the gaze and the bell suggests her paranoiac fears in general, the Mildred story, which Beckett advised the actress, Eva Katharina Schultz, to 'speak in an infantile voice' (Knowlson 1985, 127), can be seen as a manifestation of her infantile persecutory fear in general, and the castration anxiety in particular.[8] The Mildred story not only discloses Winnie's hidden castration anxiety but also provides an empirical link with Klein's work. In this story, Mildred at the age of 'four or five' sneaked out of her bedroom with her wax doll when it was still dark, 'descended all alone the steep wooden stairs', and 'entered the nursery' (*CDW*, 163). Describing the moment when Mildred 'Crept under the table and began to undress Dolly. [*Pause.*] Scolding her [doll]', Winnie stops the narration, after adding the phrase, 'Suddenly a mouse' (163). She tries to calm herself, saying 'Gently, Winnie' (163), and asks Willie to interrupt her as if she feels difficulty in continuing the story. After recomposing herself, digressing to tell other stories such as 'Mr Shower – or Cooker' (164), and when it becomes evident that Willie is not going to respond to her begging for 'Help' (165), she tells us an unusual story of a girl bitten by a mouse:

> WINNIE: Suddenly a mouse ran up her little thigh and Mildred, dropping Dolly in her fright, began to scream – [WINNIE *gives a sudden piercing scream*] – and screamed and screamed – [WINNIE *screams twice*] – screamed and screamed and screamed and screamed till all came running in their night attire, papa, mamma, Bibby and ... old Annie, to see what was the matter ... [*pause*] ... what on earth could possibly be the matter. [*Pause.*] Too late. [*Pause.*] Too late.
>
> (*CDW*, 165)

Despite her uneasy feeling about narrating the Mildred story, there is an urge to tell it, as we see that she saves it for last: 'There is my story of course, when all else fails' (163). As 'of course' indicates, the story has been told before, and is narrated to pass the time – a purpose often served by stories in Beckett's works. As the underlying compulsion indicates, it is the act of telling the Mildred story that is important for Winnie. In contrast to her other stories, in this story Winnie expects Willie to interrupt her before she reaches a climax, the part which describes the mouse running up Mildred's thigh. Before reaching the climax, Winnie calls Willie for 'Help' (165) twice, and by stating 'it is not like him to be wantonly cruel' (163), she hints that he normally does meet this specific request. The autobiographical element also implies the significance of the castration anxiety expressed in the Mildred story: as many critics have pointed out, Mildred is Winnie's childhood self. In the early manuscript, Winnie's name is Mildred, and in his theatrical notebook Beckett establishes the link between Winnie and Mildred clearly by making Mildred's 'frilly frock' and 'Pearly necklace' reflect those of Winnie.[9] The autobiographical element highlights that the castration anxiety expressed in the Mildred story is Winnie's own infantile dread of internalized persecutory objects. As Klein's theory tells us, the compulsive repetition in telling the story reveals that Winnie has never really overcome her infantile depressive position.

Remarkably, Beckett uses a name from his own childhood in the Mildred story. Bibby was the name of his nanny, and also appears in other works, including a short story, 'A Case in a Thousand' (1934;

CSP), in which a male protagonist, Dr Nye, encounters his old nanny by chance. Phil Baker reads this story as an Oedipal parody in which the nanny is 'the woman whom as a baby and a small boy [Dr. Nye] adored'.[10] More interestingly, Beckett, using Winnie's voice, also talks about his own recollection of extraordinary memories of being in 'his mother's womb at a dinner party [...] under the table' (cited in Knowlson and Knowlson 2006, 151), the 'intrauterine memories' (*DF*, 171) evoked during psychotherapy with Wilfred Bion. Winnie says: 'Beginning in the womb, where life used to begin, Mildred has memories, she will have memories, of the womb, before she dies, the mother's womb' (*CDW*, 163). This is not only the most direct reference to Beckett's intrauterine memories in his works, but the mention of the mother's womb before describing Mildred being bitten by a mouse under the table suggests the close link between the story and Klein's castration fear, explained in 'Rita's case'. As his 'Psychology Notes' show, Beckett knew both classical and Kleinian theories of the castration complex. In his notes from Stephen's *The Wish to Fall Ill*, Beckett first summarizes the castration complex, which is close to Freud, as being produced in reaction to the boy's puzzlement over the anatomical difference between the sexes: 'Horrified early discovery that women are without penes [sic], & so would want to steal the man's. Horror of intercourse, fear of penetration lest the woman should not let penis go [...] Fears concerning contact between genitals regarded as instruments of castration & mutilation' (TCD MS 10971/7/3).

The male castration fear is pervasive in Beckett's early fiction in which both Belacqua and Murphy fear entrapment by sexually provocative women. Their castration fears are manifested in the myth of the beaver – 'The beaver bites off his balls – that he may live'[11] in both *More Pricks Than Kicks* and *Murphy*. Wylie in his description of Murphy, for example, states 'Even so the beggar [Murphy] mutilate himself [...] that he may live, and the beaver bites his off' (*M*, 217). As John Pilling (1999) observes, this is a reference to Burton's *Anatomy of Melancholy*. However, this is also Beckett's attempt to use his own knowledge of psychoanalysis learned from Stephen's text as his notes – 'castration & mutilation' – indicate. In his later work, we see a different take on this issue. Whereas in Beckett's early fiction the male protagonists' castration fear contributes to their fear of and resistance to the female characters, in *Happy Days* Willie is safe from such fears because the question of making love does not arise between him and Winnie. Instead, using his psychoanalytic knowledge, Beckett makes Winnie express castration anxiety – a female castration anxiety that does not exist in Freud's theory.

Rita's case

In Freud's theory it is only in the boy's case that the castration fear arises, as a result of the discovery of the anatomical difference between the sexes and of the paternal threat. For the boy, the father acts as the castrating agent who prohibits the boy's Oedipal wish to usurp the father's place. In the case of the girl, however, Freud's theory becomes problematic since she hardly can conceive 'a threat to deprive her of what she has not got' (Laplanche and Pontalis 1980, 57). While in Beckett's early fiction, Freud's castration complex is used in order to present the male characters' flight from their women, in *Happy Days* Winnie's Mildred story not only expresses a female castration anxiety that is strikingly similar to Klein's 'Rita's case', but also expresses complicated psychological symptoms which are related to Klein's infantile depressive position. When examining Beckett's notes on Stephen's book further, we can see that he was exposed to a description of the castration complex which is close to Klein's, and that he also paid particular attention to the link between the castration fear and melancholia, which is studied in 'Rita's case':

> Fears of genital attack from parent of same sex (rival). Introjection of parent, producing internal conflict, self-hatred, -love, -denial, -fear, & perhaps melancholia & suicide. [...] With introjection the child's own sense-pleasure become 'bad', are repudiated & bring about a <u>split libido</u>. The child desires father's penis to be taken from him, or it & the mother's genitals to be injured in intercourse. Hence castration complex.
>
> (TCD MS 10971/7/3, Beckett's emphasis)

As we saw in the Introduction, Stephen not only directly refers in her own text to Klein's book, *The Psycho-Analysis of Children*, observing that 'Klein has been a leading pioneer' (Stephen 1933, 195), but also offers a substantial discussion of female castration anxiety that seems to owe a great deal to Klein.[12] For instance, infantile sadism – the child's wish to attack the genitals of both parents – introduced in the summary is a key to understanding Klein's castration theory through which the girl's castration anxiety can be explained. Through 'Rita's case', Klein discovered that the castration anxiety arises from the introjected parents and from the baby's own aggressive wish to attack its parents. It is the infantile sadism that gives rise to the feelings of remorse as well as to the fear of losing a good object and retaliation from bad objects.

Beckett's notes above correspond to Klein's castration theory, and, more importantly, to 'Rita's case' – the first case introduced on the first page of the first chapter, 'The Psychological Foundations of Child Analysis' (1923) in Klein's *The Psycho-Analysis of Children* (1975; first published in 1932). *The Grove Companion to Samuel Beckett* states that 'Bion recommended to SB [Samuel Beckett] *The Psycho-Analysis of Children*' (Ackerley and Gontarski 2004, 299). Also as mentioned in the Introduction, Beckett's 1934 letter to Nuala Costello shows his familiarity with Klein and that the theories of Klein and Stephen are connected in his mind. Whether or not Beckett read the whole book, it is likely that he must have paid attention to the case of the little girl, Rita, introduced in the first page, because she, like Beckett, grew 'strongly fixated upon her mother' and 'suffered from night-terrors' – '*pavor nocturnus*' (Klein 1975, 3–4). As both Knowlson and Baker point out, Beckett too suffered from '*pavor nocturnus*, particularly associated with obsessionals' (Baker 1997, 6), which were indeed one of the symptoms that impelled Beckett to go to see a psychotherapist in the first place. As Beckett's interest in the connection between melancholia and the castration fear indicates, Rita's symptoms must also have caught his attention: Rita showed 'all the signs of a melancholic depression' and alternation 'between feelings of remorse and uncontrollable "naughtiness"' (Klein 1975, 3) as well as the castration fear.

As 'Rita's case' helped Klein to discover the importance of introjected persecutory objects that came to terrorize the child, it is also going to help us to locate Winnie's castration anxiety in relation to her infantile depressive position. Thus, Klein's analysis of Rita will be introduced in some detail, despite its length. It is one of Rita's displays of 'obsessional neurosis' (3), which Klein called the 'bed-time ritual' (6), that exhibits the same castration fear (again in the guise of a mouse) as Winnie shows. In Rita's bed-time ritual, 'she had to be tightly tucked up in the bedclothes' because of the fear that 'a "mouse or *Butzen*" would get in through the window and bite off her own "*Butzen*" [genital]' (6). Her doll[13] also had to be tucked up in the bed alongside her, and the bed-time ritual became more and more elaborate: For instance, on 'one occasion during her analytic session she put a toy elephant to [sic] her doll's bed so as to prevent it from getting up and going into her parents' bedroom and "doing something to them or taking something away from them"' (6). Rita in the analytic session also 'used to punish her doll and then give way to an outburst of rage and fear' (7).

According to Klein's analysis, Rita's bed-time ritual is the manifestation of her fear of internal persecuting objects. Rita's 'attacks of anxiety and rage [...] turned out to be a repetition of her night-terrors', and 'were closely connected with strong feelings of guilt arising from that early Oedipus conflict' (4). Klein explains that the toy elephant in her game 'was taking over the role of her internalized parents whose prohibiting influence she [had] felt' (6) since she was fifteen months old. What the introjected parents prohibited was her Oedipal wish to usurp her mother's place, and to injure and castrate both parents. The agency of the super-ego here is not only her 'real parents', but also, and more especially her 'excessively stern introjected parents' (7). As Beckett's notes highlight, 'Excessive self-control, resulting from excessive parental control' tends to 'turn the aggression in upon the subject & produce melancholia' (TCD MS 10971/7/2). On the other hand, the infant's aggressive wish to attack its parents – it 'desires father's penis to be taken from him', and 'the mother's genitals to be injured' (10971/7/3) – also gives rise to a sense of remorse and guilt as well as melancholia. Rita's 'sadistic desire' to 'rob the mother's body of its contents, namely, the father's penis', and to 'destroy the mother herself' (*LGR*, 217), then, makes it possible to explain the girl's castration anxiety since she fears her mother's retaliation for her own aggressive wish.[14] Unlike Freud's theory, Klein's theory allows for the girl too to have castration anxiety.

In Winnie's Mildred story, the ideas of prohibition and punishment and her phantasy attack can be found beneath the dread of being bitten by the mouse. As Rita's aggression and fear of punishment are manifested while punishing her doll and giving way to outbursts of rage and fear, so Winnie describes Mildred's wrongdoing – it is 'forbidden to do so' (*CDW*, 163) – and it is when Mildred is 'scolding her' doll that she is punished by the mouse. Such prohibition and punishment in the Mildred story that is also Winnie's childhood memory can be regarded as the manifestation of her castration anxiety and also of her childhood phantasy of being persecuted by the introjected objects. In her phantasy, Mildred or Winnie, like Rita, was supposed to be in her bed, but she sneaked out from her bedroom and was bitten by the mouse. The prohibition in the story, as in 'Rita's case', is imposed not by Winnie's real mother but by 'an introjected one who treated her with far more severity and cruelty than the real one had ever done' (Klein 1975, 6). In the story, the agency of the harsh super-ego is fragmented, as in Klein's super-ego theory,[15] to 'papa, mamma, Bibby and ... old Annie' (*CDW*, 165).

While the castration anxiety expressed in both Winnie's Mildred story and Rita's case are strikingly similar, Winnie's manic symptoms contrast with Rita's melancholia. In the case of Rita, as Klein explains, there are two sets of fears: the fear of retaliation from the bad internalized mother derived from her own aggressive wish and the fear of losing the good mother who was damaged in her phantasy. It is the two sets of fears existing at the same time and oscillating that cause ambiguity and her 'melancholic depression' (Klein 1975, 3). In Mildred's story, however, the absence of a good object and the lack of inner conflicts between the good and bad objects are noticeable. In Mildred's danger of castration by the mouse, for instance, papa, mama and Bibby, who were supposed to provide love and care, all came 'Too late' (*CDW*, 165) to rescue Mildred from danger. As Winnie repeats the words 'Too late' twice, in her phantasy the internal objects' failure to protect Mildred is emphasized. Instead of love and care, they enact only prohibition and punishment as Winnie describes Mildred being 'forbidden to do so'. Such persecutory fear in Winnie's phantasy, then, further indicates her state of mind in which she suppresses the depressive position by activating the dread of bad objects in general and the introjected persecutory mother in particular, and by concealing a sense of loss for the good mother. Furthermore, her manic symptoms can also be considered as her attempt to disguise her dread of losing Willie.

The pervasive castration fear in the Mildred story suggests Winnie's persecutory fear of the bad internal objects. When examining the beginning of the story, however, we see that it also hints at the fear of the separation from the mother. Even though the story can stand by itself by starting from Mildred's age of 'four or five' when she was bitten by the mouse, Winnie starts her narration from the 'Beginning in the womb'. 'Mildred has memories, she will have memories, of the womb, before she dies, the mother's womb' (163). Winnie's reference to the memories of the womb implies that she is still haunted by her first separation from the mother, and this, together with her dread of bad internalized objects confirms again that she has never really overcome her infantile depressive position in general and the separation from the good mother in particular. According to Klein, 'the manic-depressive and the person who fails in the work of mourning' have been 'unable to establish their internal "good" objects' during the infantile depressive position, and are unable to 'feel secure in their inner world' (*LGR*, 369). When distress about the impending loss arises, in order to overcome its depressive anxiety the baby needs to go through the testing of reality that helps to assure that the loved object is not injured, and is not turned into a vengeful person. Klein also explains that when experiencing loss, 'the individual is reinstating' not only 'his actually lost loved object', but also 're-establishing inside himself his first loved objects – ultimately the "good" parents – whom, when the actual loss occurred, he felt in danger of losing as well' (369). Since Winnie has failed to establish her internal good objects during the infantile depressive position, in experiencing the impending loss of her husband her early dread of being castrated by a bad retaliating mother is reactivated along with her manic defences.

Winnie's reference to the memories of the womb echoes Beckett's own intrauterine memories and suggests another significant change in his attitude towards self and other. For the young Beckett, these intrauterine memories were closely related to – as he said to Knowlson – his 'feeling trapped, [the feeling] of being imprisoned and unable to escape, of crying to be let out but no one could hear, [and] no one was listening' (*DF*, 171), and accordingly, in early works such as *Eleutheria*, this feeling is expressed through the protagonist Victor Krap's attempt to escape from the mother and his fiancée. In Beckett's later plays, such as *Happy Days*, which were written after his mother's death, however, we see a different take on the same memories. As discussed above, the intrauterine memories not only imply the separation from the mother, but also suggest that they are more than only the writer's expression of his own cry to be heard. From *Happy Days* onwards, Beckett shows his concern for the other voices which have been repressed and 'unheard' (*CDW*, 382). What Beckett said to Martin Esslin, for instance, indicates such a shift from his concern for his own frustrated voice to others' 'unheard' voices. When Esslin asked him what motivates him to write, Beckett said, 'The only obligation I feel is towards that enclosed poor embryo' because that 'is the most terrible situation you can imagine, because you know you're in distress but you don't know that there is anything outside this distress or any possibility of getting out of that distress' (cited in Knowlson and Knowlson 2006, 151). Even though this remark is similar to what Beckett said to Knowlson, here the focus lies on the voice of the other as well as his own. The next section, thus, will further explore Beckett's portrayal of the self in relation to the psychic others and their 'unheard' voices.

IV   Flight from the 'self so-called': *Play* and *Film*

Beckett's own general introduction to *Film* (1963) begins with Irish Bishop George Berkeley's words *esse est percipi* – to be is to be perceived – and the question of ontology in this work in relation to the philosopher, Berkeley, has often been discussed in Beckett studies.[16] The theme of the screenplay is also stated in the introduction as a matter of identity: 'Search of non-being in flight from extraneous perception breaking down in inescapability of self-perception' (*CDW*, 323). Beckett remarks that 'the protagonist is sundered into object (O) and eye (E), the former in flight, the latter in pursuit', and emphasizes that the highlight of the film is to disclose that O and E are from the same being: 'It will not be clear until end of film that pursuing perceiver is not extraneous but self' (323). Critics, thus, tend to focus on the idea of the dual nature of being – the perceiver, E, who is represented as the camera, and the perceived, O, who is watched by both the spectator and by E. Although on the surface *Film* seems to centre on the self existing independently of other people, it also raises the question of identity in relation to the lost psychic others. This section will argue that in addition to philosophical and ontological questions, *Film* reveals a complex psychological duality in relation to the protagonist's loved objects. What distinguishes *Film* from Beckett's earlier works, which show a similar Cartesian mind and body division,[17] is the protagonist's awareness of the lost others in the development of the self. Using Klein's paranoid-schizoid position, this section will show that *Film* records the significant process whereby the protagonist realizes that he has been in flight from the introjected persecutory objects that he has projected outside of himself.

Examining this process will offer us an important clue to understanding the gender dynamic in *Film* and *Play* (1962) as it will unveil the way in which the condemnation of women as menacing and devouring expressed by Beckett's early male protagonists is reversed in their own projection of the dread of the internalized bad objects onto the female others. By revealing such a process in his works, Beckett demonstrates his intention of recovering the 'woman lost' who has been ridiculed and silenced in his early fiction. The process can be compared to Klein's process of reparation, which is grounded in repairing the harmed lost object in phantasy, and which is related to the creative impulse. In *Play* – which was written less than a year after *Happy Days* (*DF*, 434, 443, 444) – Beckett, as he does in *Happy Days*, juxtaposes the female characters, W1 and W2, with the melancholic male character, M, who has abandoned both women in order to achieve 'peace' (*CDW*, 308) of mind. As many critics point out, the continuity between *Happy Days* and *Play* is apparent: if Winnie is buried up to her waist and then to her neck in Act 2, the three characters in *Play* are embedded in funerary-like '*grey urns*' (307) up to their necks. However, while Winnie, despite her physical limitations, keeps herself busy by constantly bringing out the objects from her bag, the characters in *Play* are reduced solely to the act of speech, which is '*provoked by a spotlight*' (307). Considering that the single story we hear in *Play* is rather a banal one of their triangular relationship, it is worth noting that the story is narrated from three separate perspectives. As if inspired by his 'Female Solo' experiment

(cited in Gontarski 1977, 13) – the working title of *Happy Days* – in *Play*
Beckett once again endeavours to give voices to the formerly unheard
female characters, presenting more conspicuously the theme of forsaken women than in *Happy Days*.

'Before Play' and *Play*

As tracing the early manuscripts of *Happy Days* has helped to locate the
remnants of Beckett's early characters, so the early typescript of *Play*,
which is entitled 'Before Play', will show how the conception of W1 and
W2's characters is related to his attempts to retrieve the female voice.
In 'Before Play', in contrast to the two women and one man scenario in
the final version of *Play*, there are two men, called Syke and Conk, and
a woman called Nickie. Beckett's early male protagonists blame women
for interrupting their solipsistic world; similarly, both men in 'Before
Play' blame Nickie for their disruption. Like *Words and Music*, which
was written only a few months before *Play*, Conk shows how his imagination dwells the most upon the 'woman lost' than the 'woman won'.
Conk seemed to be happy when he was in casual relationships with
women: 'Women I won unwooed weekly' (UoR MS 1227/7/16/6; cited
in McDonald 2007, 220). He complains, however, that things changed
after he met Nickie, and as he only talks about her after he has lost her,
it is apparent that he is haunted by the woman he has lost. Syke, too,
talks compulsively about Nickie and displays his bitter and ambivalent
feelings over having lost Nickie, calling her 'bitch' while also claiming
her 'my sweet love … my one love' (219).

Nickie, who appears to be the 'woman lost' to both Conk and Syke, is
physically allied with Celia in *Murphy*: Nickie's head, like Celia's, combines the colours of the Irish flag – 'carrot-hair', 'milk complexion' and
'green earrings' (219–20), significantly echoing the feature of woman-as-
Ireland in Beckett's early fiction. Nickie is unfairly blamed by the male
characters for disturbing them as Murphy does in *Murphy*. However,
unlike Beckett's early fiction in which only the devouring and penetrating female gaze has been mentioned, in this manuscript the persistent
male gaze is also acknowledged. It is Conk who obsessively and voyeur-
istically chases Nickie to her house while she is dating another man.
However, Conk is as puzzled as the early male protagonists who ask how
women spy on them, and wonders: 'She got rid of him at the door […].
Then she ran up the steps and put her key in the door. I asked her afterwards what possessed you to turn, why in the name of God didn't you
go straight in? She said she felt eyes boring into her. Boring into me,
those were her words' (cited in Pountney 1988, 88). Although it is Conk

who observes Nickie with his penetrating gaze, he is bewildered by how she has perceived it. In 'Before Play' despite the male characters' claim that it was Nickie who had disturbed them, by revealing that the source of the disturbance is their own desire for her, Beckett revises his earlier condemnation of women as devouring and penetrating.

In 'Before Play' Nickie exists as a woman whom the male characters have lost for some unknown reason. In *Play*, however, the male character, M – who was torn between two women, his wife W1 and his lover W2 – abandoned both women in an attempt to attain peace of mind through solitude. This change suggests that Beckett has shifted his focus from a 'woman lost' to women as victims. It can be argued that Beckett not only criticizes the solipsistic male by positioning M as a persecutor of the women, but also recuperates the female voices which appear to have been silenced. As we see that W2 expresses her need to talk and seeks a listener by asking, 'Are you listening to me? [...] Is anyone bothering about me at all?' (*CDW*, 314), so it is important for Beckett to offer the women a chance to speak in their own voices. While M's 'moaning about his home life' (309) and abandoning his home, wife and mistress for his solipsistic world echo Beckett's early male protagonists, in *Play* he chooses a different path from his early fiction by putting the man's story together with the stories by women. The stories told by each character reveal further that M is the persecutor who has caused the women's suffering, as Willie consciously or unconsciously contributes to Winnie's 'misery' in *Happy Days*. The purgatorial setting of the play, where the characters are entrapped in '*grey urns*' (307) and are interrogated by an unknown power, indicates that they are dead. In this situation, it is hinted that both women's deaths are related to M's abandonment. W1 threatened M that she would 'cut [her] throat' (308) if he did not give up W2. M's report, 'She was looking more and more desperate' carrying 'a razor in her vanity-bag' (310), echoes the green one's 'Gillette' (*CDW*, 366) and her suicide in *Eh Joe*. Later on W1's suicide is implied as we hear that she believes M left her for W2. Similarly, after M abandoned W2, she 'made a bundle of his things and burnt them', and 'All night [she] smelt them smouldering' (*CDW*, 311). When W1 visited W2's place, however, 'it was all bolted and barred' (311), hinting at W2's tragic end.

In Klein's theory, during the reparation process the subject takes responsibility for the loss and feels a sense of guilt for it. Arising from the similar sense of guilt, it can be seen that Beckett recovers the women who have been harmed in his early fiction and criticizes the male character. For this reason, it is necessary that M, like the male protagonists in Beckett's early fiction, appears to be melancholic, and displays a narcissistic preoccupation with himself. Unlike Conk and Syke, for whom Nickie clearly exists as the 'woman lost', in the final version Beckett strengthens the link between M and his earlier melancholic males by making M unaware that he has lost something important. M's negligent attitude is further criticized when he shows that he does not recognize his contribution to the women's suffering. Instead, and despite the suggestion that both are dead, in his 'fantasies' (316) M imagines those two women whom he abandoned, 'have become friends' (313), and 'compare [...] happy memories' (314). M's wife, W1, appears only as a victim, forsaken by her husband, and in contrast to M whose guilty part is apparent, it is not certain why she suffers by the spotlight despite her pleas for mercy and for it to leave her alone. Although all the characters are exposed by the relentless spotlight in *Play*, the interrogation seems to function to let women speak in their own voices and to tell their side of the stories unlike Beckett's early fiction which is solely narrated by males.

Film

In contrast to *Play* in which the source of the relentless gaze represented by the spotlight is not identified, in *Film*, it is lost others in general and the mother in particular who contribute to the male protagonist's paranoiac perception of the gaze. As Beckett's notes taken from Freud's *New Introductory Lectures on Psychoanalysis* (1933) remark, the super-ego causes 'delusions of observation of certain psychotics, whose observing function (super-ego) has become sharply separated from the ego & projected into external reality' (TCD MS 10971/7/6; cited in Feldman 2006, 30). As his 'Psychology Notes' show, Beckett was aware of Klein's super-ego as well as Freud's. The harsh super-ego, which constitutes the persecutory fears, is formed through not only the stern real parents but also the harsher introjected parents. While 'excessive parental control' shapes the super-ego, as Beckett highlighted in his notes, in Klein's super-ego the introjection and projection of the infant's own aggression onto parents and its fear of 'retaliation' also play a significant role in causing persecutory fears. *Film*, by presenting the moment when the male protagonist revisits his memory when he was the age of '6 months' and recalls his mother's 'severe eyes devouring him' (*CDW*, 333), makes it possible for us to examine his paranoiac perception of the gaze using Klein's theory of paranoia in the early development of the infant.

Throughout *Film* the protagonist, O, displays paranoid anxieties towards 'All extraneous perception' (323) and attempts to evade such perception by hurriedly escaping from the street to a room. As soon as O enters the room, he 'suppress[es]' (323) all the possible gazes around him by drawing the curtain across the window, ejecting a 'dog and cat', destroying 'God's image', and shrouding a 'parrot', 'goldfish' (327) and even the 'mirror' (329) in order to avoid his own gaze. As Beckett emphasizes in his script that the 'pursuing perceiver is not extraneous, but self' (323), any extraneous gaze turns out to be the protagonist's own. This is, however, not enough to explain why O is in flight from his own perception and what makes him so afraid of the gaze. The psychological motivation for O's paranoid anxiety towards the unknown gaze and for his escape to the room is hinted at in the 'NOTES' of the screenplay:

> Suggestion for room.
> This obviously cannot be O's room. It may be supposed it is his mother's room, which he has not visited for many years and is now to occupy momentarily, to look after the pets, until she comes out of hospital. This has no bearing on the film and need not be elucidated.
>
> (*CDW*, 332)

According to Beckett's 'psychological explanation' (Gontarski 1985, 188), O demonstrates paranoid anxiety in this 'room full of eyes' (190) because it is not his own room but supposedly his mother's. How does the information of the room, although Beckett states it 'needs not be elucidated', help understand the protagonist's paranoid anxiety? Why does it need to be the mother's room to 'elucidate' O's anxiety? Beckett's account of the room in his pre-production discussion with the crew further suggests another 'psychological explanation' for O's anxiety: 'This place [the room] is a trap prepared for him, with nothing in it that wasn't trapped. There is nothing in this place, this room, that isn't prepared to trap him' (cited in Gontarski 1985, 190). This comment, repeated twice, is possibly the most direct association Beckett ever made between the mother and the male protagonist's feeling of being entrapped. This echoes Beckett's earlier male protagonists' flight from the devouring women who, the males believe, are intent on ensnaring them in a place they would resist staying in. What is particularly interesting in Beckett's own comment above is that he describes the room as being 'prepared to trap him' instead of O merely feeling that he is trapped there. Thus in O's mind it is the mother who prepares the room to trap him, and he, as well as Beckett, puts her in the active role as a dangerous persecutor who devours him. O's paranoid anxieties and the dread of being devoured and persecuted by the bad objects (all the mother's belongings in her room) can be explained using Klein's model of paranoia. Considering O's age – in an early version of *Film* 'O's age was set specifically, fifty' (Gontarski 1985, 106) – we can assume that his mother is an old woman. O's unusual visit to his mother's room while she is in hospital, after he has not visited for 'many years', suggests that her illness is very serious. It can be argued that O's paranoid anxiety is brought on by the fear of his mother's impending death.

As Klein's theory suggests, the poignancy of the impending loss of O's mother has reinstated his unconscious phantasies of having lost his internalized good object (his mother) in his earliest stages of psychic development, while at the same time the fears of being punished by dreaded bad objects have also been revived. The link between O's mother and the internalized bad objects becomes clear when looking at Beckett's 'NOTES' on the description of O's own photographs when he was a child:

1. Male infant. 6 months. His mother holds him in her arms. Infant smiles front. Mother's big hands. Her severe eyes devouring him. Her big old-fashioned beflowered hat.
2. The same. 4 years. On a veranda, dressed in loose nightshirt, kneeling on a cushion, attitude of prayer, hands clasped, head bowed, eyes closed. Half profile. Mother on chair beside him, big hands on knees, head bowed towards him, severe eyes, similar hat to 1.

(*CDW*, 333)

Here, the depiction of the mother's 'severe eyes devouring' the male infant and the child particularly catches our attention. The photographs described in the screenplay cannot easily be portrayed in the film: it is difficult to illustrate 'severe eyes devouring him'. These 'NOTES', therefore, function more for psychological explanation than for the actual production of the movie. The mother's eyes as bad objects and dangerous persecutors indicate O's own fears of his mother's gaze, and also that his mother exists as introjected bad objects in O's psyche. To reiterate Klein's argument, the baby perceives aspects of the mother as bad objects and as dangerous 'persecutors who it fears will devour it' (*LGR*, 262) because it projects its own aggression onto these objects which frustrate its desires. O, however, at this stage still does not realize that the mother's 'severe' and 'devouring' gaze is the projection of his own fear outside of himself. It is intriguing that Beckett's description of the second photograph is almost identical to a photograph of himself as a child.[18] Together with the autobiographical element, Beckett's focus on the devouring and menacing mother's gaze in *Film* reveals his own old anxieties and fears of his maternal imago, his internal bad objects.

Although not elucidated in the final production of the film, it is important for Beckett that the room needs to be the mother's in order to suggest that O's paranoid anxiety of the extraneous perception is specifically related to her as the source of the dangerous persecutors. In paranoia, according to Klein, the characteristic of defences is mainly aimed at 'annihilating the persecutors' (*LGR*, 264). The act of annihilating the persecutors in *Film* is evident in O's 'inspection and destruction of photographs' (*CDW*, 328), and for O this needs to be done in his mother's room. For that purpose, O carries a 'briefcase' (324) – as if suggesting carrying his lifelong burden – to his mother's room. This briefcase contains the seven photographs which portray his life events and which remind him of the loss of his loved objects: the two photographs described above, himself at '15 years' with his 'School blazer', 'Graduation day' at '20', himself at '21' with his 'fiancée', himself with a little girl in his arms when he was 'Newly enlisted' and lastly when he was '30 years. Looking over 40' with a 'Patch over left eye' (333–4). O is sitting in his mother's rocking-chair looking at each photograph, and Beckett heightens the emotional power of the 'inspection' by stilling the chair when the protagonist examines the photograph of himself with his fiancée and the little girl. O holds these photographs in 'trembling hands' (328), looking at them for twice as long as the other photographs, and touching the little girl's face with his forefinger. O's emotional reaction to the photograph of his fiancée and the little girl suggests that they are his lost objects, which in turn reminds him of the impending loss of his mother. While O's response to his already lost objects, his fiancée and the little girl, can be compared to the depressive position in which he reveals his sorrow and longing for the lost object, as the description of the mother's photographs indicates, O shows ambivalence towards his mother and projects his own fear of being persecuted by his internalized bad objects onto her. So in order to protect his ego in reaction to the impending death of his mother, and as an attempt to expel bad feelings – 'dangerous excreta' (*LGR*, 356) in Klein's term – O undertakes the process of destroying the bad objects by 'tearing' all the photographs and discarding them 'on floor' (328).

Significantly, it is after this act of 'destruction' that O falls asleep in his mother's rocking-chair and realizes that the extraneous perception to himself is his own gaze and self-perception. As most emphasis on the gaze in this film centres on the 'eyes' in O's mother's room and the 'devouring' aspect of her gaze, this ending is the moment of revelation when O also realizes that the mother's severe and devouring gaze, seen as dangerous persecutors, is in fact nothing but his projection of his own dread of his internalized bad objects onto his mother. The protagonist's journey to his mother's room in *Film* then shows a different drive from Molloy's, and has a specific purpose. Molloy looks for his mother's room without knowing the reason, and converts his sense of loss – without realizing what he has lost in himself by the separation from his mother – into creation by writing a story in her room. O/E, however, carries the briefcase which contains photographs of his loved objects all the way to his mother's room for 'inspection and destruction' (*CDW*, 328).

In *Molloy*, Molloy's denial of the loss of loved objects and repression of his emotion are understood in the light of Freud's melancholia and also of Schiesari's explanation of the male melancholic tradition, in which control of one's emotions is an important feature in aesthetic practice. In *Film*, which is 'entirely silent except for the "sssh!" in part one' (323), and thus free from any verbal expression of O/E's emotion, Beckett allows the protagonist to revisit his painful memories, which are specifically connected to the loss of the loved ones, and to display his emotional turmoil through his body language. *Film*, thus, not only presents the protagonist's emotional attachment to his lost loved ones and his mother more conspicuously than *Molloy*, but also hints at his step towards the work of mourning by showing his destruction of the internalized bad objects. After portraying the significant process whereby the male protagonist realizes that he has been in flight from the 'self so-called', the self that has internalized bad objects, Beckett in his late works endeavours to restore the lost objects as good objects – a process crucial in the mourning practice. The argument continues, therefore, with an exploration of the Kleinian work of mourning repre-sented in Beckett's late works.

5
The Kleinian Work of Mourning in Beckett's Late Works

I Introduction

In a letter to his friend Thomas MacGreevy written on 18 April 1939, Beckett describes his mother, who recently moved away from Cooldrinagh, his family home:

> In the meantime she is living in a little shanty on the harbour at Greystones, to which she seems to have become very attached, chiefly I think because she can see Redford cemetery from the sitting-room corridor, or the slopes of Bray Head across the water. She is of course lonely, but sees Frank & Jean fairly often.
>
> (*LSB*, 656)

As we see from this letter, Beckett believes the main reason for his mother's choice of New Place when she left Cooldrinagh was to be near her husband's grave. What is intriguing is that Beckett's later works such as *Mal vu mal dit/Ill Seen Ill Said* (1980/1982) and *Rockaby* (1980) not only centre on an old and lonely female figure who is in mourning like his mother, but are also set in a place that resembles his mother's home in Ireland. The setting of Beckett's manuscript, 'Kilcool', considered to be an earlier version of *Not I* (1972), is Redford by the sea, which has a 'beautiful view all bare and glitter just the tunnels through the Head [Bray Head]' (cited in Gontarski 1985, 136). The background of both *Not I* and *Company* (1979) is also distinctively Ireland as Beckett uses the names of his home town, Croker's Acres and the Ballyogan Road. Unlike his drama written in the early 1960s which tends to erase the Irish setting, in his later works, Beckett attempts to envisage the 'woman lost' in general and the mother in particular by deliberately revisiting his home in Ireland in his mind's eye.

While Beckett, in his earlier works, undergoes the process of 'undoing' and 'vaguening' autobiographical elements, his revising process in his later works shows the opposite course. For instance, the female protagonist's name in *Footfalls* (1975) is changed from Mary to May, which is the Christian name of Beckett's mother. Whereas home or the name of his home town is treated almost as taboo in his French fiction, in his late texts, when revising them, he adds the word twice with an exclamation mark. The 'typescript 4' of *Not I* reads 'on the way back', and Beckett has crossed out 'back' and adds 'home...home!' (cited in Pountney 1988, 256), which is kept in the final version. Similarly, in revising the last vignette of *Company*, Beckett changes 'refuge' to 'home. Home!' in his autograph correction.[1] *Mal vu mal dit*, the French version of *Ill Seen Ill Said*, does not have an equivalent to the English word 'home'.[2] However, when translating it back to English, Beckett uses 'home. Home!' (*ISIS*, 24, 34, 37), inserting this double word phrase three times in the English version. While the male narrators in Beckett's early fiction constantly set off on journeys from home, in his later works we see his mind's eye 'hovering' (*ISIS*, 45) over home where a lonely and ghostly female figure dwells.

After presenting in *Film* the male protagonist's recognition that his dread of woman stems from his phantasy rather than from his real mother, Beckett in his later works endeavours to recuperate the lost (m)other who has been silenced and damaged in his earlier works by returning to his home in Ireland, the place where his male characters bid farewell to the lost object. The moral torment from which Beckett suffered into later life is closely linked to his relationship with his mother as well as to his hostile portraits of women in his early fiction that echo the woman lost, such as Peggy Sinclair. Born of this sense of guilt, as Klein's artistic creation theory suggests, Beckett's later works *Not I*, *Footfalls*, *Ill Seen Ill Said* and *Rockaby* can be understood as his ongoing attempt to reconstruct the female subject that has been ridiculed in his early works. Such an attempt by Beckett is comparable to what Klein calls reparation, the process of repairing the lost loved object and restoring it from a bad to a good object inside oneself – a vital course of action in the Kleinian work of mourning. This chapter will show how Beckett, through the reparation process, recuperates the female subject on the one hand, and uses the female voice in order to express his own sense of loss and alienation on the other.

Compared to his French fiction, in which a remembered landscape becomes uncanny, Beckett's late works vividly picture his home town in Ireland, which becomes a key setting and emerges explicitly as a place on which his mind's eye hovers when envisaging his lost psychic others. In his late works Beckett attempts to restore the lost others by willingly imagining both 'woman lost' and Ireland, and as a result it seems that he is more at ease with addressing his home town. Consequently, apart from the narrators' charged reactions to the word home, it is difficult to find the moments when Beckett treats home as a lost object. In Beckett's late works Ireland exists as an indispensable background to the 'woman lost' rather than as a lost object in itself. This chapter, therefore, will focus mainly on the female as the lost psychic other and Beckett's use of the female voice and body in his late drama and prose.

II Restoring the abject entity in *Not I*

Beckett's *Not I* presents Mouth – the only part of a female body which is visible on stage – uttering fragmented phrases and sentence structures which are barely intelligible. The play, arguably the most perplexing of all Beckett's works, concerns the plight of a woman who vehemently refuses to inscribe herself as the speaking subject, speaking of herself in the third person and insisting that the story is that of 'she'. Many critics, especially French feminists and Lacanian psychoanalysts, have paid attention to this reaction of Mouth to her own words, and discussed the issue of the female subject in relation to language. For Peter Gidal, 'Mouth's resistance to constitute herself fully within the language' is seen as her refusal of the 'language of the Father', and also as subverting patriarchal discourse by disrupting the 'process of signification' (Wilson 1990, 193). Julia Kristeva's response to Mouth's language in her essay 'The Father, Love, and Banishment' is more ambiguous. On the one hand, Kristeva sees Mouth as having been expelled from the paternal 'Symbolic'. On the other hand, she also claims that '[Mouth] does not refuse the discourse of the Father' (Wilson 1990, 195), and, thus, is submissive to the order of the Father. Yet, through the work of 'mourning' of the loss of the '(paternal) love' by being exiled from the paternal Symbolic, Kristeva argues, Mouth 'experiences *jouissance* in nonsense through repression' (Kristeva 1980, 154), and disrupts the patriarchal discourse by pouring out the waste of repression, and by reminding us aurally and visually of the images of abjection.

Kristeva's double reading of Mouth as simultaneously a victim and an abject entity that disrupts the patriarchal discourse suggests the

difficulty in analysing Mouth's discourse. What the critics generally acknowledge, however, is that Beckett 'adopted the historically
excluded female position in his drama in order to explore the alienation
of the female subject in relation to self, language and representation'
(McMullan 1993, 74). While agreeing with such feminist readings of
Not I, in this section I argue that what Beckett tries to recuperate in
this play is not merely culturally and historically marginalized women
in general, but more specifically the female whom he has expelled or
tried to expel in his early fiction. In other words, Mouth in *Not I* is an
'abject' entity that Beckett's male characters have attempted to expel
in order that they might become separate and autonomous subjects. It
can be further argued that in *Not I* Beckett endeavours to embrace the
'woman lost' by using the female voice and tries to imagine what she
would have said rather than engaging in the vain struggle to exorcise
her as his earlier male characters do. This section will show how Beckett,
through a process that is comparable to Klein's 'reparation', recuperates
a female subject that has been damaged, 'unanswered' and 'unheard'
(*CDW*, 382) in his earlier works, and how at the same time he borrows
the female voice in order to express his own sense of loss and to articulate his inner voice. Before exploring Beckett's use of the female voice,
I will locate traces of his earlier female characters in *Not I*, and argue that
he repairs the female subject that was once abjected.

Vagina dentata

Mouth's use of language, the striking visual image of Mouth, the rapid
movement of her lips, teeth and tongue have aroused the interest of
many critics in relation to the representation of the female subject.
Ann Wilson's essay, '"Her Lips Moving": the Castrated Voice of *Not I*',
for example, draws attention to Mouth, the 'godforsaken hole', as 'the
image of castration' which is 'marked by the absence of the phallus'
(Wilson 1990, 198). Although acknowledging that the image of Mouth
is menacing and 'potentially castrating' (198), in this essay Wilson only
focuses on Mouth as being castrated, and sees her narrative as excluded
from the masculine Symbolic due to the lack of the phallus. While
emphasizing Mouth as a representation of woman outside the paternal
discourse, the castrating and threatening aspect of Mouth has not been
fully discussed in the studies of *Not I*. However, it is also this aspect of
Mouth that bridges the earlier and later representations of the female in
Beckett's oeuvre. Mouth's teeth 'moving with the force of articulation'
(198) are not only the very image of 'the female genital symbolized
by the *vagina dentata* or toothed vagina' (Creed 1993, 105) which is

prevalent throughout myth and legend, but are also reminiscent of Beckett's early female characters whom his male protagonists fear as devouring and castrating.

As observed earlier, the early male protagonists' resistance to women is closely related to their fear of castration, and their 'fear of penetration lest the woman should not let penis go' (TCD MS 10971/7/3) as Beckett puts it in his 'Psychology Notes'. By bringing in the image of Mouth as the *vagina dentata*, Beckett evokes the earlier characteristic of the female as devouring while also revealing more ambiguous feelings by portraying the woman as a victim and as the object expelled by the male characters. If *Film* (1963) presents a significant process whereby the protagonist realizes that he has been in flight from the introjected persecutory objects that he has projected outside himself rather than from his real mother, in *Not I* Beckett once again portrays a woman as a castrating and menacing figure in order to revise his early representation. The fact that Beckett's 'Kilcool' manuscript was written three months after *Film* was finished suggests the closeness of the conceptions of these works, and allows us to see *Not I* as part of his project of revision inspired by and continued from *Film*. By giving a voice to Mouth and by disclosing that she is a victim rather than a persecutor, Beckett shows that the visual image of Mouth as the *vagina dentata* is in fact derived from male fear rather than from a real danger.

It is the coexistence of two opposite representations of woman in *Not I* that makes this play interesting, and that are comparable to Klein's theory in which a loved object splits and is introjected as good and bad objects simultaneously. By presenting Mouth aurally as a forsaken victim at the same time as visually displaying the threatening *vagina dentata*, the woman who has been condemned as menacing has a chance to tell her side of story. The persecutory aspect of Mouth in part derives from the haunting nature of the object that is abjected from the male subject. Thus, it is first important to examine the trace of the lost loved object that has been damaged and forsaken. Beckett's 'Kilcool' manuscript is useful in locating Mouth as an old woman who has been abandoned by her lover. 'Kilcool', like *Not I*, features the image of a severed head with 'Woman's face alone in constant light. Nothing but fixed lit face and speech', and like Mouth she 'tells of herself in the 3rd person' (cited in Gontarski 1985, 135). The image of the decapitated female face, as in *Not I*, is clearly set out in this manuscript. Originally 'Kilcool' begins with describing 'papa dead' 'and then mama [dying] perhaps of grief' (135), echoing one of Mouth's first lines, 'parents unknown' and 'vanished' (*CDW*, 376). However, after having abandoned the play for some four months, when Beckett began it again, he focused on her as a victim abandoned by her 'lover', who has rejected her and '[left] her like that in the state she was in' (cited in Gontarski 1985, 138). By replacing the story of the loss of her parents with the story of the female character abandoned by her lover, Beckett shows that she is a victim of a man even if he is absent from the play.

A damaged good object

As Beckett emphasizes the male responsibility for the woman's misery in 'Kilcool', in his earlier prose piece *From an Abandoned Work* (1954–55) we find a similar process whereby a male subject suffers a growing sense of guilt for abandoning his mother. Examining the male narrator's relationship with his mother in the fiction will reveal some repressed features of the old woman in *Not I*, and enable us to see that the voice of Mouth is that of the mother who, her son claims, 'never talked, never answered' (*CSP*, 159) in *From an Abandoned Work*. As the persistent gaze in *Film* is closely associated with the male protagonist's mother, whose 'severe eyes [are] devouring him' (*CDW*, 333), in *Not I* the 'corner of the eye' (*CDW*, 381) specifically echoes 'the corners of the eyes' of the mother in *From an Abandoned Work*. The passage below from the prose piece demonstrates further resonance with the character of the old woman in *Not I*:

> Sometimes she cried out on me, or implored, but never long, just a few cries, then if I looked up the poor old thin lips pressed tight together and the body turned away and just the corners of the eyes on me, but it was rare. Sometimes in the night I heard her, talking to herself I suppose, or praying out loud, or reading out loud, or reciting her hymns, poor woman.
>
> (*CSP*, 159)

The mother's habit of 'talking to herself' or 'praying out loud' corresponds to the female character's denial, 'I am not talking to myself', and 'prayer' (cited in Pountney 1988, 97, 94) in 'Kilcool' as well as Mouth's outcry that fails to reach others and 'prayer unanswered ... or unheard' (*CDW*, 382). Moreover, as the woman in 'Kilcool' is represented as a weeping figure with tears on her face 'near beginning, briefly towards middle, longer; and the longest, to close. Curtain down on lit weeping face' (cited in Pountney 1988, 93) – one of the rare occurrences of tears in Beckett's oeuvre – so is the mother in *From an Abandoned Work*. After the male narrator leaves her and his home, the scene of his mother's 'weeping and waving' (*CSP*, 155) and 'waving, in sad helpless love' (156) haunts him, provoking a sense of guilt that even makes him feel that he has killed his mother: 'My father, did I kill him too as well as my mother, perhaps in a way I did' (159). The mother who is damaged in the male narrator's phantasy and also silenced in this text, then, can be considered as what Klein calls the internal mother who has been both lost and damaged in phantasy. In *Not I* Beckett's creative impulse once again focuses on reconstructing the female subject and the 'woman lost' who has been silenced and damaged in his previous works, in order to understand her and to try to articulate what she might have said.

While Mouth already hints at a trace of the mother as a damaged good object, the Auditor can also be seen as a representation of the good internalized mother. What is notable is the parallel between the mother's 'sad helpless love' (*CSP*, 156) in *From an Abandoned Work* and the Auditor's 'gesture of helpless compassion' (*CDW*, 375) – the only action that the audience sees on stage in *Not I*. The Auditor makes this gesture four times when Mouth vehemently denies herself as a subject of her story. Even though Beckett's stage direction states that the sex of the Auditor is '*undeterminable*' (376), critics tend to see the figure as masculine in order to discuss Mouth in relation to the patriarchal discourse. When examining the main sources of inspiration for *Not I*, however, we clearly see that the genesis of the Auditor is the maternal figure awaiting her child, from an event that Beckett recalled from his visit to Morocco:

> [While] sitting in a café in North Africa ... [Beckett] observed a solitary figure, completely covered in a djellaba, leaning against a wall. It seemed to him that the figure was in a position of intense listening – what could that lonely figure be listening to? Only later did Beckett learn that this figure leaning against the wall was an Arab woman waiting there for her child who attended a nearby school. The concept for *Not I* was, therefore, initially sparked by Beckett's preoccupation with that isolated listener, the unidentified Auditor we encounter on stage.[3]

Not only does the Auditor's appearance, '*enveloped from head to foot in loose black djellaba*' (376), resemble that of the Arab mother, but also her act of 'intense listening' as a main source for writing *Not I* indicates the significance of the role of the Auditor in the play, as Enoch Brater observes. Similarly, Knowlson emphasizes the Auditor's role as a listener and also as a good object, mentioning the other source for *Not I*,

Caravaggio's painting of the beheading of John the Baptist. Knowlson writes that, in the painting, 'Most powerful of all is an old woman standing to Salome's left. She observes the decapitation with horror', and her 'role comes closest to the Auditor in Beckett's play, reacting compassionately to what he/she hears' (*DF*, 521–2). Unlike Beckett's earlier representations of the mother as devouring, what is underlined here is the mother figure's 'helpless compassion' (*CDW*, 375) as well as the helpless nature of Mouth's agony.

Caravaggio, *The Beheading of St John the Baptist* (1608), oil on canvas, 361 cm × 520 cm, St John's Co-Cathedral, Valletta

I suggest that *The Beheading of St John the Baptist* as the 'Image of *Not I*' (*DF*, 521) – as Beckett wrote to Knowlson – can be read as a visualization of the figure of the mother divided into introjected good and bad objects in *Not I*.[4] Through this image, Beckett expresses his ambivalent feelings towards his mother, and more importantly starts to envisage an internal good mother rather than an entirely persecutory one as in *Film*. In Klein's theory, in order to overcome the work of mourning, it is important to restore the lost object as a good object inside the ego by evoking happy experiences through the reparation process. Even if what is recalled in *Not I* is far from pleasant, when considering the predominant representation of the mother as a bad object in his previous works, the presence of a good mother in the play is an important change in Beckett's works. It signals a more evident longing for the lost good mother. The representation of the castrating mother in *Not I* is also no longer so straightforward as the earlier representation of a castrating female. On the one hand, when considering the play in relation to Caravaggio's *Beheading of St John the Baptist*, we see that in its portrayal of the moment of the decapitation of St John the Baptist, the painting significantly manifests the male castration fear. Knowlson believes that the younger female figure in the painting is Salome, although this is debatable since the figure's appearance seems to suggest she is in fact a slave. It was of course Salome, the biblical epitome of a female castrator, who demanded from Herod the head of St John the Baptist.

On the other hand, while this interpretation supports the underlying theme of the castration fear in *Not I*, on stage there is no male character in flight from women, as were Beckett's early male characters. Instead, the castration fear in *Not I* is represented through the sight of the disembodied head of Mouth itself. As Freud claims in his essay 'Medusa's Head' (1922), the sight of the decapitated Medusa is analogous to the boy looking at his mother's genitals. According to Freud, the boy's sight of female genitals, together with the paternal threat of castration, is a crucial event in the activation of the boy's castration complex. This discovery of the anatomical difference between the sexes 'actualizes and validates a threat of castration which may have been a real or phantasied' (Laplanche and Pontalis 1980, 57). As Freud's formula in this essay – 'To decapitate = to castrate' (Freud 1955b, 273) – indicates, the scene of the moment of 'castrating' in Caravaggio's painting is transformed into the sight of the *vagina dentata*, which evokes the horror of castration by displaying 'lack', the absence of the phallus.

'Godforsaken hole' – the abject entity

Indeed, what is emphasized throughout the play is the image of Mouth, constantly evoking 'lack' visually and aurally by the frequent references to 'godforsaken hole' (*CDW*, 376) and her own forsaken state. While Mouth recalls Beckett's early female characters as the image of a castrator, she is depicted as threatening not because she exists as a menacing castrator on stage, but rather because, as Klein's castration theory explains, she evokes for Beckett and the audience what has been expelled and what has been damaged. (As Rita's case suggests, the castration fear in *Not I* can be seen as being related to the fear of retaliation for Beckett's attack on the female characters in his early works and his sense of guilt for the damage.) Mouth is also described as a victim precisely because she is the lost object and the abject entity, expelled from the subject. As Kaja Silverman states, 'Since the loss of the object always entails a loss of what was once part of the subject, it is – in the strictest sense of the word – a castration' (Silverman 1988, 9). The image of castration, thus, evokes not only the fear of losing the penis, but also the loss of the loved object and particularly the castrated mother arising from the guilt of the imaginary attack to her body. Similarly, in *Not I*, through the sight of the *vagina dentata*, Beckett portrays Mouth as an abject entity, the 'woman lost' in general and the mother in particular, who was once part of the self, but who was expelled.

By evoking 'lack' and 'a number of bodily orifices, on the threshold between inner and outer', Beckett not only shows Mouth as 'a disruptive force which threatens the conceptual stability and fixity established by the Symbolic' as McMullan claims (McMullan 1993, 76), but also reveals how the abject entity, the 'woman lost', haunts his own self. As Kristeva asserts, 'what is excluded can never be fully obliterated but hovers at the borders of our existence, threatening the apparently settled unity of the subject with disruption and possible dissolution' (Grosz 1989, 71). What Beckett seems to realize after numerous attempts to exorcize his memories of the loss of the loved ones is the impossibility of such an erasure. By displaying the image of abjection that disrupts the distinction between inside and outside, Beckett brings into question the boundaries between the subject and what has been abjected.

In *Not I* the transformation of the partially severed head of St John the Baptist in Caravaggio's painting into the female disembodied Mouth that echoes the *vagina dentata* further reveals Beckett's ambivalent use of the female subject, Mouth, evoking both a victim and a castrator. What is intriguing is the way in which the distinction between the subject and the object becomes blurred in this play when Beckett recuperates and appropriates the marginalized female voice at the same time. While reconstructing the female subject, Beckett seems to express his own experience of alienation, his sense of loss, and his inner voice that has been repressed by borrowing the hysterical voice of the woman who has been silenced by the male subject. Kristeva's reading in her essay on *First Love* and *Not I* reinforces the suggestion that Mouth is closely related to the male subject (hinting at Beckett). Kristeva shows that the male narrator in *First Love* takes up Mouth's position: 'Faithful to his paternal love, he has become an old lady (*Not I*)' (Kristeva 1980, 152). Even though in this essay Kristeva does not develop the statement further, it is worthy of elaboration. The early male protagonist in *First Love* narrates a painful process of separation from his female lover, foregrounding his confused feelings by using images of abjection – his contamination by excrement. In contrast to *First Love*, however, in *Not I* Beckett uses the metaphor of abjection in order to show that the distinction between the subject and the object, namely between the self and the lost other, is no longer possible.

Hysteria – deferred emotional reactions

Mouth in *Not I*, then, is the representation of both the object to be recuperated and the subject that speaks for the writer. The earlier version of *Not I*, 'Kilcool', further discloses Beckett's endeavours to talk about his own sense of alienation and his intrauterine memory in which he felt 'trapped, imprisoned and unable to escape': even if 'crying to be let out' 'no one could hear, [and] no one was listening' (*DF*, 171). As Beckett later mentioned this experience in relation to his motivation to write as an 'obligation [...] towards that enclosed poor embryo' (cited in Knowlson and Knowlson 2006, 151) whose distress went unheard, so the female figure in 'Kilcool' cries out: 'Someone in me trying to get out, saying let me out [...] someone there, – wanting out, into the light, poor creature' (cited in Gontarski 1985, 140). As the woman in 'Kilcool' displays her distress as if it is someone else's, so Beckett reveals his own agony and torment by borrowing the female voice.

Unlike 'Kilcool', however, *Not I* begins with Mouth's story of the separation from the womb, 'out ... into this world ... this world ... tiny little thing' (*CDW*, 376).[5] If his other works often present his characters in an enclosed, womb-like shelter, in *Not I* Beckett describes his traumatic experience of the severance with the mother and his sense of loss and alienation while confronting the world and people after the birth. Beckett's male narrators in his early French fiction set off on similar journeys from their womb-like shelters and encounter people on the way. Whereas the male narrators' marginalization is self-alienation arising from their desire for a solipsistic world, Mouth's sense of alienation is involuntary; she attempts to interact with people only to fail. Mouth wants to 'scream for help', but she 'couldn't make the sound' (378), and when she tries to utter some words, she only receives a cold response from people 'star[ing] at her uncomprehending' (379). While the recurring motif of the separation from the womb in Beckett's early fiction represents the narrators' desire for severing the umbilical cord properly, in *Not I* Mouth's predicament is derived from the fact that she was evicted from the womb. In 'this world' Mouth is entirely divorced from reality, and for her to be in a public space like a 'busy shopping centre' and 'court' is a matter of 'surviv[ing]' (379, 381). There, being unable to communicate with others, and being isolated from reality, all she could do was to stand motionless 'staring into space ... mouth half open as usual' (381).

Through Mouth, and the female position that is associated with marginalized and repressed aspects of culture Beckett is enabled to express his own sense of alienation. More importantly, Beckett's 'Psychology Notes' – 'The hysteric is always out of date in his emotional reactions' (TCD MS 10971/8/21) – indicate that not only was he aware of the hysteric's ability to pour out words that have been suppressed, but that he also saw this feature as helpful in displaying his deferred emotional reactions to the separation from the mother using the birth motif in *Not I*. While the memories that are recalled in *Not I* are still vague and the repressed elements are not fully disclosed, both the characteristics of the hysteric and the hysteric's linguistic symptoms can be seen as manifestation of Beckett's underlying, repressed grief over the loss of his mother. Mouth's linguistic symptoms, for instance, echo those of Josef Breuer's Anna O., with whose case Beckett was familiar: 'aphasia', 'linguistic disruptions', 'loss for words and [for] command of grammar and syntax', and 'repeating the words "tormenting, tormenting"' (Hunter 1985, 92–3).[6] Similarly, Mouth describes her 'torment', and 'sudden urge to ... tell ... then rush out stop the first she saw ... nearest lavatory ... start pouring it out ... steady stream ... mad stuff ... half the vowels wrong ... no one could follow' (*CDW*, 378, 382).

What distinguishes Mouth from Beckett's male characters is just such an outpouring of energy in her narrative and her hysterical laughter and screams.[7] In contrast, during the recording process of *Texts for Nothing* (1952) for BBC Radio, Beckett insisted the male narrator's reading 'should be no more than a murmur', and explained the reason to Patrick Magee: 'You see this is a man who is sitting at an open window on the ground floor of a flat. He is looking out into the street and people are passing a few yards away from him but to him it is as if it were ten thousand miles away' (*DF*, 535). While the text describes a sense of alienation and failure to communicate that is similar to that of *Not I*, this anecdote shows how in *Not I* Beckett specifically uses the female hysteric's suppressed but potentially 'explosive' linguistic capacity. Billie Whitelaw reports that Beckett 'used the phrase "explosive constipation" to think about Maddy Rooney. She's terribly constipated; she has all these feelings, and wants to explode, to release them, but she can't' (cited in Ben-Zvi 1990, 7). Whereas Mrs Rooney's feelings are repressed, in *Not I* – even if Mouth's screams are claimed to be those of the internalized 'she' and not her own (as Winnie screams borrowing her narrative of the story of Mildred in *Happy Days*) – such an outburst of emotion allows her (and Beckett) a momentary 'purg[ing]' (*CDW*, 381) of what is more usually bottled-up.

What is interesting is Beckett's claim that he 'actually heard' Mouth's story and thus the parallel between Mouth's denial of ownership of the story and that of Beckett:

> I knew that woman in Ireland. I knew who she was – not 'she' specifi-
> cally, one single woman, but there were so many of those old crones,
> stumbling down the lanes, in the ditches, beside the hedgerows.
> Ireland is full of them. And I heard 'her' saying what I wrote in *Not I*.
> I actually heard it.
>
> (*DF*, 522)

This not only reveals Beckett's discomfort in expressing his emotion as he does when using Mrs Rooney's voice in *All That Fall*, but also his clear intention of using the marginalized female voice, that of 'old crones' in Ireland, in a different manner from the male voice. One might ask whether Beckett speaks on the woman's behalf or merely appropriates the female voice in order to express his own anxiety. It seems to me that Beckett speaks for the 'woman lost' while Mouth also speaks for him and for the audience. W.B. Yeats similarly claimed that his 'Crazy Jane poems' included in *Words for Music Perhaps*, the title that echoes Beckett's *Words and Music* (1961), were 'founded on the sayings of an old woman, "Cracked Mary", who lived near Gort in Co. Galway [and who] "had an amazing power of audacious speech"' (Yeats 1996, 604–5). Elizabeth Cullingford states, 'Crazy Jane was both Yeats's attempt to speak the Other and a strategy for evading his own internal censor' (Cullingford 1993, 235). While this reveals Beckett's ongoing dialogue with Yeats, showing similarities in using the marginalized hysterical and crazy female voice as well as potentially disruptive female energy in order to resist patriarchal authority, what makes Beckett's voice distinct from that of Yeats is the way in which he becomes the lost other: despite his claim that *Not I* is the story of the other, by blurring the boundaries between the subject and the object in the text, Beckett makes the content more ambiguous and therefore universal.

Actresses and audiences claim to identify with Mouth in *Not I* and to relate to Mouth's experience.[8] For his part Beckett needed a medium which could deliver his sense of longing and grief for his mother. After Beckett wrote *Footfalls*, for example, he sent a note to Whitelaw describing the text as: 'The pacing is the essence of the matter. To be dramatised to the utmost. The text: what pharmacists call excipient' (cited in Whitelaw 1995, 139). 'Excipient', according to Webster's dictionary, is 'an inert or slightly active substance used in preparing remedies as a vehicle or medium of administration for the medicinal agents'. The text itself, like an excipient, might not contain the remedy for curing his sense of loss and his longing for the mother. Through the medium of the actress and the experience of the theatre, however, Beckett endeavours to continue the work of mourning. By looking at May's pacing and hearing the sounds, Beckett attempts to assuage his sorrows when recalling the 'Dying mother' in *Footfalls*.[9]

III 'Seek well': search for the lost (m)other in *Footfalls* and *...but the clouds...*

'Is it not time for my pain-killer?'[10] Hamm asks Clov repeatedly through-out *Fin de partie/Endgame* (1957/1958), first written in French. Even though Clov knows that 'There's no more pain-killer', he hides the fact, and replies '[*Violently.*] No!'; another time he tantalizes Hamm, saying 'It's too soon' (*CDW*, 127, 109, 104). Clov seems to be taking advantage of his management of the administration of pain-killers in order to con-trol the tyrannical Hamm. The abusiveness of the control is shown in Clov's disclosure of the fact that there are no pain-killers only at the end of the play, increasing Hamm's despair. If *Endgame*, the first play Beckett wrote after the death of his mother and brother, treats the subject of death and impending death[11] with emotional detachment, in *Footfalls* (1975), first written in his mother tongue, English, Beckett endeavours to revisit and revise the scenario of a dying patient with some 'warmth' (Asmus 1977, 84), as Beckett put it. In the first part, which Beckett called 'Dying mother', we encounter one of the most moving scenes in his plays, in which a female character, May, cares for her dying mother, asking a series of sympathetic questions: 'Would you like me to inject you again? [*Pause.*] Would you like me to change your position again? [*Pause.*] Change your drawsheet? [*Pause.*] Dress your sores? [*Pause.*] Sponge you down?', and the Mother answers, 'Yes, but it is too soon' (*CDW*, 400), a reverse echo of Hamm and Clov's dialogue. Whereas in *Krapp's Last Tape* (1958) Beckett attempts to cast a 'cold eye' on the scene of the death of Krapp's mother – with some autobiographical detail, such as the description of his waiting outside 'the house on the canal where mother lay a-dying' 'wishing she were gone' (*CDW*, 219) – in *Footfalls* the author assigns an entire scene to the daughter nursing or imagining nursing her dying mother. The death of Beckett's mother, briefly described with emotional remoteness by the male protagonist in *Krapp's Last Tape*, is recreated in *Footfalls* with the addition of care and concern for the sick woman.

Once again, in *Footfalls* Beckett endeavours to recuperate the 'woman lost'. This section will demonstrate that Beckett, in a project of revision that is comparable to Klein's reparation process, not only attempts to repair and restore the lost loved object as a good one, but also blurs the boundaries between the subject and the lost loved object by presenting a scene from more than two different perspectives. In *Footfalls*, using the female characters, Beckett shows how the subject re-incorporates the abject entity that has been expelled into the self. However, when portraying a similar process two years later using a male character, M, in his television play, ...*but the clouds*... (1976), Beckett focuses on M's effort and difficulty in recuperating the lost beloved woman. Yet, through the medium of television, which allows him to create the ghostly image of the lost object, Beckett illustrates how the male protagonist's imagination dwells upon the 'woman lost'.

'Never really been born'

As Beckett and later critics have noted, *Footfalls* is the writer's 'poignant recreation of [the story of] the girl who had never really been born', and who had been 'isolated' and 'totally encapsulated within herself' (*DF*, 544) – the story he heard in C.G. Jung's lecture at the Tavistock Clinic in 1935. In spite of Mrs Rooney's comment in *All That Fall*, 'it was just something he said, and the way he said it, that have haunted me ever since' (*CDW*, 196), we find the story is described rather plainly in Jung's lecture notes:

> Recently I saw a case of a little girl of ten who had some most amazing mythological dreams. Her father consulted me about these dreams. I could not tell him what I thought because they contained an uncanny prognosis. The little girl died a year later of an infectious disease. She had never been born entirely.
>
> (Jung 1977, 96)

This is an entire sketch of the little girl's case in the lecture notes, and Jung does not take any further account of her symptoms. It becomes clear then that it is rather Beckett's 'long-standing interest in abnormal psychology' (*DF*, 544) as well as his own intrauterine memory – the memory of feeling trapped and imprisoned in his mother's womb – that impels him to recreate the story. While 'not having been born properly' is a recurring motif throughout Beckett's oeuvre, for example, it appears briefly in *Watt* and *All That Fall*, in *Footfalls*, Beckett attempts more fully to illustrate the little girl, and more importantly to include the 'Voice of the Mother' and her perspective towards her own daughter who has confined herself 'in the old home' (*CDW*, 401).

When we examine how the little girl's story is used in *Footfalls*, we see that the Mother is an important component in the play. *Footfalls* consists of four parts: the dialogue between May and Voice/Mother (the 'Dying mother' scene), Voice's monologue ('Mother back'), May's monologue ('Sequel') and 'Empty Strip'. In the second scene, when the Voice of the Mother describes May, she interrupts herself while narrating 'in the old home, the same where she' and then continues, the 'same where she began' (401). According to Walter Asmus, during the rehearsals for the German premiere in 1976, Beckett explained to Charlotte Joeres, the actress who played the Mother, why she hesitates: 'She was going to say: "... the same where she was *born*." But that is wrong, she hasn't been born. She just began. "It began. There is a difference. She was never born"' (Asmus 1977, 84). Not only does this indicate the mother's keen awareness of her daughter's symptoms, but also, by introducing the story of 'not having been born' through the Mother's voice, Beckett reveals his intention. That is, the play should be not merely about the girl but also about the Mother and the relationship between them. Beckett's own explanation sheds additional light on their relationship: 'Jung said he wasn't able to help this patient' (83). Even though that might not be exactly how Jung phrased it, Beckett's account hints at his decision to portray the Mother, who tries to listen to her daughter just as the Auditor listens in *Not I*, with 'helpless compassion'. Thus the play starts with May calling the Mother, and the Voice of the Mother answering, 'I heard you in my deep sleep. [*Pause.*] There is no sleep so deep I would not hear you there' (*CDW*, 399). In contrast to the earlier representation of the Mother as one who entraps the male characters in her womb and who fails to recognize them, in *Footfalls* and also in *Not I* Beckett reconstructs the Mother as a Kleinian 'good mother' who is sympathetic and endeavours to listen to the protagonists.

Footfalls and *Not I*, then, show that the protagonists' innate problems, namely their self-alienation and a lack of communication, are beyond the Mother's capacity to help as we observe both the Auditor and the Mother's efforts to listen to the female characters on stage. Without understanding what is going on in her daughter's 'poor mind' and her compulsion to pace up and down, the Mother in *Footfalls* can only ask her daughter, 'Will you never have done ... revolving it all?' (*CDW*, 400).

The Mother's monologue reveals that she listens to her daughter even 'when [May] fancies none can hear' because that is the only time when May 'Tries to tell how it was' and to 'speak' (401). Yet, May does not tell the Mother and the audience the reason for her endless pacing and her confinement to the 'old home'. In contrast to the Mother's effort to understand her daughter, we see that it is May who estranges herself from the Mother. As Beckett explains, May's isolation is closely related to her artistic creativity. In the following conversation, Beckett and Hildegard Schmahl, who played May in the Berlin production, discuss the 'Dying mother' scene. Asmus reports:

> H[ildegard Schmahl] asks: 'Does she do that every day?' [Beckett answers] 'Yes, that is routine.' H: 'Without feeling?' 'Yes, routine.' The bedpan can express some feeling, i.e. warmth, he says. [...] H: 'The conversation between mother and daughter has something very practical and normal – it has nothing lyrical about it?' 'Yes, while May is speaking she is perhaps thinking of something quite different, perhaps she is occupied with her story.' Beckett says. [...] H: 'Is the posture [of May] supposed to express fear?' [B:] 'No, not fear. It expresses that May is there exclusively for herself. She is isolated.'
>
> (Asmus 1977, 84–5)

The 'story' is May's monologue, 'Sequel', in which she speaks of herself in the third person as Mouth does in *Not I*. According to Beckett, May's monologue is part of the story that she is composing: 'One can suppose that she has written down everything which she has invented up to this, that she will one day find a reader for her story – therefore the address to the reader' (Asmus 1977, 86) when she narrates, 'Old Mrs Winter, whom the reader will remember' (*CDW*, 402). Although Beckett 'contemplated substituting "hearer" for "reader" in order to shift the emphasis from page to stage' (Gontarski 1999, 285), the fact that he retained 'the reader' in the production implies that it was important for him to preserve the link between the process of her artistic creation – her act of writing – and her self-alienation especially in relation to the Mother. May's status as a writer, then, parallels Beckett as a creator of the play as well as his male characters who appear as writers, like Krapp.

As observed previously, *Krapp's Last Tape* describes three crucial incidents in Krapp's life: the moment of his mother's death, his revelation about his artistic approach which echoes Beckett's own experience, and his separation from his loved one in search of the solipsistic world that he saw as necessary for the creation of his 'opus…magnum' (*CDW*, 218). While almost the same topics converge in *Footfalls*, Beckett, using female characters, reconfigures and reconstructs the themes and the character's relationship with the mother. May is confined in her solipsistic world and is preoccupied with her artistic search as is Krapp. Unlike Krapp's silenced mother, however, Beckett recuperates the Mother's voice, and presents May as caring for her 'Dying mother'. Furthermore, the motif of 'not having been born properly' in *Footfalls* takes quite a different shape from its appearances in Beckett's earlier works and the story of the little girl described in Jung's lecture. In Beckett's early fiction, the motif is closely related to the male protagonists' fear of being trapped in the mother's womb, the vehement refusal of the devouring mother figure, and the attempt to sever the umbilical cord as a prerequisite for artistic search. While sustaining the connection between the mother and artistic creation, in *Footfalls* Beckett depicts a daughter who cannot or rather chooses not to leave the Mother's old home/womb. Instead of feeling that the mother is devouring and entrapping her in the womb as the male protagonists feel in Beckett's early works, May voluntarily encloses herself in the Mother's womb staying 'there exclusively for herself'.

Such a process of revision corresponds to Klein's reparation whereby one's creative impulse, arising from the sense of guilt, focuses on repairing the lost object that has been damaged in phantasy. In May's monologue, 'Sequel', she creates the story of Mrs Winter and Amy who, as many critics point out, parallel the Mother and May: Amy, 'the daughter's given name', is an anagram of May, and Amy shares May's compulsive 'revolving it all' (*CDW*, 403). Just as Beckett's comment on May's preoccupation with her own artistic creation in the nurturing scene curiously intimates a sense of guilt, so does May's 'Sequel'. In May's story, whereas Mrs Winter's act of listening is emphasized as she repeatedly says, 'But I heard you respond' and 'I heard you distinctly', her daughter claims that she 'saw nothing, heard nothing' and 'was not there' (403). May's focus on Amy's absentmindedness is imbued with May's (and Beckett's) sense of guilt: she has neglected her dying Mother for her artistic creation even though, as represented in the 'Dying mother' scene, May demonstrates her intention to nurture her mother. Beckett's comment to Schmahl that May's care is routine 'without feeling' seems to arise from his regret that it was 'Not enough' (401), as May puts it, even if in reality he must have done his best to care for his dying mother as Knowlson's biography of Beckett reveals.[12] The sense of guilt is also related to Beckett's own representations of the mother and to references such as Krapp's 'wishing she were gone' while 'mother lay a-dying' as well as the author's self-imposed exile to France, which first caused the severance with his mother. If May creates a story of the mother and daughter out of her sense of guilt, Beckett also reconstructs his previous representations of the dying mother by writing the nurturing scene and attempting to recuperate the silenced mother.

The (m)other tongue

Beckett's revision of the motif of 'not having been born' in *Footfalls*, then, reflects the change in his representation of the lost other. By staging a female character who is confined in the mother's womb, Beckett shows a character who is hardly discernable from the lost (m)other, and significantly talks in the (m)other tongue. As Asmus reports, during the rehearsals Beckett emphasized many times that scenes two and three – the Mother and May's monologues – are 'exactly parallel' and 'these parallelisms are extremely important for the understanding of the play' (Asmus 1977, 86). Part of the reason, Beckett explained, is that 'The daughter only knows the voice of the mother' (86). This statement, even if it might sound natural given that May 'has not been out since girlhood' (*CDW*, 401) and stayed in her mother's home, highlights the intentionality of Beckett's choice of the gendered context of *Footfalls*. Whereas M in *...but the clouds...* displays his difficulty in recuperating the voice of the 'woman lost', in *Footfalls* the author reveals how the subject incorporates the lost (m)other's voice using the (m)other tongue. It is not clear whether the Voice of the Mother is real or is May's creation from her memory of the dying mother – the Voice in the early manuscript says 'My voice is in her head' (cited in Pountney 1988, 281). Regardless of whether the Voice is real, ghostly or imaginary, what is interesting is the way that Beckett presents May in relation to the Voice of Mother. As Anna McMullan claims, *Footfalls* establishes 'a series of binary oppositions: self/(M)other, sound/silence, visible/invisible, but proceeds to undermine or blur such divisions' (McMullan 1993, 97): thus the way in which the voices of the Mother and May are set up works to erase the differences. In the second part (Mother's Monologue), for example, even though we hear the Mother say 'I walk here now' (*CDW*, 401), what we see on stage is May walking while the Voice speaks apart from the physical presence of the Mother.

It can be further argued that the Mother's voice functions as muse, inspiring May to write, as a voice that May recuperates in her own writing. In the second scene, Asmus states that Beckett said, 'May should move her lips twice during the mother's text, as though she were murmuring something to herself': from 'She has not been out since girlhood' until 'The same where she began [*Pause*]' and then again from 'Till one night, while still little more than a child' until '[May – the child's given name] May: Not enough' (Asmus 1977, 87). While the act of murmuring once again raises the issue of who is the real subject of the speech, May's murmuring also suggests her incorporation of the Voice of the Mother, and reproduction of the words since the murmured part is particularly resonant with May's composition in 'Sequel': May says, 'she began to – [*Pause*.] A little later, when as though she had never been, it never been, she began to walk. [...] one late autumn Sunday evening [...]' (*CDW*, 402). The part, 'Amy – the daughter's given name' and 'Not there?', also echoes the Mother's words as Beckett emphasized 'The "Not enough?" in the mother's story must sound just like the "Not there?"' (Asmus 1977, 86). Beckett in *Footfalls* then not only shows how the daughter May recuperates and incorporates the voice of the lost (m)other, but also the process of artistic creation whereby a personal experience is used in a work of art as a source of inspiration.

...but the clouds...

'Beckett stressed to Billie Whitelaw that the word "sequel" should be pronounced' like 'seek well' (Gontarsk 1999, 285), implying that May's monologue represents the process of 'seeking well' for her mother, and the same theme is considered in his television play, *... but the clouds...*, which centres on the male character M's search for his lost loved one. Using the technique that television allows, Beckett creates a ghostly image of 'Close-up of woman's face' (*CDW*, 417) that M attempts to conjure. Whereas in *Film* (1963) and *Eh Joe* (1965) the male characters are in flight from the ghostly female, in *...but the clouds...* M 'beg[s], of her, to appear' in his 'sanctum' (*CDW*, 420). In contrast to Joe in *Eh Joe* who thinks he is haunted by the 'plaguing voice' and tries to exorcise the ghostly voice by 'Throttling the dead in his head' (*CDW*, 363), in *...but the clouds...* M desperately seeks for the 'woman lost' and attempts to recuperate her. Unlike *Footfalls*, however, in which Beckett proposes a successful way of incorporating the lost (m)other by speaking with the (m)other tongue, his male character in *...but the clouds...* finds it difficult to do so.

Rather, it is the process of seeking and recuperating the lost other on which the television play focuses, a process that is close to the Kleinian work of mourning. In *...but the clouds...*, while M describes the 'moment' when the 'woman lost' does 'appear' and 'speak to' him, we see on screen the close-up of a woman's lips '*uttering inaudibly*' (*CDW*, 421). M is also '*synchronous with* [her] *lips*' (421), in the same way as May murmurs in some parts while the Mother speaks. Notably, as identified by M at the end of the play, the muted part turns out to be the lines from W.B. Yeats's 'The Tower': '... but the clouds of the sky ... when the horizon fades ... or a bird's sleepy cry ... among the deepening shades ...' (422). As Daniel Katz claims, because the lines are 'emphatically not cut and framed so as to give a readily digestible encapsulated pill of wisdom', the 'question arises as to whether these lines are not in effect what Freud would call a "screen memory" for others that the play omits' (Katz 1995, 86). Since Yeats's question in the poem, 'Does the imagination dwell the most | Upon a woman won or woman lost?' (Yeats 1996, 305), is also left unanswered, even if this question is 'immediately relevant to the central scene of ...*but the clouds...*', Katz claims that it 'should serve to remind us of that scene's central uncertainty' (Katz 1995, 88). Rather than signalling the 'central uncertainty', however, Yeats's 'The Tower', in fact, helps us to locate what 'the play omits'. Using Yeats's poem Beckett attempts to express his sense of loss and to proceed with his work of mourning.

As Anne Atik's memoir of Beckett suggests, the quoted lines from 'The Tower' are specifically related to his mourning process. 'After the cremation' of Beckett's 'old friend Con Leventhal' in 1979, Atik reports, 'Sam leaned against the wall, a glass of wine in his hand, and recited from that poem':

> Now shall I make my soul,
> Compelling it to study
> In a learned school
> Till the wreck of body,
> Slow decay of blood,
> Testy delirium
> Or dull decrepitude,
> Or what worse evil come

And here he hesitated, squared his shoulders, then went on firmly

> The death of friends, or death
> Of every brilliant eye
> That made a catch in the breath
> Seem but the clouds of the sky...

(Cited in Atik 2001, 68)

As Beckett borrows Yeats's voice in expressing his sorrow after his friend's funeral, so in *...but the clouds...* the same words reveal his work of mourning for his 'woman lost'. According to Atik, '"The Tower" was particularly significant for him', and Beckett 'remarked the congruence of language with visual imagery' (Atik 2001, 67–8). In *...but the clouds...* Beckett attempts to display a congruence between the 'Memories of the words of women' (Yeats 1996, 306), as Yeats puts it in the poem, and the visual image of his lost other through the medium of television. By portraying M's effort to hear and envisage his 'woman lost' in order to understand her, Beckett shows how his imagination dwells the most upon the 'woman lost' in his process of mourning. Pointing out how M corrects his first lines – 'When I thought of her it was always night [...] No, that is not right. When she appeared it was always night' (*CDW*, 419) – Katz asserts that the television play shows the relationships 'between obsessional memories and the apparition of ghosts, between mourning and haunting' (Katz 1995, 84). However, as M's constant effort to conjure the 'woman lost' reveals, M's words, 'she appeared', cannot be seen as 'haunting'. M's attempt to incorporate the 'woman lost' is indicated in his act of '*murmuring, synchronous with lips*' (*CDW*, 421) of the female figure who is far from persecutory, unlike the woman in *Eh Joe*. Beckett's male character, however, still seems to fail to find a healthy way of restoring the lost object and to accomplish the work of mourning. As Klein claims, 'there is a link between loneliness and the incapacity sufficiently to integrate the good object' (Klein 1997, 309). As if suggesting such difficulties in restoring the lost object as a good one in himself, Beckett's male narrator in *Company* expresses such a sense of loneliness, and implies its relation to the lost others.

IV 'On the Sense of Loneliness' and *Company*

> Ghost graves. Ghost ... he all but said ghost loved ones ... Trying to treat of other matters. Till half hears there are no other matters. Never were other matters. Never two matters. Never but the one matter. The dead and gone. The dying and the going.
>
> (*CDW*, 429)

So says the Speaker in *A Piece of Monologue* (1979). In this short play, Beckett introduces a male character who reveals the failure of his long efforts to move away from the lost loved objects. Whereas in *A Piece of Monologue* the focus is mainly on the 'Ghost graves' and 'ghost loved ones' from which the Speaker is unable to tear himself away, in *Company* (1979) – begun slightly earlier than the monologue but finished later[13] – Beckett seems to try 'to treat of other matters' by recalling his own childhood memories and by re-examining his own self. Referring to *Company*, Beckett wrote to Ruby Cohn, 'Tried to get going again in English to see me through, say for company, but broke down. But must somehow...' (*DF*, 574). If the genre of theatre has allowed Beckett to explore and recuperate the lost others through the female voice and body on stage, prose to him seems to be a place where he examines the self. Whereas Beckett's shift into French in writing his fiction reflects his wish to detach himself from memories of home and the lost others, his shift back to English in *Company* hints at his intention of revisiting such memories in relation to the self.[14] As James Knowlson asserts, '*Company* comes closer to autobiography than anything Beckett had written since *Dream of Fair to Middling Women*' (*DF*, 574).

In *Company* the 'Scenes from past',[15] as Beckett puts it, are reminiscent of his childhood, and his home town is remembered by name, unlike in his French fiction. In *Company*, however, early memories are still narrated with emotional distance in contrast to Mrs Rooney's nostalgic recollection of the scenery of Beckett's home town, which appears as a lost object in *All That Fall*. It can be argued that in *Company* Beckett once again attempts to cast 'a cold eye' on his memories, and the 'Scenes from past' are carefully selected in order to maintain detachment and to prevent him from falling into the 'depressive position' (to borrow Klein's term) in talking about them. The recollections mostly centre on the narrator's sense of being neglected by his parents. Yet, underneath the feeling of forsakenness, as I will demonstrate using Klein's theory, there is also a sense of guilt arising from the feeling that it is himself who has neglected them. The narrator's overemphasis on the sense of loneliness suggests 'the incapacity sufficiently to integrate the good object as well as parts of the self which are felt to be inaccessible' (Klein 1997, 309). At the heart of the self there are remnants of the lost objects that have been abjected from the subject, who feels they are inaccessible. In his attempt to see himself through *Company*, Beckett inevitably encounters the lost objects, his parents. This section therefore will examine the narrator's self in relation to his lost others and show how Beckett successfully exploits psychoanalytical ideas in both obscuring and hinting at his sense of loss and guilt in *Company*. I begin, however, by introducing Klein's 'On the Sense of Loneliness' (1963) and comparing her male patient's case with the symptoms of Beckett's narrator and other male characters.

'On the Sense of Loneliness'

In 'On the Sense of Loneliness', the unfinished paper that Klein was working on just before her death, she analyses a patient whose symptoms are strikingly similar to those of the narrator in Beckett's *Company*. This male patient, 'who was not unhappy or ill, and who was successful in his work', had 'always felt lonely as a child', and 'this feeling of loneliness had never entirely gone' (Klein 1997, 307). As the narrator of *Company*, like most of Beckett's male characters, compulsively takes walks 'plodding along a narrow country road' 'since break of day' till 'evening' (*C*, 18), so Klein's male patient had an 'obsessional need to be out of doors' walking 'through hilly country' and felt 'revulsion', as Belacqua does, 'when he entered the town' (Klein 1997, 307–8). The patient was fond of his mother, yet displayed 'his resentment about her rather disciplinarian attitude' that made him feel, as Beckett's male characters and the author himself do, 'hemmed in at home' (308). Klein also remarks that 'for unconscious reasons', he felt responsible for his mother's frailty, and 'there was a great deal of guilt' (308).

According to Klein, the patient's 'urgent longing to be out of doors' (308) is connected to his claustrophobia which 'derives from two main sources: projective identification into the mother leading to an anxiety of imprisonment inside her; and reintrojection resulting in a feeling that inside oneself one is hemmed in by resentful internal objects' (308). Such an explanation reminds us of Beckett and his characters' feeling of being confined in the mother's womb on the one hand, and their claim, 'Someone in me trying to get out, saying let me out' (cited in Gontarski 1985, 140) on the other. It also confirms that the male characters' fear of a devouring woman in fact stems from their projection of their dread of the internalized bad objects onto her. Klein explains that her patient's 'flight into nature was a defence' against these anxieties: to him nature represented 'beauty' and 'the good object that he had taken into himself' because his 'de-idealization' of the mother 'led to his transferring his idealization on to nature' (Klein 1997, 308). We can find a similar account in *From an Abandoned Work* when the narrator comments on the 'Great love in [his] heart' for nature such as 'bushes', 'boulders' and 'flowers of the field' (*CSP*, 155) immediately after describing the moment of departure from his mother's home. With regard to home and his mother, 'the patient felt very lonely, and it was this sense of loneliness which was at the root of his revulsion against town' (Klein 1997, 308). Klein further remarks that the patient's idealization of nature was 'derived from a strong sense of beauty and linked with appreciation of art' as well as 'a means of counteracting the fundamental loneliness which had never entirely gone' (308).

Like Klein's patient, in *Company* the narrator's sense of loneliness is emphasized through his 'craving for company' (*C*, 77) and his need of a listener. According to Klein, loneliness can be alleviated through the internalization of the good object. 'This identification with the good object mitigates the destructive impulses and in this way also diminishes the harshness of the super-ego' (Klein 1997, 309–10). The narrator in *Company*, however, emphatically resists any such alleviation by consistently recalling the memories that reveal the sense of being neglected by his parents as well as the parental control that shapes self-control and the super-ego. Describing the day of his birth, for instance, the narrator focuses on his father's emotional detachment. Rather than remaining near his wife during her labour, his father leaves home due to 'his aversion to the pains and general unpleasantness of labour and delivery' (*C*, 16). When his father comes back, his mother 'moves aside to let the father look' (66) at the newborn baby. Here what the narrator stresses again is the father's detachment towards his own son: 'In his turn he murmurs to the newborn. Flat tone unchanged. No trace of love' (66). While such an occasion can hardly be seen as the narrator's real memory, as no one can recall their own birth – as is the case with Beckett's intrauterine memory – it can be considered as his phantasy, in which his father represents an introjected bad object that has neglected him.

What Beckett attempts in *Company*, then, is to activate the bad objects in order to control his own feelings when talking about his childhood memories of his parents. As Klein claims, the 'harsher the super-ego, the greater will be loneliness, because its severe demands increase depressive and paranoid anxieties' (Klein 1997, 313). Thus, by emphasizing the presence of the 'harsher' super-ego, in *Company* Beckett intensifies the sense of loneliness. Unlike his earlier works in which male characters show either melancholic (depressive) or paranoiac symptoms, in *Company* Beckett finds his own way of dealing with those anxieties by saturating his narrator in his loneliness instead of allowing him to surrender to his anxieties. To recall the memories that strengthen the super-ego, 'resulting from the excessive parental control', as Beckett puts it in his 'Psychology Notes', is one way to do this. One such recollection, which is autobiographical according to Knowlson, describes the narrator as a young boy, throwing himself from 'the top of a great fir' (*C*, 28) while Mrs Coote was visiting his mother. The mother's prohibition and possible punishment are implied as the narrator recalls his mother saying, 'He has been a very naughty boy' (28). Some 'Scenes from past' that distinctively manifest the harsh super-ego recur several times in Beckett's different works. The scene of his father urging his son to 'jump' off the 'high [diving] board' (23) in *Company* also occurs in *Eleutheria* and briefly in *Embers*, as Elizabeth Barry asserts, 'as an image of the son's failure to gain his father's approval and the correspond-ing sense of self-worth' (Barry 2006, 82). Similarly, in *Company*, even though the father presses him, calling again saying, 'Be a brave boy. Many eyes upon you', the young narrator fails to make the jump, and his 'father's upturned face' haunts him throughout the prose piece, implying the demand of the super-ego and the failure of identification with the parental agency.

Displacement

Another memory evoked in *Company*, which has also been used in *Malone Dies* and 'The End', as often cited by critics, is of an incident when the narrator, as a young boy out walking with his mother, asks her how far away the sky is. This episode bears a particular significance, not only because it is summoned up first among the 'Scenes from past', fore-shadowing the atmosphere of the following memories that the narrator evokes, but also because it manifests the mother as a bad object, inter-nalized in his childhood, which continues to affect his phantasy. The narrator recalls: 'For some reason you could never fathom this question must have angered her exceedingly. For she shook off your little hand and made you a cutting retort you have never forgotten' (*C*, 13). Whereas this memory is connected to his super-ego as he wonders about why the question caused her anger, what is also emphasized in the incident are the 'cutting retort' and withdrawn affection that have left an indelible imprint on his mind and phantasy.

While this distressing memory clearly indicates that it is the narrator's mother who has neglected him, its value as a constant reminder of the bad object is also a displacement with a defensive function which aims to hide his sense of loss and guilt in order to conceal his longing for the lost object. This first recollection is closely linked to another poignant memory, the hedgehog story, as we see that Beckett deliberately adds 'You have never forgotten' attached to these two memories only. In this incident, the young boy takes 'pity on a hedgehog [that is] out in the cold and put[s] it in an old hatbox' (*C*, 41, 38). He completely forgets about it and some weeks later he finds it dead. This experience, like the first memory recalled, has a huge impact on the narrator who says, 'You have never forgotten what you found then. You are on your back in the dark and have never forgotten what you found then. The mush. The stench' (41).

The memory of the hedgehog is, according to Knowlson, Beckett's own indelible childhood memory, and as Anne Atik reports, Beckett told the story several times and also attempted to write his 'first poem in French' called 'Petit sot' using the same story.[16] The hedgehog memory can be argued as a screen memory 'characterized both by its unusual sharpness and by the apparent insignificance of its content' (Laplanche and Pontalis 1980, 410). As Laplanche and Pontalis explain, the screen memory hides important things, and by analysing the memory we can identify the concealed 'unconscious phantasy' (410). While it might be argued that Beckett's hedgehog memory is too significant in itself to be a screen memory, it can still be considered as one because it displaces a more important feature, his hidden sense of guilt towards the lost mother. Furthermore, Beckett, knowing psychoanalysis in depth, uses the psychoanalytical idea of the screen memory as 'a formation produced by a compromise between repressed elements and defence' (410) in order to control his emotion and protect his feelings while still hinting at something that is concealed in the 'Scenes from past'.

From the early manuscript of *Company*, it is evident that Beckett attempted to understand his past deeds and the recurrence of the hedgehog memory using psychoanalysis. I argue that Beckett intended to engage such psychoanalytical concepts in describing the memory. In the manuscript, after pondering whether perhaps he should have let 'the hedgehog free to continue on his way' instead of having taken it and let it die, the narrator says:

> Rather than face up to which and make amends ($$+) put things right if necessary you banished the whole episode from your thoughts. All this beneath the threshold of course. This much later when steeping in the works of Freud and his followers was the nearest you ever came to an explanation.[17]

One of the 'nearest' explanations Beckett mentions here is likely to be displacement, which is the 'predominant mechanism' (Laplanche and Pontalis 1980, 411) of the screen memory and the super-ego. Those concepts are studied in detail in Beckett's 'Psychology Notes' under the 'Freud's Psychology' section of Freud's chief disciple, 'Freudchen',[18] Ernest Jones's *Papers on Psycho-Analysis*. Klein's 'On the Sense of Loneliness' would have offered Beckett an even better explanation of his behaviour than the works of Freud and his followers.

Klein's male patient mentioned earlier told her of an incident that was remarkably similar to Beckett's memory of the hedgehog. Examination of this case will thus further reveal what the memory truly signifies in *Company*. On his trip to the country, Klein's patient 'had caught a field-mouse and put it in a box in the boot of his car, as a present for his young child, who, he thought, would enjoy having this creature as a pet' (Klein 1997, 309). Like the boy in *Company*, the patient also 'forgot about the mouse' and found 'it had died' (309). Klein reports that his 'guilt about having forgotten the field-mouse' and causing 'its death led in the course of subsequent sessions' to him talking about 'dead people for whose death he felt to some extent responsible though not for rational reasons' (309). According to Klein's analysis, on the one hand, the field-mouse 'stood for a split-off part of himself, lonely and deprived' (309). On the other hand, Klein explains that the field-mouse also represented 'his good object, which he had enclosed in his inside – represented by the car – and about which he felt guilty and also feared that it might turn retaliatory' (309). What is remarkable in Klein's analysis is how she links his own sense of being forsaken to the good object that he felt he neglected. Klein describes how:

> One of his other associations, referring to neglect, was that the field-mouse also stood for a neglected woman [...] The link with similar feelings towards his mother became clear in the material, as did the conclusion that he contained a dead or lonely object, which increased his loneliness.
>
> (Klein 1997, 309)

Given this, while the narrator of *Company* persistently recalls the memories that activate the bad objects that have deserted him in order not to fall into the depressive position, as the memory of the hedgehog suggests, he also reveals his sense of guilt for having forsaken his 'ghost loved ones' and his feeling of being responsible for them. Beckett, thus, intentionally connects the memory of the hedgehog to that of the mother's 'cutting retort' by adding 'You have never forgotten' (*C*, 13, 41) exclusively to two memories. The young narrator put the hedgehog 'in an old hatbox' believing that he offered 'the poor creature' 'warmth and security', and that it was a 'good deed', expecting 'a word of praise from [his] parents or mentors' (38–9). What comes up later, however, is a sense of guilt and regret: 'you entered its life. [...] That rather than do as you did you had perhaps better let good alone and the hedgehog pursue its way' (40–1). This short story compresses and expresses the narrator's hidden anxiety and desire in relation to his mother. As observed above, the narrator obsessively takes a walk on a 'country road' (18), presumably responding to his anxiety that the mother imprisons him in his home – an anxiety shared also by Beckett and his other male characters. Is the narrator here pondering whether his mother also meant to provide him 'warmth and security'? If the narrator presents himself as a figure seeking 'an explanation for [his] lapse' (cited in Krance 1993, 81) and cannot entirely justify his deed in the hedgehog memory, we see also that he 'could never fathom' (*C*, 13) the reason why his mother reproached him. Such unknowns defy answers, and impel Beckett through the narrator to seek the lost others and to understand them by repeatedly recuperating them in his works.

What is also concealed in the hedgehog memory is the wish to be recognized by the agency of the super-ego; the little boy expects to hear 'a word of praise from [his] parents or mentors'. Beneath the feeling of maternal neglect, there is the narrator's desire for recognition, as Beckett's work written immediately after *Company* suggests. 'Un soir'/ 'One Evening', 'originally conceived [as an] opening fragment of *Mal vu mal dit*' (Krance 1996, 163), significantly starts with an episode of a man found by an old woman: 'HE WAS FOUND lying on the ground. No one had missed him. No one was looking for him. An old woman found him. To put it vaguely. It happened so long ago. She was straying in search of wild flowers. Yellow only' (*CSP*, 253).

As if counterbalancing the predominant tone of desertion in *Company*, in 'One Evening' the narrator shows his wish to be recognized by the old woman, who can be seen as an imago of the lost mother and also as reminiscent of Beckett's other female characters. The narrator explains that the old woman, 'wearing the black she took on when widowed young', 'strays in search of the flowers he had loved' 'to reflower the grave' (254). The search is 'for the need of yellow' flowers in an 'April evening' (254). Echoing the old woman in *Not I* who is 'looking aimlessly for cowslips [yellow flowers]' in an 'April morning' (*CDW*, 376), Beckett in *Ill Seen Ill Said* and *Rockaby* attempts to recuperate his earlier female characters, especially the mother. For instance, in his abandoned piece, 'J.M. Mime' (1963), discussed in the Introduction, the son reveals his feeling that he has been neglected by his mother. Here he explains that his mother has 'lagged behind' looking for flowers: 'She would give all she has for a daisy. But she has nothing. She has me. Am I not of more value than a flower? No, not now. When there were flowers, yes. But not now, when there are none' (cited in McMullan 2006, 337). In this piece Beckett focuses on the son and his displacement of the feeling of being overlooked by his mother to jealousy towards flowers, disclosing his true feeling of loss, and refuses to continue his narration on this topic. In the following section, however, we will see how Beckett endeavours to push forward his work of mourning by recuperating the lost mother as a good object in *Ill Seen Ill Said* and *Rockaby*.

V 'Foreknell': *Ill Seen Ill Said* and *Rockaby*

David Farrell Krell begins his book, *The Purest of Bastards: Works of Mourning, Art, and Affirmation in the Thought of Jacques Derrida*, with the following statement:

> Mourning demands both a keeping in mind or memory and a releasing or letting go. How could we mourn our friend if we forgot him? And how could mourning do its work if we adamantly refused to let her go?
>
> (Krell 2000, 1)

In the works of Beckett studied so far, we have seen that his characters find it difficult to balance such contradictory tasks. In *Embers* and *Eh Joe*, for example, even though the male protagonists try to tear themselves away from some 'old grave' (*CDW*, 258), they fail to do so because they do not realize that it is in fact themselves who unyieldingly refuse to release their lost others, and also that the haunting nature of the ghostly lost objects stems from their desire to keep them alive in mind. For the male protagonists, recalling memories of the lost loved objects becomes painful since the lost others often appear as persecutory figures. As the haunting and persecutory features indicate, many of Beckett's characters tend to compulsively remember their lost others as if torturing and punishing themselves through a sense of guilt arising from their belief that it is themselves who have caused the separation from the lost objects. Their process of remembering, then, is hardly seen as mourning since it lacks not only a healthy way of keeping the lost other in mind that would help them let her/him go, but also the ritual of mourning that affirms the lost object no longer exists. The work of mourning in Beckett's earlier works, thus, has been endlessly deferred.

In his fiction, *Mal vu mal dit/Ill Seen Ill Said* (1980/1982), and a short play, *Rockaby* (1980), however, Beckett finally attempts the belated work of mourning his mother, the 'old so dying woman' (*ISIS*, 20). Phil Baker claims that *Rockaby* is a 'belated death rite' that 'spells her dying out as if to witness it again' and to 'confirm that she really is dead' (Baker 1997,

164–5). Charles R. Lyons asserts that the 'emphasis' in *Ill Seen Ill Said* is not 'upon the death of the woman as an event in her story but, rather, as the opportunity for the speaker to complete the process of telling the story and release himself from this female figure as object' (Lyons 1990, 159). Yet, the focus in those works, I argue, is not merely on bidding farewell to the 'woman lost', but also on showing how to keep the lost others in mind. In other words, in *Ill Seen Ill Said* and *Rockaby* what Beckett portrays is precisely the work of mourning Krell describes, by showing the oscillation between the desire for letting the 'woman lost' go and for keeping her in mind. Furthermore, Beckett suggests here a Kleinian way of restoring the lost loved one in his mind as a good object. In order to complete the work of mourning, we first need what Freud calls 'reality-testing' to confirm 'the loved object no longer exists' (Freud 1991, 253). More importantly, however, mourning also requires Klein's 'testing of reality' that involves repairing and restoring the lost object from a bad to a good one inside oneself by recalling happy memories and regaining the trust in the lost object that affirms she or he is not 'turned into a vengeful person' (*LGR*, 346–7). Using Klein's theory, this last section will show the process of mourning represented in Beckett's *Ill Seen Ill Said* and *Rockaby* and argue that his attempt to recreate the 'old so dying woman' is comparable to Klein's theory of artistic creation in which the creative impulse is closely related to 'reinstating' one's lost loved objects and 're-establishing inside himself his first loved object – ultimately the "good" parents' (*LGR*, 369).

'But harmless, no harm in her'

Pointing out the narrator's struggle in 'bringing a dead woman back to life' in *Ill Seen Ill Said*, both Lawrence Graver and James Knowlson claim that 'Beckett would have been aware of Melanie Klein's theory of artistic creation, according to which the writer is driven by the "desire to rediscover the mother of the early days, whom [he] has lost actually or in [his] feelings"' (*DF*, 589). When reading *Ill Seen Ill Said*, however, Graver and Knowlson neither mention Klein's theory any further nor explain the psychological process behind the author's urge to reproduce the mother's death over and over again. Beckett's creative impulse to seek the 'woman lost' in *Ill Seen Ill Said* and *Rockaby* needs to be understood as a process of mourning that affirms the death of the mother figure, and also as his attempt to restore her from a bad to a good object in himself. For instance, in *Rockaby* we see on stage a 'Prematurely old' woman, dressed in a 'Black lacy high-necked evening gown' (*CDW*, 433). She rocks a chair rhythmically while listening to her '*recorded voice*' that repeatedly tells her the moment, the 'day' that 'in the end came' (435). It is only towards the end of the play that the narration discloses what the event is about – the moment of her mother's death:

> mother rocker
> where mother rocked
> all the years
> all in black
> best black
> sat and rocked
> rocked
> till her end came
> in the end came
> off her head they said
> gone off her head
> but harmless
> no harm in her
> dead one day
> no
> night
> dead one night
> in the rocker
> in her best black
> head fallen

(CDW, 440)

The rhythmical rocking and the soothing narration that resembles a lullaby – as the title of the play suggests – can be seen as a ceremony geared towards alleviating the pain in accepting her mother's death. More significantly, immediately before uttering 'dead one day', the voice asserts that her mother is 'harmless | no harm in her', as if it is very important for the narrator to emphasize that the dead mother is not going to hurt her. Recalling the lost other in *Rockaby* is then a highly ritualized mourning process which confirms that the lost object no longer exists and helps the character to restore her lost mother as a good object.

In *Ill Seen Ill Said*, the narrator's constant effort to illustrate the 'old so dying woman' also needs to be understood as a mourning process intended to recreate the lost other to keep her as a good object and to avow she is dead. The narrator claims, 'No shock were she already dead. As of course she is. But in the meantime more convenient not' *(ISIS,* 41). This shows that the repeated narration of creating and abolishing the old woman is like a 'Child's play [...] to restore' (18) the old woman, as a 'way for remembrance' of the dead woman 'Till all recalled' (52) and for bidding farewell to her. In contrast to Beckett's earlier works in which the male characters are often haunted by the 'woman lost', in *Ill Seen Ill Said* the narrator obsessively seeks for the ghostly old woman who keeps appearing and disappearing. The 'devour[ing]' (23) and 'relentless eye' (29), the feature more usually assigned to the persecutory mother figure in Beckett's earlier works, is given to the narrator. When she reappears the narrator attempts to capture her: 'But quick seize her where she is best to be seized' (15). 'Finally the face caught full in the last rays. Quick enlarge and devour before night falls' (22–3).

The narrator's attempt to create a series of portrayals of the 'old so dying woman' that bear 'a dignity' (Graver 1990, 143) can be analysed in relation to Klein's case of a Danish painter called Ruth Kjär, introduced in 'Infantile Anxiety-Situations Reflected in a Work of Art and in the Creative Impulse' (1929). Klein describes how Ruth who fell into the 'deepest melancholia', claiming her inner void, 'an empty space' in herself, conquers her melancholia through the act of drawing a succession of portraits of an 'old woman on the threshold of death' even though she had never painted before (*LGR*, 215, 218). One of them is 'an old woman, bearing the mark of years and disillusionments' and 'a look that seems to say', 'My time is so nearly at an end!' (217). The portrait of Ruth's Irish-Canadian mother shows a kind of dignity similar to that of the 'old so dying woman': 'Head haught now she gazes [...] the tomb' (*ISIS*, 37). Klein reports the description of the painting of the mother: 'What a chin! What force there is in the haughty gaze!' (*LGR*, 217).[19] As the parallel with Ruth's case shows, the narrator's repeated attempts to recreate the old woman can be seen as Beckett's desire 'to make reparation, to make good the injury psychologically done to the mother and also to restore [...] her mother' (218) as intact and also harmless in himself. Three vignettes out of sixty-one in the prose work, thus, are allocated to imagining the old woman's lips smiling:

> The thin lips seem as if never again to part. Peeping from their join a suspicion of pulp. [...] Impressive above all the corners imperceptibly upcurved. A smile? Is it possible? Ghost of an ancient smile smiled finally once and for all.
>
> (*ISIS*, 48–9)

We have observed that in the last part of *Rockaby* the recorded voice confirms that the woman's mother is dead after assuring her(self) that the mother is 'harmless'. Similarly, in *Ill Seen Ill Said*, as if assuring himself that the 'old so dying woman' is harmless, shortly after envisaging her smile the narrator tries to say good-bye to her: 'Quick say it suddenly can and farewell say say farewell. If only to the face. Of her tenacious trace' (59).

Beckett in *Ill Seen Ill Said* endeavours to recreate not only the mother of his childhood, whom he has lost actually or in his feelings as Graver claims, but also the representation of the mother in his earlier works. Baker sees the old woman as 'an instance of Beckett's maternal imago – a phantasy figure emerging in several texts', comparing her with the mother who is 'distinguished by viduity and blackness' (Baker 1997, 154) in *Krapp's Last Tape* and the woman in *Rockaby*. Whereas Baker does not relate this 'instance' to Klein's artistic theory, I argue that in *Ill Seen Ill Said* Beckett attempts to restore the mother seen in *From an Abandoned Work* where he significantly describes the moment of the departure from home and his mother. The mother's 'poor old thin lips pressed tight together' (*CSP*, 159) in *From an Abandoned Work* are echoed in the 'thin lips [that] seem as if never again to part' in *Ill Seen Ill Said*, but are repaired later in the text as ones that 'smiled'. Whereas *From an Abandoned Work* describes the relatively recent experience of the painful severance with the mother using a melancholic voice, in undertaking a belated mourning process in *Ill Seen Ill Said*, it seems it was necessary for the author to revisit a site that resembled his mother's home in Ireland, and to employ similar metaphors to those used in *From an Abandoned Work*.

The use of white is one such metaphor. The mother in *From an Abandoned Work* is not only centrally linked to whiteness, but also the narrator's peculiar attention to whiteness throughout the journey is closely related to his separation from his mother. In the prose piece, as he leaves home, the narrator sees his 'white mother' 'in the window waving [...] in sad helpless love', and hears 'faintly her cries' (156). It is from this moment that the narrator obsessively channels his view on 'all white things' such as 'sheets, walls, [...] flowers', and a 'white horse' (157). While the narrator spells out the significance of white to him by saying, 'White I must say has always affected me strongly' and 'there is that word white again' (157, 161), as Baker claims, he also 'pre-empts' a 'psychoanalytic reading' (Baker 1997, 17) of the text by stating, 'the white horse and white mother in the window, please read again my descriptions of these' (*CSP*, 160–1). Despite the series of associations (white mother – white horse – 'savage rage'), the narrator suppresses the white mother in the link when he blatantly states 'the white horse and then the rage, no connexion I suppose' (157–8). In *Ill Seen Ill Said* whiteness also intriguingly dominates the atmosphere from the very beginning, suggesting a thematic link to *From an Abandoned Work*. First, the narrator describes Venus rising, stating 'How whiter and whiter as it climbs it whitens more and more the stones' (*ISIS*, 9). The narrator also mentions, 'White stones more plentiful every year. [...] Everywhere every instant whiteness is gaining' (26–7). 'There had to be lambs' in the imaginary scenery as the narrator explains: 'Lambs for their whiteness' (11). If whiteness in *From an Abandoned Work* is used as a way of both hinting at the 'savage rage' after his severance with the mother, in *Ill Seen Ill Said* white imagery is carefully selected and collected in correspondence with *From an Abandoned Work* for a belated ritual of farewell to the old woman whose 'whiteness' is also emphasized by her 'long white hair' (28) and the 'white body' (37) beneath her black clothes. It is then, not just the dead (m)other that the narrator mourns and restores. In *Ill Seen Ill Said* Beckett also revisits and revises his literary memory which describes the moment of the painful separation from the mother in Ireland.

Unlike *Company* in which the narrator says 'To whom here in any case farewell' (*C*, 85), in *Ill Seen Ill Said* and *Rockaby* the lost object is identified as the 'old so dying woman' and the mother respectively. Those old women, as Baker points out, share affinities: in *Rockaby* the 'Prematurely old' woman 'in white expressionless face' with 'white hands' is dressed in a 'Black lacy high-necked evening gown' (*CDW*, 433), and the 'old so dying woman' in *Ill Seen Ill Said* wears black clothes with 'Nape under frill of black lace' (*ISIS*, 29).[20] What is also notable is that the old woman is often read as having some biographical relevance to Beckett's own mother. Knowlson's interview with Beckett shows how the author associates his mother with perpetual mourning. Immediately after Beckett mentions the year of his parents' births to Knowlson, he adds: 'My father died in 1933 and my mother died seventeen years later. She was seventeen years a widow. In fact, she hardly left off mourning for the whole time, in the little house, "New Place", when she left "Cooldrinagh"' (cited in Knowlson and Knowlson 2006, 6). Like Beckett's remark in his letter to MacGreevy mentioned above, his cousin, Ann Beckett's description of his mother also echoes the 'old so dying woman' with 'the widowed eye' 'hovering' above the tomb (*ISIS*, 22, 44): 'When Sam's father, Willie, died', his mother 'rented a house in Greystones so that she could see Willie's grave in the graveyard' (cited in Knowlson and Knowlson 2006, 7–8). This is not to overemphasize the autobiographical link in *Ill Seen Ill Said* and *Rockaby*. Yet, in contrast to Baker's argument that the 'old so dying woman' is 'independent of "real" biographical concerns' (Baker 1997, 154), I argue that it is important to note how Beckett's real mother, who was in constant mourning for her husband, influences the representation of the lost loved object in his works as well as his emotional reactions to the subject. In the rest of the section, therefore, I am going to explore the complex way of incorporating the lost (m)other as a mourning process in *Ill Seen Ill Said* and *Rockaby* and Beckett's devices for maintaining some emotional detachment in undertaking the process.

'Farewell to farewell'

As Krell observes, mourning is a process which inevitably involves affect and emotion.[21] In *Ill Seen Ill Said* as if suggesting difficulty in controlling emotion in illustrating the sites of the old woman's 'little house' and the 'graveyard' with their biographical resonances, the narrator repeatedly utters 'Careful' and 'Gently gently' in order to encourage himself to keep talking 'Till all recalled' (*ISIS*, 52). While the 'trembling fingers' (54) and the narrator's preoccupation with the site of the grave represent 'a highly charged attempt to say farewell to' (*DF*, 590) the old woman in *Ill Seen Ill Said*, in this prose work and in *Rockaby* Beckett devises a way of achieving a certain emotional distance in recalling the memories of the lost others. As James Olney claims that 'Beckett decided, when memory became in all ways central to his work to write in French [in order to be] safer' (Olney 1998, 347), his decision to write *Ill Seen Ill Said* in French implies the author's emotional engagement with the memory represented in this prose piece.[22] Similarly, the use of a *'recorded voice'* in *Rockaby* can also be seen as an 'apparatus' (Roof 2000, 147) devised to maintain some emotional detachment from the painful memory of the mother's death.

While such devices indicate Beckett's need and determination in continuing the mourning process, the process represented in *Ill Seen Ill Said* and *Rockaby* is by no means simple. In *Rockaby*, her *'recorded voice'* reveals that the woman is yearning for and mourning her own mother. However, it is not clear whether the woman is talking about her dead mother obsessively searching for 'another like herself' or whether she is speaking of her own experience in the third person, as do Mouth in *Not I* and May in *Footfalls*. The distinction between the speaking subject and the lost object described is equally uncertain. Because of the parallel between the mother depicted by the voice and the woman on stage, it becomes ambiguous whether the woman on stage is the mourner of the lost mother or whether the audience (and Beckett) are put in the position of 'witness[ing]' (Baker 1997, 164) the scene of the mother dying. The voice's portrayal of the moment of the mother's death (quoted above) eerily resembles the last scene of the play: the woman's 'head slowly sinks, come to rest' (*CDW*, 433) as she sits in her black evening gown on a rocking chair 'where mother rocked' (440), as if implying her own death.

This resemblance leads Baker to claim that the woman's 'identification with the mother', in a 'melancholic' way reminiscent of Krapp or Molloy, shows that the 'envisioning of her death fails to achieve finite discharge, and the dead mother imago continues her "old so dying. So dead" existence' in *Ill Seen Ill Said*.[23] This, however, is questionable since *Rockaby* was conceived later than the prose work,[24] and the woman and Molloy's reactions to their loss are different. As Baker asserts, Molloy's return to his mother's room stating, 'I am in my mother's room. [...] I have taken her place. I must resemble her more and more' (*T*, 7), displays a narcissistic identification with his lost mother, which as discussed in Chapter 2 derives from the fact that Molloy is not consciously aware of his loss, causing an 'object-loss' to be 'transformed into an ego-loss' (Freud 1991, 258). This, as Freud claims, is a crucial feature that differentiates melancholia from mourning. In *Rockaby*, however, the centre of the narration addresses the death of the woman's mother, and also the ambiguous distinction between the woman and the lost mother is relevant to the woman's act of incorporating the lost (m)other as a good object in her mourning.

According to Klein, in 'the mourner's state of mind, the feelings of internal objects are also sorrowful', and the objects 'share his grief in the same way as actual kind parents would' (*LGR*, 359). As 'the poet tells us that "Nature mourns with the mourner"', Klein goes on, 'I believe that "Nature" in this connection represents the internal good mother' (359). In *Rockaby* the old woman, who wears similar black clothes to that of her dead mother, sitting in a rocking chair 'where mother rocked' (*CDW*, 440) is both mourning her lost mother and imagining or desiring her mother mourning with her. Beckett's use of the recorded voice, rather than making the woman on stage talk to herself, also reflects such a wish. As if showing the woman's desire to hear the voice of the mother that confirms she is dead, the recorded voice gently urges her to let the lost object go, repeating 'time she stopped' and asking her to proceed with the mourning process. The woman on stage also joins the procedure by 'echo[ing]' and synchronizing with the voice's words, 'time she stopped'.

Similarly, in *Ill Seen Ill Said* the narrator is simultaneously engaged in the process of mourning and recollection of the mother in perpetual mourning. In the several vignettes that describe 'the eye [that] fills with tears' (*ISIS*, 17), Beckett seems to make deliberately ambiguous whether it is the narrator or the old woman who is the subject of 'Weeping over as weeping' (18) as if implying that they mourn together.[25] While 'weeping' also reminds us of the mother who weeps for her son's leaving in *From an Abandoned Work*, the narrator in *Ill Seen Ill Said* shows his desire to be recognized by the old woman, and his wish for her to be mourning with and for him. As the old woman in *Rockaby* imagines her mother's 'famished eyes' desire 'to see | be seen' (*CDW*, 439), so in *Ill Seen Ill Said* the narrator, whose eyes 'relentlessly' seek for the old woman, also exhibits his wish to be recognized by her by asking 'does she see him?' (*ISIS*, 42). Unlike *Ill Seen Ill Said*, which omits the context of the encounter between the old woman and the narrator,[26] in 'One Evening', as observed in the previous section, the desire to be seen and 'missed' by her is indicated: 'HE WAS FOUND lying on the ground. No one had missed him. No one was looking for him. An old woman found him. To put it vaguely. It happened so long ago' (*CSP*, 253). The narrator goes on, 'She was straying in search of wild flowers' and found him 'lying there' (253). Shortly after this, the narrator changes the tense from past to present, and says she, 'widowed young', 'strays in search of the flowers he had loved' 'to reflower the grave' (254). Beckett's vague use of the pronoun 'he' on the two different occasions as well as the apparent parallel between the old women's repeated act of 'straying in search of the wild flowers' both now and in the past hints that the narrator expresses his longing to be missed by the woman, to be her lost object. Underneath the narrator's desire to be recognized by the old woman, then, there is his urge to restore the lost (m)other as a good object and his wish for her to be mourning with him and to show sympathy towards him.

So, in *Ill Seen Ill Said* and *Rockaby* Beckett painstakingly portrays the process of the work of mourning in the Kleinian way of keeping the lost (m)other as a good object. As Krell states, the process, both keeping the lost others in mind and releasing them at the same time, is not an easy task. In *Ill Seen Ill Said* and *Rockaby* Beckett shows such a 'paradox' (*ISIS*, 36) by frankly revealing the contradictory desires. In *Rockaby*, the woman's scarce utterances on stage vacillate between 'time she stopped' and 'More'. The woman on stage expresses her wish to release the lost mother by repeating and synchronizing with the voice's words, 'time she stopped', the affirmation of her mother's death, gently encouraged by the lost mother's voice. 'More', her begging to hear the lost mother, however, is the woman's own word, not from the tape, displaying her difficulty in releasing the lost object. Likewise, in *Ill Seen Ill Said* immediately after saying, 'Farewell to farewell. Then in that perfect dark foreknell darling sound pip for end begun', the narrator ends the story by revealing his contradictory desire to hold on to the process a bit longer: 'No. One moment more. One last. Grace to breathe that void. Know happiness' (*ISIS*, 59). As the last words of the text, 'Know happiness' and the description of 'foreknell' as 'darling sound' highlight, *Ill Seen Ill Said* presents mourning as a process that involves recalling and restoring the lost (m)other as a good one. In *Rockaby*, through the genre of theatre and the female voice and body, Beckett portrays the mourning ritual more successfully. In the final scene of *Rockaby*, by showing how the woman's head 'slowly sinks, [and] come[s] to rest' in her mother's rocking chair whose 'curving arms to suggest embrace' (*CDW*, 433), Beckett manages to incorporate as well as release the lost (m)other. As the concluding point of discussion of this study, such distinctions in Beckett's dramatic (female) language and prose piece will be addressed.

Conclusion: *Stirrings Still*

'ONE NIGHT AS he sat at his table head on hands he saw himself rise and go' (*CSP*, 259): so begins Beckett's *Stirrings Still* (1988),[1] his last prose work. According to Lawrence Shainberg, it was 'a sentence that haunted [Beckett]' for a long time as Beckett commented, 'It won't go away, and it won't go further [...] It's like the situation I spoke of in my book on Proust. "Not just hope is gone, but desire"' (Shainberg 1987, 132). As Beckett goes on to talk about his 'writing' (132) in this conversation, the sentence indicates the tension between his desire to speak, or rather his obligation to speak, and his desire to put an end to speaking. The man in the story, although imagining 'himself rise and go', fails to do so: 'First rise and stand clinging to the table. Then sit again. Then rise again and stand clinging to the table again' (*CSP*, 259). Such contradictory desires for detachment from and attachment to the place where one belongs are familiar ones in Beckett's oeuvre. What is interesting in this short prose piece is that the man repeatedly sees himself 'disappeared only to reappear later' (259), just as in *Ill Seen Ill Said* the narrator sees in his mind's eye the 'old so dying woman' appearing and disappearing. If, as observed earlier, the mourner of *Ill Seen Ill Said* and *Not I* is merged with the dead, in *Stirrings Still* Beckett curiously situates the man alongside the dead in the 'same place' where the lost 'others' 'died and left him':

So again and again disappeared again only to reappear again later at another place again. Another place in the place where he sat at his table head on hands. The same place and table as when Darly for example died and left him. As when others too in their turn before and since. As when others would too in their turn and leave him till he too in his turn. Head on hands half hoping when he disappeared again that he would not reappear again and half fearing that he would not. Or merely wondering. Or merely waiting. Waiting to see if he would or would not. Leave him or not alone again waiting for nothing again.

(CSP, 260)

It is implied here – 'leave him till he too in his turn' – that the man anticipates his impending death, and his 'half hoping' and 'half fearing' reflect his ambiguous feelings towards his attempt to detach himself from life. Such ambivalence towards his own departure echoes the narrator's attitude towards his bidding farewell to the 'old so dying woman' in *Ill Seen Ill Said*, and highlights the fact that the man in *Stirrings Still* is not only contemplating his own impending death but is recalling the lost others. As James Knowlson points out, Beckett's friend, Arthur Darley, commemorated in his poem 'Mort de A. D.', is alluded to in *Stirrings Still*: 'The same as when among others Darly once died and left him' (*CSP*, 260).[2] Knowlson's interpretation of the inclusion in this story of the death of Darley, who died in 1948, is rather telling: The death 'was already very remote. But it is emblematic of those more recent – "among others" – whose death it would be too painful (and indelicate) to evoke' (*DF*, 613).

Finding it too poignant to utter the rest of the names of the lost others, the narrator of *Stirrings Still* can only mention the ceaseless 'cries' that he hears, just as the narrator of *First Love* hints at his sense of loss by recalling the ceaseless cries of Lulu during her labour. The narrator of *Stirrings Still* says, 'The cries. The same as ever', and confesses that he 'was sorry that [the cries] did not' 'cease' (*CSP*, 261, 263). Until the very last prose piece he wrote, Beckett remains agitated by the loss of loved ones, and seems to experience great difficulty in displaying his sorrow. In *Stirrings Still*, as he does in his French fiction, Beckett locates the man in the melancholic tradition: 'To this end for want of a stone on which to sit like Walther and cross his legs the best he could do was stop dead and stand stock still' (263).[3] As *The Grove Companion to Samuel Beckett* points out, this reference is to Walther von der Vogelweide, whose poetry exemplifies the literary tradition of melancholia, and the same image recurs in 'The Calmative' and *Molloy*.[4]

The narrator's 'want of stone' and need to appropriate the melancholic posture indicate Beckett's ongoing efforts to achieve emotional detachment in writing about his personal memories, especially in his prose work. However, there is another intertextual reference to *Ill Seen Ill Said* that hints at the narrator's emotion. The man expresses his 'want of a stone' after recalling memories of 'indoor' and 'outdoor' (*CSP*, 263). As if implying that those memories particularly stir him, he needs a stone on which to sit to calm himself. He imagines the man in 'his memory of indoor' 'hastening westward at sundown to obtain a better view of Venus' (*CSP*, 262–3), just as the 'old so dying woman' in *Ill Seen Ill Said* does in her house. His 'memory of outdoor' echoes the scenery of Beckett's home town remembered in *Ill Seen Ill Said*: 'the short green grass he seemed to remember eaten down by flocks and herds but long and light grey in colour verging here and there on white' (263). As observed in Chapter 5, white is specifically associated with the narrator's separation from his 'weeping' mother in both *Ill Seen Ill Said* and *From an Abandoned Work*, and it is at this moment, following the mention of the animals verging on white, that the narrator of *Stirrings Still* stops describing the scenery and wishes only to 'sit like Walther' to 'set out to take thought' (*CSP*, 263). This intertextuality suggests that Beckett is self-consciously thinking of the loss of his mother, while the man's wish to imitate the melancholic brooding posture suggests his ambivalence towards expressing feelings.

There is, however, evidence that at this stage Beckett also attempted to express his sorrow through the medium of drama and by borrowing a female voice once again. As Knowlson writes, the 'theme of a man seeing himself rise and disappear was developed, intermittently', over a 'few years in several short manuscript fragments' (*DF*, 612). In one of the manuscripts in his so-called 'Super conquérant' notebook, Beckett alternates the theme of *Stirrings Still* and the fragment of an unpublished play, 'Bare Room'.[5] On the first page of the notebook, on the back of which Beckett wrote the haunting sentence that developed into *Stirrings Still*, he starts 'Bare Room', which begins with W's speech about 'a kind of ritual | Ritual, yes that's the word' and her trying to remember the 'words that came to [her]' (UoR MS 2934/f.1v). Intriguingly, the ritual that she mentions is connected to a mourning ritual. On the next page, following the sentence that developed into *Stirrings Still*, Beckett inserts the dialogue between two speakers, who are subsequently identified as 'W' and 'M'. The conversation between them in the second draft reveals that what W is trying to recall is Shakespeare's Sonnet LXXI, 'No longer mourn for me when I am dead'. In this holograph, however, Beckett interestingly replaces the word, 'mourn' with 'weep':

Come & read to me.
What?
That ~~Shakespeare~~ sonnet we ~~once~~ 'used' to love~~d~~.

> You mean 'No longer weep ...'
> What? (P.) No longer what?
> Weep. (P.) [']No longer weep ...'
>
> (UoR MS 2934/f.1v; cited in Van Hulle 2004, 489)

In this dialogue, it is ambiguous whether it is M or W who wants to remember Shakespeare's line since the speakers are not designated in the draft. The ambiguity is even more intriguing when considering that in *Stirrings Still* it is equally uncertain whether the narrator mourns his lost others or his own impending death. The draft moves to M at the window. Looking out of the window M tells W, 'The snow. (P.) all the land is white' (f.3r). It is difficult to ignore the similarity between the images that Beckett uses in *Stirrings Still* and *From an Abandoned Work*: 'white', the colour that agitates the narrator, and his description of the 'weeping' mother when he leaves her. The repeated phrase, 'No longer weep ...', in 'Bare Room', together with the intertextual elements with *From an Abandoned Work* (and Shakespeare's 'No longer mourn for me when I am dead') suggests that Beckett here might be expressing a contradictory wish for his mother to stop weeping for him and mourning with him (as in the case of *Not I* and *Ill Seen Ill Said*) while he ponders his own impending death, just as in *Stirrings Still*. Perhaps the cries that agitate the man in *Stirrings Still* are poignant to Beckett because they are so closely linked to the sound and image of the lost mother's weeping which he connects with the severance from his own mother.

Until his very last works, then, Beckett writes about his lost (m)other and expresses his difficulty in letting her go, while also thinking about 'a kind of ritual' for releasing her and also himself using the dramatic form. Even though *Stirrings Still* cannot utter the names of the lost 'others' apart from 'Darly', as the last sentences of the prose piece – 'Time and grief and self so-called. Oh all to end' (*CSP*, 265) – indicate, it is not just the self that the man attempts to release, but also the 'self so-called', the self that has incorporated the lost psychic others. It does not seem to be merely the deaths of loved ones that affect Beckett, but also his departure from his mother and from his homeland through his long-ago self-imposed exile to France. As Klein writes, 'We keep enshrined in our minds our loved people' (Jacobus 2005, 69), and Beckett's works endeavour to describe his relationship with these lost psychic others who are imprinted in his mind at the moment of departure.

The young Beckett's statement in *Proust* (1931), 'the dead are only dead in so far as they continue to exist in the heart of the survivor' (*P*, 44), prefigures his later works, which exhibit his faith to his own words as he keeps his lost others in the heart of himself. While this statement reveals Beckett's innate attitude towards the loss of the loved ones, it is given neutrally because it comes in the context of an essay on Proust. Also, at that time Beckett had not experienced any great loss. As this study has revealed, however, Beckett's works written after his exile delve painstakingly into what strategies to undertake when the memories of the lost others refuse to go away. Beckett's male narrators in his French fiction claim that 'you must think of them for a while, a good while, every day several times a day, until they sink forever in the mud. That's an order' (*CSP*, 46–7), while disavowing the importance of their loss. In his early English drama, when the repressed memories of lost objects, woman and Ireland, 'came over' him 'like a flood' (*CDW*, 176), triggered by his mother tongue, Beckett borrows Mrs Rooney's voice in order to express his sorrow. In his dramatic works of the 1960s, Beckett moves away from the melancholic male voice, and attempts to recuperate the lost others as well as revealing the characters' sense of loss through various symptoms such as mania and paranoia. Beckett's late works more specifically endeavour to restore the 'woman lost' in general and the mother in particular, and undertake the Kleinian work of mourning by revisiting in his mind's eye his home in Ireland.

Beckett's poetics of grieving, as I have demonstrated, cannot be merely 'described as a melancholy one' without a 'single event that may be identified as the cause of loss' (Hill 1992, 15) in his works. Instead, his texts need to be understood beyond the melancholic tradition in which, as Schiesari claims, melancholic males turn their 'woman lost' 'into the abstract principle of his loss' (Schiesari 1992, 176), leaving her as an oppressed and nameless other while he converts his loss into the cultural prestige of heightened artistry. In his late works, as Beckett's efforts to recuperate the lost (m)other underline, his poetics of grieving addresses his previous failure to understand the lost object. Beckett's works also display a sense of guilt arising from the fact that he has willed the losses through abjecting the (m)other in his search of the self. Consequently, his late works focus on restoring the 'woman lost' who has been ridiculed in his early fiction.

In this study, psychoanalytic theories and Beckett's 'Psychology Notes', which provide empirical links with such theories, have offered a useful framework in identifying the lost others as woman and Ireland and demonstrating the way in which these elements intersect in his oeuvre. As the young Beckett's statement in *Proust* – which implies his interest in psychic lost others – shows, there are many possibilities for examining his early fiction using a Kleinian approach. I have limited myself here, however, to those suggested by the empirical links to Beckett's own reading. For instance, regarding the title of *First Love*, *The Grove Companion to Samuel Beckett* interestingly comments that it 'defines love in psychoanalytical terms deriving from Melanie Klein, that between the child and the breast, as conducive to the first awareness of otherness' (Ackerley and Gontarski 2004, 197). Indeed, the narrator's painful and repeated act of separation from Lulu can be compared to a weaning process, which is significantly connected to the infant's depressive position comparable to the adult melancholia in Klein's theory. Much work could fruitfully be done in this area in the future.

Referring to Beckett's use of 'Irish related raw materials' in late works such as *That Time*, Rodney Sharkey claims, 'Beckett eventually had to squeeze out "site specific" Irishness, [for] the instigation of the search for "self"', and goes on to say, 'Too often a study such as this succeeds in tying down an author to a set of convenient historical and cultural moments and so limits the scope of interpretation' (Sharkey 1994, 15–16). Rather than squeezing out 'site specific' Irishness, however, as Gontarski asserts, Beckett attempted to 'undo' what were already abundant Irish references in his texts. In fact, as this study has shown, in his late works Beckett chose to revisit Ireland in his mind in order to recall the 'turning-point' (*CDW*, 390), the moment when he departed from the 'woman lost' and turned to a quest for the self as well as towards a recuperation of the lost others. By exploring the representation of women and Ireland using a psychoanalytic framework indicated by Beckett's own research into this area, this study has laid the groundwork for further psychoanalytical investigations in Beckett studies while offering its own new reading of his creative work.

Notes

Introduction

1. Throughout the book, the word 'object' will be used to refer to the psycho-analytical concept of another 'person'.
2. This theme is further developed in Beckett's prose-poem, 'neither'.
3. *More Pricks Than Kicks* was written between 1931 and 1933 and published in 1934. *Murphy* was completed in 1936, and published in 1938.
4. Hereafter, the term 'lost others' is going to be used when referring to the lost objects that have been expelled or abjected from the self during its formation.
5. *Dream of Fair to Middling Women* was written in 1932 but first published in 1992. Beckett 'resisted entreaties to have the novel published until 1986', when he 'allowed Eoin O'Brien and Edith Fournier to edit it and to bring it out after he had died' (Ackerley and Gontarski 2004, 150).
6. See Ackerley and Gontarski (2004, 75). John Pilling has thoroughly identified the sources in *Beckett's Dream Notebook* (1999).
7. According to Mark Nixon, 'no residua pertaining to this aborted work survives', but 'Beckett outlined his ideas regarding its possible form and tone' in his 'German Diaries' (Nixon 2004, 19).
8. These are the years when the *Nouvelles/Novellas* and *Molloy* were written in French, not the years of publication. By *Novellas*, I mean the four short stories, 'L'Expulsé'/'The Expelled', 'Le Calmant'/'The Calmative', 'La Fin'/'The End' and *Premier amour/First Love*. The short stories (except *First Love*) were first published in 1955 as *Nouvelles et textes pour rien* and *Premier amour/First Love* was published in 1970 in French and 1973 in English. *Molloy*, first of the *Three Novels*, was published in French in 1951.
9. According to Matthew Feldman, 'the Institute of Medical Psychology' is wrongly called the Tavistock Clinic when referring to Beckett's thrice-weekly sessions there (Feldman 2006, 85). The Institute was burned during the Second World War along with its official records.
10. As the MacGreevy correspondence shows, according to Feldman the 'Psychology Notes' are 'unmistakably traceable to the period of Beckett's therapy with Wilfred Bion' (Feldman 2006, 95).
11. Feldman (2006, 100 and 2). As Feldman points out, Beckett calls Ernest Jones, 'Freudchen'. The nine texts include Karin Stephen's *Psychoanalysis and Medicine: a Study of the Wish to Fall Ill*, Sigmund Freud's *New Introductory Lectures on Psychoanalysis*, Robert Woodworth's *Contemporary Schools of Psychology*, Ernest Jones's *Papers on Psycho-Analysis* and *Treatment of the Neuroses*, Wilhelm Stekel's *Psychoanalysis and Suggestion Therapy*, Alfred Adler's *The Neurotic Constitution* and *The Practice and Theory of Individual Psychology* and Otto Rank's *The Trauma of Birth* (see Feldman 2006, 29–30).

12. See Feldman (2006, 30, 100 and 79). Beckett summarized the third edition of Jones's *Papers on Psycho-Analysis* (1912), published in 1923.
13. Psychoanalytic literary criticism available on Beckett's works is summarized well in Feldman's book, and such criticism diverges between (a) 'the textual demonstration of a theoretical approach' as the case of Baker and O'Hara's works, and (b) 'psychological readings of Beckett', the writer himself, typi-fied by Didier Anzieu in his 'Beckett and the Psychoanalyst' (Feldman 2006, 81–4). Since 2002 when Beckett's 'Psychology Notes' started to be avail-able for consultation, more varied psychoanalytical approaches have been offered. These include Lois Oppenheim's neuro-psychoanalytic approach in her book, *A Curious Intimacy: Art and Neuro-Psychoanalysis* (2005). In her chapter on Beckett, Oppenheim explores how his art reflects his interest in the 'relation between psyche and soma' (71) and also how 'the obsession with illness functioned' in his art as 'a stabilizing force' (60).
14. Jonathan Boulter shares Hill's view. (See Boulter 2004, 332–50.)
15. TCD MS10971/8. The first three sentences are cited in Tonning (2007, 151). I am indebted to Matthew Feldman (2004), whose Appendix B transcribes Beckett's 'Psychology Notes', and am extremely grateful to him as all of the citations from the 'Psychology Notes' used herein are from this source.
16. Freud (1991, 258). As James Strachey indicates in his editor's notes, Freud seemed not quite certain about the link when he wrote the essay. Strachey writes, 'Freud seems to have been inclined at first to regard [the nature of identification] as closely associated with, and perhaps dependent on, the oral or cannibalistic phase of libidinal development' (Freud 1991, 249). Freud's essay, however, as Strachey remarks and also as Jones recognizes, 'called for an examination of the whole question of the nature of identifica-tion' as it implies the 'process by which in melancholia an object-cathexis is replaced by an identification' (249–50).
17. John Keller, a practising psychoanalyst, uses the Kleinian model of object-relation theory in exploring the relationship between what he calls the 'narrative-self' and internal objects in his book, *Samuel Beckett and the Primacy of Love* (2002). Keller reads longing for a primary 'good mother', who repre-sents care and love, as fundamental in Beckett's works. However, I argue that Beckett's texts explore the sense of loss, and restore the lost mother not out of longing for love, but out of the sense of guilt that is important in Klein's theory. Also, Keller uses an 'analytical term "mother"' that is stretched too far to cover any person including the male and even a thing that performs a 'mothering' or 'caring' function. My focus, however, lies on the representa-tion of the mother in Beckett's works. (See Keller 2002, 1–7.) While Keller attempts to examine Beckett's works carefully, he consistently misspells Miss Carridge in *Murphy* as 'Miss Clarridge', although her name is significant in relation to the function of 'mothering'.
18. Steven Connor disagrees with Deirdre Bair's view that Bion was a Kleinian in the mid-1930s. See 'Beckett and Bion', a paper written for the 'Beckett and London' conference held at Goldsmiths College, London in 1998.
19. Chris Ackerley and S.E. Gontarsky, the authors of the *Grove Companion*, acknowledge that the source of this information is not certain. Nonetheless, Stephen highly values *The Psycho-Analysis of Children* as a source, and quotes

from the book in her *Psychoanalysis and Medicine: a Study of the Wish to Fall Ill*.

20. I am very grateful to Professor Knowlson for kindly alerting me to this reference.

21. The 'List of Members of the International Psycho-Analytical Association' in the *Bulletin of the International Psycho-Analytic Association* (1931 and 1933), however, indicates that Stephen's professional address changed from 140 Harley Street to 50 Gordon Square around 1933.

22. Cited in Knowlson (1985, 16).

23. This description of his symptoms is based on Beckett's letters to Thomas MacGreevy, 1 January and 10 March 1935 (cited in *DF*, 169, and 651).

24. Beckett noted, '<u>Super-ego</u>: heir to Oedipus complex' (cited in Feldman 2006, 30; Beckett's emphasis).

25. In the case of the girl, for instance, Freud's theory becomes problematic since she can hardly conceive 'a threat to deprive her of what she has not got' (Laplanche and Pontalis 1980, 57).

26. It is also interesting to note that Beckett keeps using the words 'parental' or 'parents' when Stephen writes 'adult' in order to suggest that the agent of control is not solely limited to parents. (See Stephen 1933, 150–1.)

27. The term 'phantasy' is widely used in psychoanalysis, and refers to an 'imaginary scene in which the subject is a protagonist, representing the fulfilment of a wish in a manner that is distorted to a greater or lesser extent by defensive processes' (Laplanche and Pontalis 1980, 314–19). In Klein, 'phantasy' refers to 'a kind of primitive thinking consisting of what the baby makes of experience both inside and outside itself'. For Klein, 'phantasies of loving and hating form the basis of a rudimentary sense of identity consisting of impulse, defence and relationships', which distinguishes her 'concept of phantasy from Freud's concept of the unconscious' (Minsky 1996, 79). Instead of 'fantasy', I am going to use the spelling 'phantasy' in reference to the Kleinian unconscious phantasy.

28. To 'introject' is 'close in meaning to incorporate', which 'provides it with its bodily model, but it does not necessarily imply any reference to the body's real boundaries'. The notion plays a significant part in Klein who 'sought to describe the phantasied comings and goings of "good" and "bad" objects' (Laplanche and Pontalis 1980, 229–30). In Klein's theory, 'introjection as a phantasy is a defence adopted to preserve the ego or the good objects' (Hinshelwood 1989, 333).

29. See Baker (1997, 175) and Laplanche and Pontalis (1980, 211).

30. Even though Freud first used the concept of projection, 'the joint concept of projection and projective identification are particularly associated with the work of Melanie Klein'. In Klein's theory, the baby projects itself onto the mother and then re-identifies with her. Due to this process of projection, the infant perceives the mother in phantasy as good when it is full and satisfied by the mother, and as bad when it feels frustrated and empty. (See Minsky 1996, 7.)

31. Knowlson describes the moment when May Beckett 'disliked intensively' her son's works: when she encountered his writing, which Knowlson assumes to be a story from *More Pricks Than Kicks* or *Dream of Fair to Middling Women*,

she was 'shocked', and told him 'she would not have him writing such monstrous work under her roof' (*DF*, 131–2).

32. The French version was written in 1946, but was not published until 1970. The English translation was completed in 1973.

33. Joshua D. Esty, drawing attention to Kristeva's analysis of abjection, examines *First Love* as a postcolonial work in that excremental images 'redress a history of debasement by displaying the failures of development' in the postcolonial era (Esty 1999, 24).

34. While I am aware that in French feminist theories, Kristeva's *chora* is a very important concept that is closely related to the 'semiotic', my study focuses on the representation of the women and the mother in their relation to the self in Beckett's works rather than looking at the aspect of *écriture féminine* in Beckett's writing that the French feminist readings offer. For further discussion of Kristeva's concept of the semiotic *chora* in Beckett's later drama, see McMullan (1993, Chapter 4). For the analysis of *écriture féminine* in *écriture Beckettienne*, as Bryden puts it, see Bryden (1993, Chapter 6).

35. When Linda Ben-Zvi asked Billie Whitelaw, Beckett's favourite actress (and muse), why she thinks 'Beckett has so many women on the stage in the later works', Whitelaw answered, 'There were what I call the Beckett triplets: two actors and an actress, of which I was the actress. Jack MacGowran and Patrick Magee [Beckett] adored, and they are gone. And I'm left. And based on nothing at all, I wonder if perhaps at times he writes with a voice in his head' (Ben-Zvi 1990, 10). While Whitelaw's comment is interesting, it needs to be understood that Patrick Magee died in August 1982. Significantly he is the one who reads Beckett's late prose work, *Ill Seen Ill Said*, which features an old woman who can be considered as the imago of Beckett's mother in the BBC radio production, directed by Ronald Mason in 1982. All Beckett's later plays featuring female protagonists were written before Magee's death.

36. After opening such a fascinating debate on intertextual elements in Beckett's own texts, however, Connor mainly concentrates on Beckett's use of repetition within individual texts rather than among texts in his otherwise excellent study on how repetition plays a crucial part in the formation of the self and the power relationships of authorship and authority.

37. Gontarski states that in the second typescript of *Happy Days*, Beckett jotted down the word 'Vaguen' in the margin of a page which characterizes his revision process in eliminating detail (Gontarski 1977, 36).

38. See Admussen (1978, 113). 'J.M. Mime' is published in facsimile in Gontarski's *The Intent of Undoing* (1985).

39. The first text written in English after *Watt* (1948) is *From an Abandoned Work* (1954–55).

40. Lawrence Shainberg states that Beckett 'tried to describe the work he wanted to do now. It has to do with a fugitive "I" [or perhaps he meant "eye"]. It's an embarrassment of pronouns. I'm searching for the non-pronounial' (Shainberg 1987, 134).

41. *More Pricks Than Kicks* is often compared to Joyce's *Dubliners*. For further examinations of the literary relationships between Joyce and Beckett, see Carey and Jewinski (1992).

1. Severing Connections with Ireland: Women and the Irish Free State in Beckett's Early Fiction

1. Here, by inserting extra inverted commas in the Alba's speech, Beckett emphasizes that she is quoting the lines from works on Deirdre and 'Kawthleen' (*DFMW*, 197).
2. Beckett also lectured on Racine in 1931. For the details of the lecture, see 'Appendix: Beckett on Racine' in Knowlson and Knowlson (2006, 306–13).
3. One of the 'antiquarians' who is attacked by Beckett is Austin Clarke, who is accused of being a poet trading in 'fully licensed stock-in-trade from *Aisling* [or vision poems from the Gaelic tradition] to Red Branch Bundling' (*D*, 73). Later on, Beckett satirizes this aspect of Clarke by caricaturing him as 'Austin Ticklepenny Pot Poet | From the County of Dublin' in *Murphy* (*M*, 84).
4. See Harrington (1991, 32). In the 1960s, when examination of Beckett's early work began, he assisted his bibliographers, Raymond Federman and John Fletcher, by describing a lost essay later revealed to be 'Recent Irish Poetry' as a review of a 'late work by W.B. Yeats'.
5. 'It is time that I wrote my will; | I choose upstanding men | That climb the streams until | The fountain leap, and at dawn | Drop their cast at the side | Of dripping stone; I declare | They shall inherit my pride' (Yeats 1996, 305–6). Here, the 'upstanding men' particularly refers to the 'people of Burke and of Grattan', who often appear in Yeats's writing and represent the Anglo-Irish Protestants. Even though the Anglo-Irish Protestants and their tradition, with which Yeats strongly identifies, need to be differentiated from the majority Irish Catholics and the Irish Free State, the young Beckett at this stage emphasizes Yeats as a leader of the Celtic twilighters. There is also an intertextual reference to James Joyce's 'Scylla and Charybdis' chapter in *Ulysses* in which Stephen debates his theory about Shakespeare and his 'second-best bed' with his friends.
6. Bair (1993, 526–7). John Montague recorded the conversation. See also Armstrong (1990, 31).
7. The title is also 'an Irish expression for courting, yet Belacqua walks out on his fiancée before a celibate marriage' (Ackerley and Gontarski 2004, 624).
8. Harrington (1991, 63). Here, Harrington compares the story with *Cathleen ni Houlihan*, but it is *The Countess Cathleen* that Beckett attacks.
9. The definite article in front of the names of 'the' Alba and 'the' Smeraldina, who also appear as important characters in *Dream of Fair to Middling Women*, indicates that Beckett objectifies those two characters more completely than is the case with his other female characters.
10. Lady Gregory in *Our Irish Theatre: a Chapter of Autobiography*. Cited in Harrington (1991, 99).
11. In Yeats's *Deirdre*, it is the Musicians who 'give a wail' during Deirdre's passionate speech over Naoise's death, and 'keen with low voices' over her death (Yeats 1952, 198, 202). Keen ('*caoineadh*') refers to an Irish funeral song accompanied with wailing and lamentation for the dead (see Kiberd 1989, 292). For more details about keening represented in the Irish theatre, see Bourke (2000, 67–79).

12. This particular passage was presented by James Knowlson during the 'Beckett at 100: New Perspectives' conference held at Florida Sate University, USA in 2006, accompanied by the photograph of Peggy Sinclair that is included in Knowlson and Knowlson (2006, 38).

2. Memories and Melancholia in Beckett's Early French Fiction

1. In 'The End', the narrator says, 'She wanted to take it away, but I told her to leave it. She wanted to buy me another, but I told her I didn't want another' (*CSP*, 84–5).
2. Beckett, in the French version, 'L'Expulsé', uses the exact translated version of the song. This song is also cited in Joyce's *Ulysses*.
3. *Malone Dies*, the second of the *Three Novels*, also suggests a way of dealing with a loved object, again mentioning a very small object. While talking about his 'possessions', Malone suddenly remembers the 'bowl of [his] pipe' that he found 'somewhere, on the ground', and says the previous owner must have 'thrown away because it could no longer serve, the stem having broken off'. Malone comments, 'he must have said, Bah, I'll buy myself another' although the 'pipe could have been repaired' (*T*, 247–8).
4. 'Cathexis' refers to the concentration or accumulation of 'psychical energy' in a particular channel, which is 'attached to an idea' or 'to a part of the body, to an object'. See Laplanche and Pontalis (1980, 62).
5. TCD MS 10971/8/12. The underlined parts are cited in Feldman (2006, 108).
6. Also in 'The Expelled', the narrator is given money by a woman whose 'name that [he has] forgotten' (*CSP*, 55). However, further details, such as 'swaddling clothes', suggest that she is his mother (ibid.).
7. The word 'mother' appears very frequently in *Molloy*. Yet, as Knowlson points out, Molloy's quest for the mother offers a useful structure for the book rather than a theme (*DF*, 340), and his wordplay with his mother's name can be considered as being similar to the narrators' taboo treatment of the names of the female and Ireland in the *Novellas*.
8. Moran also mentions that 'like the inhabitants of Blackpool' 'their town was on the sea' (*T*, 134), as if further reminding us of the etymology of Dublin.
9. Phil Baker shows how the conception of past time in *Krapp's Last Tape* is treated as excrement, and argues that Krapp's wordplay with spool and stool exhibits a scatological joke showing a loathing for the personal past. See Baker (1997, 49–50).
10. As Feldman has shown, together with Watt and Mercier who are 'explicitly noted as having their backs to the engine', this is another example of Beckett's exploitation of Rank's concept: the 'disinclination of many persons to travel with their backs to engine' is due to the anxiety caused by the first separation from the mother. See Feldman (2006, 31).
11. (Cited in *DF*, 686.) Beckett said to Israel Shenker: 'The more Joyce knew the more he could. He's tending towards omniscience and omnipotence as an artist. I'm working with impotence, ignorance.'
12. According to Deirdre Bair, Beckett 'alternated between writing *Fin de partie*' and *From an Abandoned Work* (Bair 1993, 451).

13. Molloy recalls his memory of an intrauterine experience as 'the only endurable, just endurable, period of [his] enormous history' (*T*, 18).
14. (See *CSP*, 42 and 84; *T*, 46.)
15. 'The End' has almost the same storyline as 'The Expelled': the narrator is ejected from a house, is given a room by the Greek/Turkish woman, is expelled from her house, changes dwellings several times, and ends his story in a womb-like boat.
16. See Baker (1997, 69).
17. Near to the end of the story 'The End', there is a strong suggestion that the narrator might have committed suicide in the womb-like boat, which floats towards the sea with a hole in its bottom. However, as the last sentence suggests, he comes back to life and tells us his memory of the severance.
18. See Connor (1988, 9–10). Henk Hillenaar also discusses that the narrator here can be seen as playing a kind of *fort-da* game as a kind of 'mastery' over painful situations (Hillenaar 1998, 419–37).
19. Molloy's description of the rooms, 'These different windows that open in my head' (*T*, 51), echoes the scene of the birth in 'The End'.
20. In 'The End', after the narrator has been expelled from the charity house, he is lost 'In the street', and recalls 'Whole buildings had disappeared, [and] the palings had changed position' but the 'general impression was the same as before' (*CSP*, 81). His 'bench' near the river which 'seemed at first sight more or less as [he] had left it' echoes the bench in *First Love*: the 'bench on the bank of the canal, one of the canals for our town boasts two, though I never knew which was which' (*CSP*, 30). Indeed, Dublin has two canals; the Grand Canal and the Royal Canal, and these canals often appear in other Beckett works, such as *Molloy* and *Krapp's Last Tape*.

3. The Gendering of Mourning and Melancholia in Beckett's Early Drama

1. Cited in Knowlson and Knowlson (2006, 252) and *DF* (347). 'Undated personal conversation' with Beckett *c*. 1980 (*DF*, 692).
2. Here Beckett consciously/subconsciously suppresses the word, '*Homeward*', from the original title *Homeward Songs by the Way* (1894) while indicating that Mr Case's course is clearly homeward. As Francis Doherty points out, this title itself was not something to be easily forgotten because 'it had caused more than a little trouble when it first appeared' (Doherty 1991, 197).
3. For further discussion of representations of the Anglo-Irish Protestant in *All That Fall*, see Grene (1999, 170–93) and Kennedy (2003, 247–61).
4. As Chapter 5 will show, a lonely female mourner in Beckett's later works is reminiscent of Beckett's mother, May Beckett. She was 'seventeen years a widow' and 'hardly left off mourning for the whole time' alone in her house (Knowlson and Knowlson 2006, 6). It is interesting to note that after Mrs Rooney's comments, 'All alone in that great empty house. She must be a very old woman now', Mr Rooney suddenly bursts into tears.
5. Phil Baker also connects Dan's 'feeling of being confined' to the womb metaphor, and points out 'the carriage container of Rooney entrained is in

parallel with the underground backstreet velvet-hung container of Rooney's office', which signifies womb. See Baker (1997, 67–8).

6. According to Beckett's own summary of Proust's work, presented in his *Proust*, Marcel's grandmother is the one who offers him 'comfort' when 'he suffer[s]' from sleepless nights in a hotel at Balbec (*P*, 24–5). When his grandmother dies, he represses his emotion: 'Now, a year after her burial, thanks to the mysterious action of involuntary memory, he learns that she is dead [...] For the first time since her death, he knows that she is dead, he knows *who* is dead. He had to recover her alive and tender before he could admit her dead and for ever incapable of any tenderness' (*P*, 41–2).

7. Gontarski, 'Genesis of the Play and Notes on the Text', in Knowlson (1980, 17).

8. A version of the same word also appears in *Murphy*: 'eleutheromania' (*M*, 131).

9. Its two English versions were published in 1995 and 1996, translated by Michael Brodsky and Barbara Wright respectively. 'These were controversial' as Beckett 'to the end wished the play withheld' (Ackerley and Gontarski 2004, 165–6).

10. Beckett wrote in his theatre notebook under the 'Psychological' section: 'Krapp – tape-recorder relationship both fundamental and almost impossible to convey through the acting without descending to the level of the sentimental' (cited in Knowlson 1992, 181).

11. Katherine Kelly compares the Orpheus myth with Beckett's *Not I*. See Kelly (1980).

12. For the evidence of Beckett's reinstatement, see his letter to Bray, dated 11 March 1959 (TCD MS 10948/1/22).

13. Cluchey, 'Beckett's San Quentin Theatre Workshop production: Berlin, September, 1977', in Knowlson (1980, 127).

4. Beyond Mourning and Melancholia: Kleinian Approaches

1. TCD MS. 4664, 11v. The word in square brackets is illegible. Gontarski reads it as 'tell' (Gontarski 1985, 137) whereas Rosemary Pountney reads it as 'seen' (Pountney 1988, 95).

2. The term 'position' designates a configuration of object relations and its characteristic anxieties and defences. Klein uses the term instead of 'phase' or 'stage' because anyone, as an adult, can find themselves operating within one or other position at any time. However, although Klein compares paranoid anxieties with melancholia and mania in detail in her essay above, she did not theorize the 'paranoid-schizoid position' until 1946. For more discussion about the 'position', see Kristeva (2001, 73–81).

3. Beckett stated at rehearsal, 'She's a bit mad. Manic is not wrong, but too big ...' (See Knowlson 1985, 16.)

4. In his transcriptions from Stephen's book, Beckett noted concepts that are similar to Klein's good and bad objects: 'the idea of them [parents] to be split, into the familiar easy person & the terrifying sexual monster' (TCD MS 10971/7/3).

5. See note 37 of the Introduction.
6. Eoin O'Brien explains that *Reynolds' News* is 'a once popular Sunday news-paper' in Ireland (O'Brien 1986, 373).
7. See Benstock (1990, 185).
8. Some critics explain the sexual implication in the Mildred story, referring to a mouse as a phallic symbol in Freudian terms. John Fletcher, for example, sees it as the 'burlesque tale of how little Mildred was deflowered by a mouse' (Fletcher and Spurling 1972, 102).
9. See Pountney (1988, 145) and Knowlson (1985, 54).
10. See Baker (1997, 1–5).
11. This is Beckett's own citation from Burton's *Anatomy of Melancholy*, which he studied and from which he took extensive notes in his 'Dream Notebook' in the early 1930s. The beaver myth also appears in *Dream of Fair to Middling Women* (63) and in 'What a Misfortune' in *More Pricks Than Kicks* (160). (See Pilling 1999, 116.)
12. In her book, Stephen analyses Miss M who is jealous of her mother and suf-fers from 'the guilt concerning her rivalry with her mother' (Stephen 1933, 85). Miss M, as Klein's Rita does, displays aggression derived from her 'disap-pointment at not getting the longed-for physical pleasure and the baby from her father' (85). This 'led to revengeful impulses against him which took the form of fantasies of genital injury' (85). Miss M's 'jealousy which, together with fear, lay at the root of the whole conflict and forced its dissociation was twofold, directed against her mother' (86). This further strengthened her sense of guilt 'because, in spite of everything, her love for her mother was real and deep' (86).
13. Here the doll also 'stood for her little brother whom she had wanted to steal from her mother during the latter's pregnancy' (Klein 1975, 6). Both Rita and Miss M were very jealous of their mother's pregnancy and desired to rob their mother of the baby. (See Stephen 1933, 83.)
14. The ideas introduced in Klein's analysis of Rita can be seen as precursors to her later more formulated descriptions of the mechanism of introjection and projection, which challenged the classical theory of the castration complex and the super-ego. Klein had not developed her theory fully at this stage, and I have applied some of Klein's later theory in analysing 'Rita's case'. Klein's 'combined parent figure', for instance, is useful in explaining Rita's Oedipus conflict. It refers to the baby's phantasy of the 'mother with the father inside her' (Hinshelwood 1989, 242), and more specifically, the phan-tasy of the father's penis contained in some phantasmic body of the mother. While there is Rita's Oedipal desire to usurp her mother's place, which leads her to wish to attack her mother's inside and rob the father's penis, through the process of introjection and projection, she feels that it is the mother who attempts to castrate her. Klein's combined parent figure, thus, explains Rita's wish to attack both her mother and father and her fixation on her mother since her phantasy attack centres on her mother's body due to her wish to rob her father's penis from inside her mother.
15. Whereas Freud's super-ego is a 'monolithic amalgam of introjected Oedipal parents' in general and the father in particular, in Klein's theory, the con-stituents of the super-ego are multiple and varied, and the mother figure

becomes more central than in Freud since the baby incorporates the father as part of its phantasy about the mother (Hinshelwood 1989, 98).

16. Branka Arsic's *The Passive Eye: Gaze and Subjectivity in Berkeley (via Beckett)* (2003) discusses Berkeley's theory and applies this to Beckett's *Film*.

17. To quote examples of this body and mind division, *From an Abandoned Work* ends with the narrator's affirmation, 'my body doing its best without me' (*CSP*, 164), and Malone comments at one point 'My body does not yet make up its mind' (*T*, 198).

18. See Bair (1993, 114–15) for the photograph.

5. The Kleinian Work of Mourning in Beckett's Late Works

1. 'Unpublished manuscript, Boston College, John J. Burns Library, ts I. (Inscribed to Calvin and Joann [Israel], April 1980).' Cited in Krance (1993, 107 and 122).

2. While the English version reads as 'At this rate it will be black night before she reaches home. Home! But time slows all this while', the French version states, 'Soudaines stations et redéparts éclair. De ce train il fera nuit avant qu'elle arrive. Mais le temps freine le temps qu'il faut' (cited in Krance 1996, 12–13).

3. Brater (1987, 24). Even though acknowledging the importance of the maternal figure as a genesis of the Auditor, Wilson claims that 'Whatever the stage directions indicate, [...] the discursive structure of *Not I* constructs the Auditor as masculine' (Wilson 1990, 193–4).

4. It is important to note the similarity between *Not I* and Caravaggio's painting in terms of composition. As the Auditor stands left to Mouth, the old woman is also on the left to the partially severed head of John the Baptist in the painting.

5. The first holograph of *Not I* begins with 'birth into the world ... this world ... of a ~~small~~ tiny baby' (cited in Pountney 1988, 254).

6. In his 'Psychology Notes' Beckett summarized numerous symptoms of the hysteric, and noted Anna O.'s case (TCD MS 10971/8/34).

7. Similarly, Mrs Rooney in *All That Fall*, '*laughs wildly*' (*CDW*, 177), and in *Play* W2's '*wild low laughter*' (*CDW*, 317) is also noticeable.

8. Referring to *Happy Days* and *Not I*, Whitelaw states, 'Whenever I've read anything of Beckett's that I've been asked to do, the first thing that I've always wondered is how is it that everything he writes seems to be about my life' (cited in Ben-Zvi 1990, 3–4).

9. In the early manuscript of *Footfalls*, Beckett wrote 'an explicit description of the play's structure' as following: 'A Dying mother', 'B Mother back', 'C ~~Epilogue~~ appendix', 'D Empty Strip' (cited in Pountney 1988, 283).

10. *CDW*, 95, 97, 109, 115 and 127. On page 104, Hamm says, 'Give me my pain-killer.'

11. The play is full of images of death: Hamm can be seen as a dying patient, Nell appears to die on stage, and there are frequent comments on burial and death including the death of Mother Pegg.

12. According to Knowlson, '[Beckett] sat watching over her for an entire week, leaving the nursing home only when it was absolutely necessary in order to eat or, when he could no longer bear to watch her suffer' (*DF*, 345).

13. The earliest holograph of *Company* dates back to 5 May 1977 and 2 October 1977 for *A Piece of Monologue*. (See Krance 1993, 121 and 179.)

14. Following *Watt*, most of Beckett's fiction was first written in French, with the exception of the short prose pieces, *From an Abandoned Work*, *All Strange Away* (1963–64) and *As the Story was Told* (1973).

15. In his early manuscript, Beckett outlines the 'Scenes from past' that the narrator recalls (Krance 1993, 119).

16. Atik (2001, 7). The manuscript of 'Petit sot' was found in a book by Kant ('the classical Cassirer edition of Kant') that Beckett lent to Avigdor Arikha in 1956.

17. UoR MS 1822. Cited in Krance (1993, 82). '($$+)' is a symbol which Krance uses for referring to the 'preceding two words [which were] crossed out', and revised 'in margin' (Krance 1993, 61).

18. See the Introduction, note 12.

19. According to Ole Andkjær Olsen, Klein analysed Ruth's case through reading 'a newspaper article' on Ruth's paintings (Olsen 2004, 34).

20. As '*Her recorded voice*' describes how she sits and fixes her eye on 'her window' in *Rockaby* (*CDW*, 435), *Ill Seen Ill Said* also portrays her 'eye glued to one or the other window' while sitting on a chair watching 'Venus' ris[ing]' (*ISIS*, 12, 7).

21. See Krell (2000, 5).

22. Interestingly, Knowlson reports how Beckett found it difficult to translate the prose piece into English: 'for a welcome spell to revise and retype *Ill Seen Ill Said* … Never had such difficulty with a translation. Or I forget, I forget' (*DF*, 590).

23. See Baker (1997, 153 and 164–5).

24. See *DF*, 582–90.

25. *Ill Seen Ill Said*, vignettes twelve, thirteen, twenty-one and twenty-three.

26. While the male figures who appear briefly in *Ill Seen Ill Said* and 'One Evening' are cryptic, they can be seen not only as identical, wearing the same 'greatcoat', but also as the narrator playing a cameo role.

Conclusion: *Stirrings Still*

1. Beckett began *Stirrings Still* in 1983, and finished it in 1987. Knowlson reports that at first 'Beckett did not seem to have known whether to write his text in French or English' as manuscripts show he 'attempted both' (*DF*, 612).

2. The name of Beckett's friend was Darley, and 'Darly' was the publisher Barney Rosset's error according to Ackerley and Gontarski (2004, 544).

3. This image is closely linked to Albrecht Dürer's famous etching, 'Melancholia I', which epitomizes the melancholic tradition. As the description of the etching in the catalogue for the exhibition of 'Samuel Beckett: a Passion for Paintings' suggests, Beckett had this painting in mind when alluding to this reference.

The exhibition was held in National Gallery of Ireland between 15 June and 17 September 2007.

4. See Ackerley and Gontarski (2004, 625).

5. UoR MS 2934. 'Bare Room', a holograph manuscript of an unpublished play fragment. It was written in the first three pages of Beckett's 'Super conquérant' notebook which also contains the poem, 'Brief Dream' and material relating to *Stirrings Still*. As in between the different versions of the piece there is material relating to *Stirrings Still* (written between 1983–87), we can assume that it was written around 1983. See Bryden et al. (1998, 15 and 175).

Bibliography

Primary sources

Beckett, Samuel (1957[1938]) *Murphy* (New York: Grove Press).

―――― (1958) *Three Novels: Molloy, Malone Dies, The Unnamable* (New York: Grove Press).

―――― (1965) *Proust and Three Dialogues with Georges Duthuit* (London: John Calder).

―――― (1980) *Company* (London: John Calder).

―――― (1981) *Ill Seen Ill Said* (London: John Calder).

―――― (1983) *Disjecta: Miscellaneous Writings and a Dramatic Fragment*, ed. Ruby Cohn (London: John Calder). (Contains 'Recent Irish Poetry'.)

―――― (1990[1986]) *The Complete Dramatic Works* (London: Faber and Faber).

―――― (1993[1934]) *More Pricks Than Kicks* (London: Calder Publications).

―――― (1995) *The Complete Short Prose 1929–1989*, ed. S.E. Gontarski (New York: Grove Press).

―――― (1996) *Dream of Fair to Middling Women* (London: John Calder).

―――― (1996) *Eleutheria*, trans. Barbara Wright (London: Faber and Faber).

―――― (1998[1963]) *Watt* (London: John Calder).

Unpublished material

'Bare Room' (holograph, written in 'Super Conquérant' notebook), Beckett International Foundation Archives, University of Reading Library, MS 2934, ff. 1–3.

'Before Play' (typescript), UoR MS 1227/7/16/6, ff. I–IV.

'Kilcool' Manuscript (holograph, contained in exercise book described under 'Paroles et Musique A'), Trinity College Dublin, MS 4664, ff. 10–19.

'Psychology Notes', TCD MS 10971.

'Samuel Beckett – Thomas MacGreevy Correspondence', TCD MS 10402.

Secondary sources

Works about Beckett

Critical studies of Samuel Beckett's manuscripts

Admussen, Richard L. (1978) *The Samuel Beckett Manuscripts: a Study* (Boston: G.K. Hall & Co.).

Bryden, Mary et al. (eds) (1998) *Beckett at Reading: Catalogue of the Beckett Manuscript Collection at the University of Reading* (Reading: Whiteknights Press and the Beckett International Foundation).

Feldman, Matthew (2004) 'Sourcing Aporetics: an Empirical Study on Philosophical Influences in the Development of Samuel Beckett's Writing', unpublished doctoral thesis, Oxford Brookes University.

198   *Bibliography*

Feldman, Matthew (2006) *Beckett's Books: a Cultural History of Samuel Beckett's 'Interwar Notes'* (London: Continuum).

Gontarski, S.E. (1977) *Beckett's Happy Days: a Manuscript Study* (Columbus, OH: Ohio State University Libraries).

—— (1985) *The Intent of Undoing in Samuel Beckett's Dramatic Texts* (Bloomington, IN: Indiana University Press).

—— (1999) *The Theatrical Notebooks of Samuel Beckett Vol. IV: the Shorter Plays* (New York: Faber and Faber).

Knowlson, James (1980) *Theatre Workbook 1: Samuel Beckett: Krapp's Last Tape* (London: Brutus Books).

—— (1985) *Happy Days: the Production Notebook of Samuel Beckett* (London: Faber and Faber).

—— (1992) *The Theatrical Notebooks of Samuel Beckett, Vol. III: Krapp's Last Tape* (London: Faber and Faber).

Krance, Charles (1993) *Company/Compagnie and A Piece of Monologue/Solo: a Bilingual Variorum Edition* (London: Garland).

—— (1996) *Mal vu mal dit/Ill Seen Ill Said: a Bilingual Variorum Edition* (London: Garland).

Lake, Carlton (1984) *No Symbols Where None Intended: a Catalogue of Books, Manuscripts and Other Material Relating to Samuel Beckett* (University of Texas at Austin: Humanities Research Center).

Pilling, John (1999) *Beckett's Dream Notebook* (Reading: Beckett International Foundation).

Pountney, Rosemary (1988) *Theatre of Shadows: Samuel Beckett's Drama 1956–1976* (Gerrards Cross: Colin Smythe).

Critical studies of Samuel Beckett's works

Abbott, H.P. (1996) *Beckett Writing Beckett: the Author in the Autograph* (New York: Cornell University).

Ackerley, C.J. (1998) *Demented Particulars: the Annotated Murphy* (Tallahassee: Journal of Beckett Studies Books).

—— and S.E. Gontarski (2004) *The Grove Companion to Samuel Beckett* (New York: Grove Press).

Anzieu, Didier (1994) 'Beckett and the Psychoanalyst', trans. Thomas Cousineau, *Journal of Beckett Studies*, 4: 23–34.

Armstrong, Gordon (1990) *Samuel Beckett, W.B. Yeats, and Jack Yeats: Images and Words* (London: Associated University Press).

Arsic, Branka (2003) *The Passive Eye: Gaze and Subjectivity in Berkeley (via Beckett)* (Stanford: Stanford University Press).

Asmus, Walter (1977) 'Practical Aspects of Theatre, Radio and Television: Rehearsal Notes for the German Premiere of Beckett's "That Time" and "Footfalls" at the Schiller-Theater Werkstatt, Berlin (directed by Beckett)', *Journal of Beckett Studies*, 2: 82–95.

Atik, Anne (2001) *How it Was: a Memoir of Samuel Beckett* (London: Faber and Faber).

Bair, Deirdre (1993[1978]) *Samuel Beckett: a Biography* (New York: Touchstone).

Baker, Phil (1997) *Beckett and the Mythology of Psychoanalysis* (London: Macmillan).

Barry, Elizabeth (2006) *Beckett and Authority: the Uses of Cliché* (London: Palgrave Macmillan).

Ben-Zvi, Linda (1990) 'Billie Whitelaw – Interviewed by Linda Ben-Zvi', in L. Ben-Zvi (ed.), *Women in Beckett: Performance and Critical Perspectives* (Urbana: University of Illinois Press), pp. 3–10.

Benstock, Shari (1990) 'The Transformational Grammar of Gender', in L. Ben-Zvi (ed.), *Women in Beckett: Performance and Critical Perspectives* (Urbana: University of Illinois Press), pp. 172–86.

Boulter, Jonathan (2004) 'Does Mourning Require a Subject? Samuel Beckett's Texts for Nothing', *Modern Fiction Studies*, 50/2: 332–50.

Brater, Enoch (1987) *Beyond Minimalism: Beckett's Late Style in the Theatre* (New York: Oxford University Press).

Brienza, Susan (1990) 'Clods, Whores, and Bitches: Misogyny in Beckett's Early Fiction', in L. Ben-Zvi (ed.), *Women in Beckett: Performance and Critical Perspectives* (Urbana: University of Illinois Press), pp. 91–105.

Bryden, Mary (1993) *Women in Samuel Beckett's Prose and Drama: Her Own Other* (Basingstoke: Macmillan).

Carey, Phyllis and Ed Jewinski (eds) (1992) *Re: Joyce'n Beckett* (New York: Fordham University Press).

Cohn, Ruby (1973) *Back to Beckett* (Princeton: Princeton University Press).

——— (1998) 'The "F—" Story', *Samuel Beckett Today/Aujourd'hui*, 7: 41–5.

Connor, Steven (1988) *Samuel Beckett: Repetition, Theory, and Text* (Oxford: Basil Blackwell).

——— (1998) 'Beckett and Bion', http://www.bbk.ac.uk/english/skc/beckbion/, accessed 26 April 2009.

Cronin, Anthony (1997) *Samuel Beckett: the Last Modernist* (London: HarperCollins).

Doherty, Francis (1991) 'Watt in an Irish Frame', *Irish University Review: a Journal of Irish Studies*, 21/2: 187–203.

Doll, Mary A. (1989) 'The Demeter Myth in Beckett', *Journal of Beckett Studies*, 11–12: 109–22.

Esty, Joshua D. (1999) 'Excremental Postcolonialism', *Contemporary Literature*, 40/1: 22–5.

Federman, Raymond (1965) *Journey to Chaos: Samuel Beckett's Early Fiction* (Berkeley and Los Angeles: University of California Press).

—— and Lawrence Graver (eds) (1979) *Samuel Beckett: the Critical Heritage* (London: Routledge and Kegan Paul).

Fletcher, John and John Spurling (eds) (1972) *Beckett: a Study of His Plays* (New York: Hill and Wang).

Graver, Lawrence (1990) 'Homage to the Dark Lady: *Ill Seen Ill Said*', in L. Ben-Zvi (ed.), *Women in Beckett: Performance and Critical Perspectives* (Urbana: University of Illinois Press), pp. 142–9.

Grene, Nicholas (1999) *The Politics of Irish Drama: Plays in Context from Boucicault to Friel* (Cambridge: Cambridge University Press).

Harrington, John P. (1991) *The Irish Beckett* (New York: Syracuse University Press).

Hill, Leslie (1992) 'Late Texts: Writing the Work of Mourning', *Samuel Beckett Today/Aujourd'hui: 1970–1989*: 10–25.

Hillenaar, Henk (1998) 'A Psychoanalytical Approach to "First Love"', *Samuel Beckett Today/Aujourd'hui*, 7: 419–37.

Katz, Daniel (1995) 'Mirror Resembling Screens: Yeats, Beckett and ... *but the clouds ...*', *Samuel Beckett Today/Aujourd'hui*, 83–92.

———— (2003) 'Beckett's Measures: Principles of Pleasure in *Molloy* and "First Love"', *Modern Fiction Studies*, 49/2: 246–60.

Keller, John (2002) *Samuel Beckett and the Primacy of Love* (Manchester: Manchester University Press).

Kelly, Katherine (1980) 'The Orphic Mouth in *Not I*', *Journal of Beckett Studies*, 6: 73–80.

Kennedy, Seán (2003) '"A Lingering Dissolution": *All That Fall* and Protestant Fears of Engulfment in the Irish Free State', in L. Ben-Zvi (ed.), *Drawing on Beckett: Portraits, Performances, and Cultural Contexts* (Tel Aviv: Assaph Books, Tel Aviv University), pp. 247–62.

Knowlson, James (1996) *Damned to Fame: the Life of Samuel Beckett* (New York: Simon and Schuster).

———— and Elizabeth Knowlson (eds) (2006) *Beckett Remembering Remembering Beckett: a Centenary Celebration* (New York: Arcade Publishing).

Lloyd, David (1993) *Anomalous State: Irish Writing and the Post-Colonial Moment* (Dublin: Lilliput Press).

Lyons, Charles R. (1990) 'Male or Female Voice: the Significance of the Gender of the Speaker in Beckett's Late Fiction and Drama', in L. Ben-Zvi (ed.), *Women in Beckett: Performance and Critical Perspectives* (Urbana: University of Illinois Press), pp. 150–61.

McDonald, Rónán (2007), '"What a male!": Triangularity, Desire and Precedence in "Before Play" and *Play*', *Samuel Beckett Today/Aujourd'hui*, 18: 213–25.

Mays, J.C.C. (1984) 'Young Beckett's Irish Roots', *Irish University Review: a Journal of Irish Studies*, 14/1: 18–33.

McMullan, Anna (1993) *Theatre on Trial* (London: Routledge).

———— (2004) 'Irish/Postcolonial Beckett', in Lois Oppenheim (ed.), *Palgrave Advances in Samuel Beckett Studies* (London: Palgrave), pp. 89–109.

———— (2006) 'Samuel Beckett's "J.M. Mime": Generic Mutations of a Dramatic Fragment', *Samuel Beckett Today/Aujourd'hui: Notes diverse Holo*, 16: 333–45.

Nixon, Mark (2004) 'Writing "I": Samuel Beckett's German Diaries', *Journal of Beckett Studies*, 13/2: 10–23.

O'Brien, Eoin (1986) *The Beckett Country* (Dublin: Black Cat Press).

O'Hara, J.D. (1997) *Samuel Beckett's Hidden Drives: Structural Uses of Depth Psychology* (Gainesville: University Press of Florida).

Olney, James (1998) *Memory & Narrative: the Weave of Life-Writing* (Chicago: University of Chicago Press).

Oppenheim, Lois (2001) 'A Preoccupation with Object-Representation: the Beckett-Bion Case Revisited', *International Journal of Psycho-Analysis*, 82/4: 767–84.

———— (2005) *A Curious Intimacy: Art and Neuro-Psychoanalysis* (New York: Routledge).

———— (2008) 'Life as Trauma, Art as Mastery: Samuel Beckett and the Urgency of Writing', *Contemporary Psychoanalysis*, 44/3: 419–42.

Piette, Adam (1996) *Remembering and the Sound of Words: Mallarmé, Proust, Joyce, Beckett* (Oxford: Clarendon Press).

Pilling, John (2003) *Journal of Beckett Studies – Special Issue: a Companion to Dream of Fair to Middling Women*, 12.

Robinson, Michael (1970) *The Long Sonata of the Dead: a Study of Samuel Beckett* (New York: Grove Press).

Roof, Judith (2000) 'Playing Outside with Samuel Beckett', in Stephen Watt et al. (eds), *A Century of Irish Drama: Widening the Stage* (Bloomington and Indiana: Indiana University Press), pp. 146–59.

Sharkey, Rodney (1994) 'Irish? Au Contraire!: the Search for Identity in the Fictions of Samuel Beckett', *Journal of Beckett Studies*, 3/2: 1–18.

Shainberg, Lawrence (1987) 'Exorcising Beckett', *The Paris Review*, 104: 100–36.

Tonning, Erik (2007) *Samuel Beckett's Abstract Drama: Works for Stage and Screen 1962–1985* (Bern: Peter Lang).

Van Hulle, Dirk (2004) '"(HIATUS IN MS.)": *Watt* and the Textual Genesis of *Stirrings Still*', *Samuel Beckett Today/Aujourd'hui*, 14: 483–94.

Whitelaw, Billie (1995) *...Who He?* (London: Hodder and Stoughton).

Wilson, Ann (1990) '"Her Lips Moving": the Castrated Voice of *Not I*', in L. Ben-Zvi (ed.), *Women in Beckett: Performance and Critical Perspectives* (Urbana: University of Illinois Press), pp. 190–200.

Wolff, Ellen (1995) 'Watt...Knott...Anglo-Ireland: Samuel Beckett's *Watt*', *Journal of Beckett Studies*, 5: 107–41.

Worth, Katharine (1978) *The Irish Drama of Europe from Yeats to Beckett* (London: Athlone Press).

Other works

Alford, C. Fred (1990) 'Melanie Klein and the "Oresteia Complex": Love, Hate, and the Tragic Worldview', *Cultural Critique*, 15: 167–89.

Alighieri, Dante (1995) *The Divine Comedy*, trans. Allen Mandelbaum (London: Everyman's Library).

Anderson, Robin (ed.) (1992) *Clinical Lectures on Klein and Bion* (London: Tavistock/Routledge).

Benjamin, Andrew and John Fletcher (eds) (1990) *Abjection, Melancholia, and Love: the Work of Julia Kristeva* (London: Routledge).

Bourke, Angela (2000) 'Keening as Theatre: J.M. Synge and the Irish Lament Tradition', in Nicholas Grene (ed.), *Interpreting Synge: Essays from the Synge Summer School 1991–2000* (Dublin: Lilliput Press), pp. 67–79.

Cixous, Hélène (1990) 'Difficult Joys', in *The Body and the Text: Hélène Cixous, Reading and Teaching*, eds Helen Wilcox et al. (New York: Harvester Wheatsheaf), pp. 5–30.

Creed, Barbara (1993) *The Monstrous-Feminine: Film, Feminism, Psychoanalysis* (London: Routledge).

Cullingford, Elizabeth (1993) *Gender and History in Yeats's Love Poetry* (New York: Cambridge University Press).

Freud, Sigmund (1933) *New Introductory Lectures on Psychoanalysis*, trans. W.J.H. Sprott (London: Hogarth Press).

—— (1955a) *Studies on Hysteria*, in *The Standard Edition of the Complete Psychological Works of Sigmund Freud Vol. 2 (1893–1895)*, trans. James Strachey (London: Hogarth Press).

—— (1955b) 'Medusa's Head', in *The Standard Edition of the Complete Psychological Works of Sigmund Freud Vol. 18 (1920–1922)* (London: Hogarth Press), pp. 273–4.

Freud, Sigmund (1985) 'The "Uncanny"', in *The Penguin Freud Library Vol. 14* (Harmondsworth: Penguin), pp. 335–76.

—— (1991) 'Mourning and Melancholia', in *The Penguin Freud Library Vol. 11* (Harmondsworth: Penguin), pp. 251–68.

—— (2003) 'Beyond the Pleasure Principle', in *Beyond the Pleasure Principle and Other Writings*, trans. John Reddick (Harmondsworth: Penguin), pp. 45–102.

Gregory, Lady (1995) *Grania*, in *Selected Writings*, ed. Lucy McDiarmid et al. (Harmondsworth: Penguin), pp. 383–421.

Gross, Elizabeth (1990) 'The Body of Significance', in Andrew Benjamin and John Fletcher (eds), *Abjection, Melancholia, and Love: The Work of Julia Kristeva* (London: Routledge), pp. 80–103.

Grosskurth, Phyllis (1987) *Melanie Klein: Her World and Her Work* (London: Maresfield Library).

Grosz, Elizabeth (1989) *Sexual Subversions: Three French Feminists* (Sidney: Allen and Unwin).

Hinshelwood, R.D. (1989) *A Dictionary of Kleinian Thought* (London: Free Association Books).

—— (1997) 'The Elusive Concept of "Internal objects" (1934–1943): its Role in the Formation of the Klein Group', *International Journal of Psychoanalysis*, 78: 877–97.

—— (2000) 'Responses: Karin Stephen and the Superego', *Psychoanalysis and History*, 2/2: 287–91.

Howes, Marjorie (1996) *Yeats's Nations: Gender, Class and Irishness* (New York: Cambridge University Press).

Hunter, Dianne (1985) 'Hysteria, Psychoanalysis, and Feminism: the Case of Anna O.', in Shirley Nelson Garner et al. (eds), *The Mother Tongue: Essays in Feminist Psychoanalytic Interpretation* (Ithaca: Cornell University Press), pp. 89–115.

Jacobus, Mary (2005) *The Poetics of Psychoanalysis: in the Wake of Klein* (Oxford: Oxford University Press).

Jones, Ernest (1923[1912]) *Papers on Psycho-Analysis* (London: Ballière, Tindall and Cox).

Jung, C.G. (1977) *The Collected Works of C.G. Jung, Vol. 18. The Symbolic Life: Miscellaneous Writings*, ed. Sir Herbert Read et al., trans. R.F.C. Hull (London: Routledge).

Kiberd, Declan (1989) 'Irish Literature and Irish History', in R.F. Foster (ed.), *The Oxford Illustrated History of Ireland* (Oxford: Oxford University Press), pp. 275–337.

—— (1996) *Inventing Ireland* (London: Vintage).

Klein, Melanie (1975[1932]) *The Psycho-Analysis of Children*, trans. Alix Strachey (London: Hogarth Press).

—— (1988) *Love, Guilt and Reparation and Other Works 1921–1945* (London: Virago Press).

—— (1988[1935]) 'A Contribution to the Psychogenesis of Manic-Depressive States', in *Love, Guilt and Reparation and Other Works 1921–1945* (London: Virago), pp. 262–89.

—— (1988[1940]) 'Mourning and its Relation to Manic-Depressive States', in *Love, Guilt and Reparation and Other Works 1921–1945* (London: Virago, 1988), pp. 344–69.

―――― (1997) *Envy and Gratitude and Other Works 1946–1963* (London: Vintage).

Krell, David Farrell (2000) *The Purest of Bastards: Works of Mourning, Art, and Affirmation in the Thought of Jacques Derrida* (University Park, PA: Pennsylvania State University Press).

Kristeva, Julia (1980) *Desire in Language: a Semiotic Approach to Literature and Art*, ed. Leon S. Roudiez, trans. Thomas Gora et al. (Oxford: Blackwell).

―――― (2001) *Melanie Klein*, trans. Ross Guberman (New York: Columbia University Press).

Laplanche, Jean (1999) *Essays on Otherness*, ed. John Fletcher (London: Routledge).

―――― and J.B. Pontalis (eds) (1980) *The Language of Psychoanalysis* (London: Hogarth Press).

Minsky, Rosalind (ed.) (1996), *Psychoanalysis and Gender: an Introductory Reader* (London: Routledge).

Mitchell, Juliet (1986) *The Selected Melanie Klein* (New York: Free Press).

Olsen, Ole Andkjær (2004) 'Depression and Reparation as Themes in Melanie Klein's Analysis of the Painter Ruth Weber', *Scandinavian Psychoanalytic Review*, 37: 34–42.

Orr, Douglas, W. (2004) 'Psychoanalysis and the Bloomsbury Group', ed. Wayne K. Chapman (South Carolina: Clemson University Digital Press), http://www.clemson.edu/caah/cedp/Virginia%20Woolf%20PDFs/Orr_Bloomsbury.pdf, accessed 26 April 2009.

Ramazani, Jahan (1994) *Poetry of Mourning: the Modern Elegy from Hardy to Heaney* (Chicago: University of Chicago Press).

Rank, Otto (1929) *The Trauma of Birth* (London: Kegan Paul, Trench, Trubner & Co.)

Russell, George (A.E.) (1907) *Deirdre* (Dublin: Maunsel).

Sánchez-Pardo, Esther (2003) *Cultures of the Death Drive: Melanie Klein and Modernist Melancholia* (Durham, NC: Duke University Press).

Schiesari, Juliana (1992) *The Gendering of Melancholia: Feminism, Psychoanalysis, and the Symbolics of Loss in Renaissance Literature* (Ithaca and London: Cornell University Press).

Silverman, Kaja (1988) *The Acoustic Mirror: the Female Voice in Psychoanalysis and Cinema* (Bloomington, IN: Indiana University Press).

Stephen, James (1923) *Deirdre* (New York: Macmillan).

Stephen, Karin (1933) *Psychoanalysis and Medicine: a Study of the Wish to Fall Ill* (Cambridge: Cambridge University Press).

―――― (1934) 'Introjection and Projection: Guilt and Rage', *British Journal of Medical Psychology*, XIV: 316–31.

―――― (1939) 'Aggression in Early Childhood', *British Journal of Medical Psychology*, XVIII: 178–90.

―――― (2000[1945]) 'Relations between the Superego and the Ego', *Psychoanalysis and History*, 2: 10–28.

Synge, J.M. (1996[1941]) *Collected Plays and Poems and the Aran Islands*, ed. Alison Smith (London: Everyman).

―――― (1996) *Deirdre of the Sorrows*, in *Collected Plays and Poems and the Aran Islands*, ed. Alison Smith (London: Everyman), pp. 175–220.

Taylor, David (1994) 'Clinical Lectures on Klein and Bion: Edited by R. Anderson, London and New-York: New Library of Psychoanalysis, Tavistock/Routledge. 1992', *International Journal of Psychoanalysis*, 75: 627–32.

Watkin, William (2004) *On Mourning: Theories of Loss in Modern Literature* (Edinburgh: Edinburgh University Press).

Watson, G.J. (1994) *Irish Identity and the Literary Revival – Synge, Yeats, Joyce, and O'Casey* (Washington DC: Catholic University of America Press).

Winnicott, D.W. (1975) *Through Paediatrics to Psycho-Analysis* (London: Hogarth Press).

Yeats, W.B. (1952[1934]) *The Collected Plays* (London: Macmillan).

——— (1952) *Deirdre*, in *The Collected Plays* (London: Macmillan), pp. 1–50.

——— (1996[1989]) *Yeats's Poems*, ed. A. Norman Jeffares (London: Macmillan).

Index

Abbey Theatre, 25, 43
Abbott, H.P., 16, 64
abjection, *see* Kristeva
Ackerley, C.J., 6, 31, 105, 128, 184,
    185 n.5, 186 n.19, 189 n.7, 192
    n.9, 195 n.2
aggression, 9–11, 53, 111–13, 129,
    135, 137, 193 n.12
    see also Klein, Melanie, infantile
    sadism
Aisling, 189 n.3
Anglo-Irish Protestant, 84–5, 189 n.5,
    191 n.3
Anna O., 151, 194 n.6
Anzieu, Didier, 186 n.13
Asmus, Walter, 153, 155–6, 158–9
Atik, Anne, 26, 160–1, 166, 195 n.16

bad object, *see* Klein, Melanie
Bair, Deirdre, 26, 29, 186 n.18, 189
    n.6, 190 n.12, 194 n.18
Baker, Phil, 4, 69–71, 126, 128, 169,
    173–6, 186 n.13, 187 n.29, 190
    n.9, 191 n.5, n.16, 193 n.10,
    195 n.23
Barry, Elizabeth, 165
Beckett, Samuel
    'A Case in a Thousand', 125
    A Piece of Monologue, 161, 195 n.13
    Act Without Words (*Actes sans*
      paroles), 115
    All That Fall, 17, 20–1, 62, 66, 67,
      76–92, 98, 107, 123, 152,
      154–5, 162, 191 n.3, 194 n.7
    'Bare Room', 181–2, 196 n.5
    'Before Play', 133–4
    ...but the clouds..., 26, 153–4,
      158–61
    'Censorship in the Saorstat', 32
    Company, 19, 98, 112, 140–1,
      161–8, 174, 195 n.13
    'Dream Notebook', 185 n.6, 193
      n.11

Dream of Fair to Middling Women, 2,
    23, 102, 162, 185 n.5, 187 n.31,
    189 n.9, 193 n.11
Eh Joe, 77, 97–106, 109, 120, 134,
    159, 161, 169
Eleutheria, 93–5, 98, 114, 131,
    165
Embers, 77, 97–106, 165, 169
Endgame (*Fin de partie*), 153
'Female Solo', 132
Film, 6, 8, 108–10, 112–13, 131–2,
    135–9, 141, 144, 145, 147, 159,
    194 n.16
Footfalls, 18, 82, 141, 152–9, 175,
    194 n.9
From an Abandoned Work, 67–9,
    80, 145–6, 163, 173–4, 176–7,
    181–2, 188 n.39, 190 n.12, 194
    n.17, 195 n.14
'German Diaries', 185 n.7
Happy Days, 8, 10, 27, 77, 107–10,
    113–34, 152, 188 n.37,
    194 n.8
Ill Seen Ill Said (*Mal vu mal dit*),
    140–1, 168–82, 188 n.35, 195
    n.20, n.22, n.25, n.26
'J.M. Mime', 19, 168, 188 n.38
'Kilcool', 108, 140, 144–5, 150
Krapp's Last Tape, 3, 67, 76–7, 90–8,
    105, 153–4, 156, 173, 190 n.9,
    191 n.20
'Malacoda', 46
Malone Dies (*Malone meurt*), 165,
    190 n.3
Molloy, 3, 5, 16, 48–52, 54–7, 59,
    66–75, 82, 88, 94, 118, 139,
    176, 180, 185 n.8, 190 n.7, 191
    n.13, n.19, n.20
More Pricks Than Kicks, 2, 13–15,
    23–30, 34–9, 42, 44–7, 49, 51,
    58, 64, 81, 92, 102, 114, 119,
    126, 185 n.3, 187 n.31, 188
    n.41, 193 n.11

Beckett, Samuel – *continued*
　Murphy, 2, 13–15, 23–5, 29–35,
　　39–47, 49, 56–9, 64, 92–4, 105,
　　118–19, 126, 133, 185 n.3, 186
　　n.17, 189 n.3, 192 n.8
　'neither', 185 n.2
　Not I, 108, 140–52, 155–6, 168, 175,
　　179, 182, 192 n.11, 194 n.3,
　　n.4, n.5, n.8
　Nouvelles et textes pour rien, 185 n.8
　Novellas (*Nouvelles*): 'The Calmative'
　　('Le Calmant'), 73, 180, 185
　　n.8; 'The End' ('La Fin'), 50,
　　57, 70, 165, 185 n.8, 190 n.1,
　　191 n.15, n.17, n.19, n.20; 'The
　　Expelled' ('L'Expulsé'), 52, 54,
　　71, 73, 101, 185 n.8, 190 n.6,
　　191 n.15; *First Love/Premier
　　amour*, 16, 50, 52–5, 57–63,
　　68–74, 99, 149–50, 180, 184,
　　185 n.8, 188 n.33, 191 n.20
　'Petit sot', 166, 195 n.16
　Play, 107–9, 114, 120, 131–5, 192
　　n.7, 194 n.7
　Proust, 24, 42, 53, 92, 103, 179, 182,
　　183, 192 n.6
　'Psychology Notes', 3–7, 9–12, 16,
　　63, 65, 70, 89, 110–12, 126–7,
　　129, 135, 144, 151, 164, 166,
　　183, 185 n.10, 186 n.13, n.15,
　　190 n.5, 192 n.4, 194 n.6
　'One Evening' ('Un soir'), 168, 177,
　　195 n.26
　Quad, 1, 19
　'Recent Irish Poetry', 25–6, 189 n.4
　Rockaby, 18, 140–1, 168–78, 195
　　n.20
　Stirrings Still, 2, 179–83, 195 n.1,
　　196 n.5
　'Super conquérant' notebook, 181,
　　196 n.5
　That Time, 184
　The Unnamable (*L'Innommable*),
　　62–3, 89
　Waiting for Godot (*En attendant
　　Godot*), 17, 20, 75, 98, 107
　Watt, 67, 70, 82–3, 88, 155, 188
　　n.39, 190 n.10, 195 n.14
　Words and Music, 107, 133, 152

Ben-Zvi, Linda, 107, 188 n.35
Berkeley, George, 131, 194 n.16
Bion, Wilfred Ruprecht, 6, 9, 11,
　65–6, 126, 128, 185 n.10, 186
　n.18
birth trauma, 63, 65, 70, 89
　see also Rank, Otto
Brater, Enoch, 146, 194 n.3
Bray, Barbara, 102, 192 n.12
Brienza, Susan, 28
Bryden, Mary, 2, 17, 34–6, 188 n.34,
　196 n.5
Burton, Robert, 2–3, 78, 126, 193 n.11

Cailleac Beare (Crone of Beare), 25,
　34, 40
Caravaggio (*The Beheading of St John
　the Baptist*), 147–9, 194 n.4
castration, *see under* Freud, Sigmund;
　Klein, Melanie
cathexis, 54, 95, 186 n.16, 190 n.4
Celtic revival (Celtic twilight), 21,
　23–5, 29–30, 34–6, 42–4, 60,
　94, 189 n.5
　see also Irish literary revival
censorship/self-censorship, 25, 32–3,
　49, 56–9
Censorship of Publications Act of
　1929, 32–3
chora, *see under* Kristeva, Julia
Cixous, Hélène, 21
Clarke, Austin, 189 n.3
Cohn, Ruby, 48, 162
Connor, Steven, 6, 18, 186 n.18, 188
　n.36, 191 n.18
Costello, Nuala, 6, 128
creative impulse, *see under* Klein,
　Melanie
Cronin, Anthony, 18, 47, 114
Cullingford, Elizabeth, 34, 152

death drive, *see under* Freud, Sigmund
Deirdre, 23, 25–6, 34–6, 39–40, 42–3,
　52–3, 84, 189 n.1, n.11
depressive position, *see under* Klein,
　Melanie
Descartes, René, 13, 43, 120, 132
Deschevaux-Dumesnil, Suzanne,
　48–9, 114

0

displacement, 46, 50, 55, 165–9
Dürer, Albrecht, 195 n.3

écriture feminine, 188 n.34
Esslin, Martin, 48, 131

'F–' story, 48–9, 53
faeces, 59–60
Federman, Raymond, 48, 73–4, 189 n.4
Fehsenfeld, Martha, 1, 6
Feldman, Matthew, 3–4, 9, 61, 63–4,
    70, 89, 135, 185 n.9, n.10,
    n.11, 186 n.12, n.13, n.15,
    187 n.24, 190 n.5, n.10
Feldman, Morton, 2
Fletcher, John, 48, 189 n.4, 193 n.8
Freud, Sigmund, 3–5, 7–11, 21–2,
    42, 46, 49–51, 53–7, 69, 71–5,
    77–9, 83–4, 87, 95, 100, 103,
    108–9, 113, 126–7, 129, 135,
    139, 148, 160, 166, 170, 176,
    185 n.11, 186 n.16, 187 n.25,
    n.27, n.30, 193 n.8, n.15
  castration complex, 9–10, 37, 126–7,
    143–4, 148–9, 193 n.14
  death drive, 72
  Elisabeth von R, 87
  fort-da (*Beyond the Pleasure Principle*),
    71–3, 191 n.18
  id, ego, super-ego, 4: *see also* super-
    ego
  identification, 5, 46, 50, 53, 61,
    176, 186 n.16
  melancholia, 3–6, 8, 20–2, 42, 46,
    48–57, 61, 74, 76–9, 83, 92,
    98–100, 108–9, 139, 180, 176,
    186 n.16
  mourning, 4, 8, 20, 22, 43–6, 49–55,
    75, 77–9, 84–8, 90–2, 95–7, 109,
    113
  Oedipus complex, 9–10, 126–7, 187
    n.24, 193 n.15
  oral phase, 5
  return of the repressed, 74–5, 80
  screen memory, 160, 166
  uncanny, 69

gaze, 36–7, 39, 58, 104, 109, 112, 124,
    133–9, 145, 172, 194 n.16

Geulincx, Arnold, 73–4
Gontarski, S.E., 1, 6, 19, 27, 105, 108,
    118–19, 123, 128, 133, 136–7,
    140, 144–5, 150, 156, 163, 184,
    185 n.5, n.6, 188 n.37, n.38,
    189 n.7, 192 n.7, n.9, n.1, 195
    n.2, 196 n.4
good object, *see under* Klein, Melanie
Grainne legend, 35
Graver, Lawrence, 170, 172–3
Grene, Nicholas, 84, 85, 87, 191 n.3
Gregory (Lady), 35, 43, 189 n.10
Grosz (Gross), Elizabeth, 16, 60, 74,
    149
guilt, *see under* Klein, Melanie

Harrington, John P. 2, 25, 29, 43, 189
    n.4, n.8, n.10
Hill, Leslie, 2–4, 183, 186 n.14
Hinshelwood, R.D., 6–8, 18, 111, 114,
    187 n.28, 193 n.14, 194 n.15
home, 3, 14, 20, 23, 24, 39–41, 43,
    48, 55, 61–3, 69, 74, 76–7,
    80–4, 88–90, 92–4, 97, 99, 107,
    116–17, 123, 134, 140–2, 145,
    155–8, 162–4, 168, 173, 181–3,
    191 n.2, 194 n.2
hysteria, 21, 78–9, 84, 86–7, 149,
    150–2, 194 n.6

identification, *see under* Freud,
    Sigmund; Klein, Melanie
imago, *see under* Klein, Melanie
introjection, *see under* Klein, Melanie
Intoxicating Liquor Acts of 1927, 30
Ireland-as-woman, 24–34
Irish Free State, 15, 21, 23–5, 29–33,
    37, 42, 56, 59, 84, 189 n.5
Irish literary revival, 25, 29
    see also Celtic revival

Jones, Ernest, 4–5, 7, 50, 55, 70, 166,
    185 n.11, 186 n.12, n.16
Joyce, James, 21, 61, 66, 188 n.41,
    189 n.5, 190 n.2, n.11
Jung, C.G., 4, 66, 90, 154–5, 157

Kant, Immanuel, 195 n.16
Katz, Daniel, 72, 160–1

Keats, John, 27
keening, 43–4, 52, 84, 189 n.11
Kiberd, Declan, 41, 189 n.11
Klein, Melanie, 5–12, 17–18, 22,
    103, 107–17, 119–39, 140–78,
    182–4, 186 n.17, n.18, 187
    n.27, n.28, n.30, 192 n.2, n.4,
    193 n.12, n.13, n.14, n.15,
    195 n.1
  bad object, 12, 110–13, 119, 121,
    123–4, 127, 129–32, 137–9,
    141, 144, 147, 163–7, 170, 187
    n.28, 192 n.4
  castration anxiety, 10, 37, 121,
    124–30, 143–4, 148–9,
    193 n.14
  combined parent figure, 193 n.14
  creative impulse, 18–19, 114, 119,
    132, 146, 157, 170, 172
  depressive position (melancholia),
    8, 11, 20, 108–14, 117, 120–25,
    127–30, 138, 162, 164, 167,
    172, 184, 192 n.2
  good object, 12, 18, 103, 109–13,
    119, 123–4, 127, 130, 137, 139,
    141, 144–8, 154–5, 161–4, 167,
    169–72, 176–8, 186 n.17, 187
    n.28, n.30, 192 n.4
  guilt, 7, 9, 11, 17–18, 47, 104,
    112–14, 120, 128–9, 134–5,
    141, 145–9, 157–8, 162–9, 183,
    186 n.17, 193 n.12
  imago, 11–13, 112, 138, 168, 173,
    176, 188 n.35
  infantile sadism, 7, 10, 127; *see also*
    aggression
  internal object, 7, 113, 123–4, 130,
    163, 176, 186 n.17
  introjection, 7, 11, 14, 17, 110–11,
    127, 135, 187 n.28, 193 n.14
  mania, 8, 22, 78, 109–13, 121–4,
    183, 192 n.2
  manic-depressive position, 8, 109,
    117, 121, 124, 130
  mourning, 8, 20, 22, 43–6, 75, 77,
    84–8, 90–2, 103–4, 108–13,
    124, 130, 139, 140–78, 182–3
Oedipus complex, 10, 126–7, 129,
    193 n.14, n.15

paranoia/paranoid position, 8, 22,
    103–5, 109–13, 121, 124, 132,
    135–8, 164, 183, 192 n.2
phantasy, 12, 17, 18, 114, 116, 119,
    129–30, 132, 141, 146, 157,
    164–6, 173, 187 n.27, n.28,
    n.30, 193 n.14, 194 n.15
position, 192 n.2
projection/projective identification,
    17, 163–5, 187 n.30
reparation, 17–18, 22, 109–10,
    113–17, 119–21, 124, 132, 134,
    141–3, 147, 154, 157, 172
Rita's case, 121, 126–31, 148, 193
    n.12, n.13, n.14
Ruth Kjär, 172, 195 n.19
Knowlson, James, 3, 11, 12, 13, 27,
    44, 47, 54, 64, 66, 76, 78, 80,
    93, 95, 96, 102, 120, 121, 122,
    124, 126, 128, 131, 146–8, 150,
    158, 162, 164, 166, 170 174,
    180, 181, 187 n.20, n.22, n.31,
    189 n.2, 190 n.12, n.7, 191 n.1,
    n.4, 192 n.7, n.10, n.13, n.3,
    193, n.9, 195 n.12, n.22, n.1
Krance, Charles, 168, 194 n.1, n.2,
    195 n.13, n.15, n.17
Krell, David Farrell, 169–70, 175, 177,
    195 n.21
Kristeva, Julia, 14–17, 60, 74, 142–3,
    149–50, 188 n.33, n.34, 192 n.2
  abjection, 14–17, 60, 142, 149–50,
    188 n.33
  chora, 17, 188 n.34
  jouissance, 142
  the language of the Father, 142
  the Semiotic, 188 n.34
  the Symbolic, 142–3, 149

Laclau, Ernesto, 15
Laplanche, Jean, 10, 55, 98, 127, 148,
    166, 187 n.25, n.27, n.28, n.29,
    190 n.4
Lloyd, David, 61
lost other(s), 2, 4, 13–17, 18–20, 22,
    24, 42, 98, 100, 105–6, 108,
    114–15, 132, 135, 142, 150,
    152, 158–61, 162, 168–71,
    175–8, 180–4, 185 n.4

MacGreevy, Thomas, 12, 41, 64, 140, 174, 185 n.10, 187 n.23
mania, *see under* Klein, Melanie; Winnicott, D.W.
manic-depressive position, *see under* Klein, Melanie
Mays, J.C.C., 2, 24, 31
McMullan, Anna, 14–15, 17–18, 143, 149, 158, 168, 188 n.34
melancholia, *see under* Freud, Sigmund; Klein, Melanie
memory, 10, 16, 19–22, 48–9, 54–7, 60–2, 65–70, 73–5, 76–84, 87–101, 105, 107, 110, 117, 126, 129–31, 135, 139, 149–51, 154, 158, 160–70, 174–5, 180–3, 191 n.13, n.17, 192 n.6
Milton, John, 27, 78
Minsky, Rosalind, 17, 187 n.27, n.30
Mitchell, Juliet, 108
Moore, Thomas, 52
mourning, *see under* Freud, Sigmund; Klein, Melanie

nanny, 125–6
nationalism, 21, 24–5, 29, 42, 84
Nixon, Mark, 185 n.7

O'Brien, Eoin, 185 n.5, 193 n.6
O'Hara, J.D., 4, 186 n.13
Oedipus complex, *see under* Freud, Sigmund; Klein, Melanie
Olney, James, 19, 67, 175
Oppenheim, Lois, 6, 186 n.13
oral phase, *see under* Freud, Sigmund
Orestes, 13
Orpheus myth, 102–3, 192 n.11

paranoia, *see under* Klein, Melanie
pastiche, 29–30, 38
phantasy, *see under* Klein, Melanie
Piette, Adam, 19
Pilling, John, 102, 126, 185 n.6, 193 n.11
position, 192 n.2
  see also Klein, Melanie
Pountney, Rosemary, 19, 108, 119, 133, 141, 145, 158, 192 n.1, 193 n.9, 194 n.5, n.9

Proust, Marcel, 92, 179, 192 n.6
  see also Beckett, Samuel: *Proust*

Racine, Jean, 23, 189 n.2
Ramazani, Jahan, 20, 43–6, 77–9, 84, 92
Rank, Otto, 63, 65, 69–70, 185 n.11, 190 n.10
reparation, *see under* Klein, Melanie
repetition, 18, 72, 75, 104, 125, 128, 188 n.36
repression, 9–10, 19, 55, 88, 99, 105, 139, 142
Robinson, Michael, 20
Russell, George (A.E.), 35, 83

scatology, 60, 190 n.9
Schiesari, Juliana, 20, 78, 87, 139, 183
screen memory, *see under* Freud, Sigmund
self-translation, 48, 141, 190 n.2, 195 n.22
Semiotic, the, *see under* Kristeva, Julia
Shainberg, Lawrence, 179, 188 n.40
Shakespeare, William, 26–7, 181–2, 189 n.5
Sheela-na-gig, 34
Shenker, Israel, 190 n.11
Silverman, Kaja, 149
Sinclair, Peggy, 18, 44–7, 102, 105, 114, 117, 141, 190 n.12
solipsism, 38–9, 88, 95, 133–4, 150, 157
Stephen, James, 35
Stephen, Karin, 6–12, 16–17, 60–1, 110–12, 126–9, 144, 185 n.11, 186 n.19, 187 n.21, n.26, 192 n.4, 193 n.12, n.13
Strachey, James, 186 n.16
super-ego, 9–10, 111–12, 129, 135, 164–8, 187 n.24, 193 n.14, n.15
Synge, J.M., 23, 25, 35, 38–9, 42–3, 52–3, 84

Tonning, Erik, 186 n.15

uncanny, *see under* Freud, Sigmund

vagina dentata, 143–5, 148–9
Vogelweide, Walther von der, 180

Watkin, William, 53
Watson, G.J., 15, 30, 38
Whitelaw, Billie, 151–3, 159, 188
    n.35, 194 n.8
Wilson, Ann, 142, 143, 194 n.3
Winnicott, D.W., 122
woman-as-Ireland, 24, 34–42, 57,
    117–19, 133
womb, 63–75, 88–90, 126, 130–1,
    150, 154–8, 163, 191 n.15,
    n.17, n.5
Woolf, Virginia, 7
Worth, Katharine, 27

Yeats, W.B., 21, 23, 25–35, 38, 40,
    42–3, 52, 76, 79, 84, 94, 107,
    152, 160–1, 189 n.4, n.5, n.11
At the Hawk's Well, 26–7
Cathleen ni Houlihan, 23, 25, 29–34,
    40, 94, 189 n.8
The Countess Cathleen, 23, 26, 29–30,
    189 n.8
Deirdre, 35, 42–3, 189 n.11
'Easter 1916', 79
'The Stolen Child', 94
'The Tower', 26–7, 107, 160
Words for Music Perhaps, 152